SERGEI N. TRUBETSKOI

An Intellectual Among the Intelligentsia
in Prerevolutionary Russia

SERGEI N. TRUBETSKOI
An Intellectual Among the Intelligentsia
in Prerevolutionary Russia

MARTHA BOHACHEVSKY-CHOMIAK

NORDLAND PUBLISHING COMPANY
BELMONT, MASSACHUSETTS 02178
1976

BY THE SAME AUTHOR

*Spring of a Nation. Ukrainians in
Eastern Galicia in 1848* (1967)

Library of Congress Catalog Card No. 75-27492
ISBN 0-913124-21-4

Printed in the United States of America

ABOUT THE AUTHOR

Dr. Martha Bohachevsky-Chomiak, Associate Professor of History at Manhattanville College in Purchase, New York, received her M.A. and Ph.D. from Columbia University. Recipient of several grants and fellowships, Dr. Bohachevsky-Chomiak has written extensively in scholarly journals, contributed to several books, and translated for *Four Ukrainian Poets*, edited by George Luckyj. She is the author of *Spring of a Nation: Ukrainians in Eastern Galicia in 1848*.

CONTENTS

INTRODUCTION

by Georges Florovsky

Forty-five years ago in Paris I wrote an article on Sergei Trubetskoi, stressing his importance for Russian philosophy and for religious thought, indeed stressing their integral connection. Trubetskoi's political role, the importance of his university activity, the significance of the work of his closest collaborators in the Moscow Psychological Society, was then overlooked, as were many aspects in Russia's past. This was particularly the case with those philosophers in Russia who did not fit the preconceived mold of progressive philosophy, as well as those who did not pose issues dramatically. My own book, *Puti russkogo bogosloviia* [*Ways of Russian Theology*], was then met with stony silence.

Today the situation has changed, and continues to change. The present book on Trubetskoi is an example of this process. Whatever the limitations of Trubetskoi's philosophy, his historical importance is incontestable. Martha Bohachevsky-Chomiak has written a valuable book on an overlooked aspect of Russia, on the turbulent and hopeful epoch at the beginning of the century. For the story of Trubetskoi — his life, his thought, and his activity — constitutes an integral chapter in the history of Russia and in the history of Russian thought.

In the history of Russian thought Trubetskoi is above all an inspired historian of philosophy. His first

5

book, *Metaphysics in Ancient Greece*, will remain an example of a genuinely philosophical study in the field. Trubetskoi became a historian because he was a philosopher. He saw philosophy as history. He felt keenly the universal and all-encompassing character of philosophical thought; and he believed that only in the total experience and combined striving of all times and of all generations is it possible for human thought to penetrate the meaning of truth. Above all he rejected individualism in knowledge. He considered the "protestant principle," the absolutism of the individual beginning, the notion of individualized knowledge, to be the greatest sin of modern European philosophy. Either skeptical or pessimistic conclusions are inevitable from such an analysis.

But Trubetskoi demonstrated that men philosophize precisely in history, in the historical element. That does not mean that man is bound by tradition. Rather, it reflects a feeling of universal solidarity, of overall mutual trust in philosophical strivings and tasks; and it is defined by the consciousness of responsibility, the consciousness of the sacredness and glory of philosophical activity. Everyone philosophizes on behalf of all and for the benefit of all, seeking and arriving at the truth, which is the same for all.

Trubetskoi viewed the philosophical past critically and freely, but always with sympathetic understanding, trying to understand each theory, even each wrong interpretation, from its own point of view as well as from the real, even if yet unsolved problems of the spirit. He could not live in the world of mistaken ideas, could not have lived if it had seemed that the entire past was in a hopeless darkness. He would not have felt justified to engage in philosophy if the history of philosophy were devoid of meaning. Hence there loomed before him the task of the justification of the history of philosophy. He was able to demonstrate that each philosophical system had its grain of truth, which was often unrecognized by its own followers, which was even deformed by them, but which nevertheless demonstrated almost always the truth of the search.

Trubetskoi believed in the goodness of the human mind, the divine image in man; and hence he could not admit that human thought would consciously seek or will falsity or self-deception. In this respect he was almost a naive optimist. This optimism at times blinded him, prevented his recognizing in the history of philosophy its severe tragic element.

Trubetskoi did not construct a philosophical system. His philosophical activity was broken off rather early. But throughout his whole life he was a teacher, almost a preacher, of philosophy. In his philosophical approach, Trubetskoi based himself on German idealism, German mysticism. In this respect he is most similar to Vladimir Soloviev, with whom he was very close. From German idealism he backtracked into the ancient world. This was his second great love. For him it was a clear world of joy and triumphant thought, a world still strong enough and young enough to overcome doubt and anxiety. But the most important factor in the ancient world for Trubetskoi was that antiquity represented the historical path toward Christianity. He saw in ancient philosophy that "evangelical preparation" which the early Christian writers recognized and accepted, considering Plato and even Heraclitus as "their own."

In Hellenic philosophy Trubetskoi saw the movement of natural human thought toward the Revelation, a type of natural prophecy, a premonition and a foreboding. He always stressed that the truth of Hellenism was sanctified and accepted by Christianity — least of all did Trubetskoi want to deduce Revelation from philosophy.

Above all, however, Christianity is the teaching about God-manhood. For the Christian, therefore, it is impossible to be oppressed by the human as such. The Incarnation of the Word attests the purity of the human being, the human potential for purity. The best in the human is his mind — and Trubetskoi found affirmation of that contention in the fathers of the Church. The mind, man's highest quality in his natural striving, is also sanctified in the Incarnation of the Word. It was no accident that Christian truth was expressed in terms of Hellenic wisdom. Yet Hellenism was incapable of demonstrating the truth, for the Truth is Divine. Hellenic thought could receive the truth and recognize it since it had striven toward it. Wisdom could only be revealed — the word became flesh.

But it was revealed to those who loved wisdom, for the love of wisdom, philosophy, had yearned for it. It was precisely in Christianity, as the religion of the Word, that Trubetskoi saw the final justification and sanctification of philosophy. One can even say that he was and strove to be a philosopher because he was a Christian.

It is quite symptomatic that Trubetskoi was apparently not attracted to the greatest of the ancient philosophers. He did not write about Plato and Aristotle, and in his textbook on the history of philosophy the chapters about them are not among the best. He was interested in beginnings and endings — the birth of thought from religiosity and myth, and in the course of Hellenic philosophy. This is very illustrative. Antiquity was for Trubetskoi only a prelude, an introduction, the first act. He tried to avoid reducing philosophical movements to plain formulae. Nevertheless, antiquity is transformed in his philosophy into a moment in the universal enunciation of thought. There was much truth in that formulation.

In Russian consciousness, Trubetskoi, for the first time
and quite correctly, raised the issue of Hellenism as a
Christian problem. But he did not raise it clearly or sharply
enough. It is also characteristic that Trubetskoi did not
feel the tragedy of antiquity. Trubetskoi seemed not to
notice the problems which Nietzsche raised so painfully
in his own early works on Greek philosophy. The Hellenic
tragism and the peculiar, never-repeated and very stubborn
rationalism of the ancient spirit also remained foreign
to Trubetskoi. Therefore he somehow simplified the
issue of the confrontation of the Gospel with philosophy.
In this respect he could not overcome if not the influence
of, then the mood of liberal German Protestantism. This
does not lessen Trubetskoi's achievements as a historian
of thought. In his time he posed the important question
and was able to demonstrate its religious and secular
relevance. And, most importantly, he studied the history
of philosophy in the consciousness that he was performing
a religious task, that he was serving the Church.

Perhaps Trubetskoi was too much of a Hellene
himself. But he was a Hellene who recognized and accepted Christ. He remained a philosopher. He was a wise
man of his age, but in this very wisdom he proclaimed and
wanted to proclaim the glory of the Incarnate Wisdom of
God.

Prince Trubetskoi belongs to a previous generation
of Russian thinkers, a bit calm and well-meaning. By
nature he was an old Russian liberal who remained a
Westerner despite the many Slavophile motifs which he
brought into his thought. This prevented Trubetskoi
from recognizing the full depth of the Russian crisis,
a crisis which always tried him sorely. He did not raise
the issue of the crisis of culture. It was as if he did not
recognize the depth of the contradictions of Russian
life, which in his time were only beginning to surface.

His books and his publicistic articles now seem a bit dated. But the philosophical love which imbues them has not aged, nor can this philosophical eros age, this love and attraction toward the truth. Nor can his firm will toward the sanctification of life, customs and thought through the Church age. And the memory of Prince Sergei Trubetskoi as a man who sought and found, and encouraged others to seek and find the truth in Christ, Incarnate Wisdom and Word, will never fade.

Georges Florovsky

Princeton, 1975
Paris, 1930

PREFACE

Sergei Nikolaevich Trubetskoi (1862-1905) was universally acclaimed as the man "who bridged the chasm between the Tsar and the people." He was the man who addressed Nicholas II in person on behalf of Russian society. He was the man who argued before the Tsar the inevitability of immediate reform for the welfare of the Empire. He was the man who, according to Pavel Miliukov, the leader of the liberals, extracted from the Tsar a definite promise of reforms.

Yet Trubetskoi shunned political activity and was primarily an academic philosopher in the idealist tradition. The two disparate trends merged within his worldview and his personality. Trubetskoi's philosophy shaped his worldview, and that, in turn, necessitated his involvement in the turbulent intellectual and political life of the Russian Empire. His philosophy, closely enmeshed with religion, aided in the decline in the popularity of radical positivism, contributed to the growth of interest in metaphysics and eventually in philosophical idealism. That the crisis of rationalism in Russia did not lead to the pessimism which marked a similar development in Western Europe, was due largely to the activist interpretation of both religion and philosophy. Trubetskoi's theories helped bridge the gap between the political radicalism of the Russian intelligentsia and its acceptance of an equally committed but less radical political liberalism, one reconciled with Russian traditions.

Trubetskoi was not a member of the intelligentsia;
he was primarily an intellectual. The distinction between
the intelligentsia and the intellectuals is always tenuous
and depends as much on the person using the characterization as upon the object of the discussion. In Russia in
the twenty years preceeding the revolution the situation
was complicated by the fact that the intelligentsia was
undergoing a drastic reevaluation of its own views, its
negative relationship to the government in general and its
glorification of the people. The discussion also generated
a still ongoing debate on the definition of the term
intelligentsia, and unwittingly led to the slighting of
research not integrally connected with that highly
articulate group. In this book, the term intelligentsia is
used to refer to those people who shared a future-oriented,
optimistic and largely materialistic outlook, who were
democratic in their political convictions, hostile to the
regime and to the church, and who tended to glorify the
people and to value highly an active involvement in various
forms of oppositional activity.

Some intellectuals — if they fitted the above
characteristics — could be members of the intelligentsia
and were generally considered to be that. But this does
not encompass all the intellectuals in pre-revolutionary
Russia. For the average educated person the term intellectual had the usual mildly pejorative connotation of referring to someone dedicated only to scholarship with
slight regard to "politics" or to the real issues of life.

That is why, when Trubetskoi suddenly burst upon
the national political scene in the Russian Empire in 1905
as the spokesman for liberalism, the overall reaction was
one of surprise that a foremost academic philosopher
would play such a role. That this should be the case is an
indication of the self-centeredness of the intelligentsia.

Trubetskoi could not but play such a role. All the threads
in his life — philosophy, religion, university teaching,
political writing — pointed to a growing political involvement.

Trubetskoi articulated the political and social
ideals of a middle-class Russian: the possibility of a
rational solution to the problems of poverty in the
villages and in the cities; reform of the government;
patriotism in the conduct of the affairs of the country;
toleration in religious matters.

He tried to implement these views in the university
where he taught while successfully prodding the government into granting the university autonomy; in his
writing, by which he hoped to shape educated public
opinion; and, most dramatically on the political level
during the Revolution of 1905.

That he has remained relatively little known is due
to the greater drama of the Russian revolutions and to the
role which the radical activist intelligentsia had played in
the events. The function of the intellectuals like
Trubetskoi has been overshadowed by the bloody events
of 1917 and 1918. Trubetskoi not only predicted the
violence which in the last analysis destroyed the revolutions and paved the way to the new dictatorship; he tried
with all his strength to prevent the ripening of the
situation which would make the revolution — and the
anarchy that would follow it — inevitable.

It is the involvement of the intellectual in
political matters which constitutes the major interest of
the present work. Thus, it is not only a story of a little
known chapter in Russian history; it provides another
poignant tale of what happens to intellectuals who
realize that their commitment to ethical norms
necessitates an actual involvement in the affairs of the
community, but whose intellect sees through their own

hopes into a reality which is grimmer than that with which they would care to cope.

The interests of some of the current Russian thinkers bear a striking similarity to those of Trubetskoi — striking in that there can be little possibility of direct influence. But the search for the lost dimension of man, the resurgence of interest in religion, will lead to a closer study of men of the type of Trubetskoi.

This study grew out of a doctoral dissertation at Columbia University. Marc Raeff was a most helpful and understanding sponsor and I gratefully thank him for all the guidance he has given me. During 1971-1972, with the aid of the Young Humanist Award of the National Endowment for the Humanities, I was able to expand my research. My greatest gratitude goes to Fr. Georges Florovsky of Princeton University, whose unparalleled grasp of the processes characteristic of transitional Russia is matched by a ready willingness to share his expertise. Ania Savage has proven to be an excellent friend and a most competent editor of the original dissertation. I have received valuable comments from Professors Donald Treadgold, Loren Graham, and Leopold Haimson.

Most of the research for this book was done at Columbia University Library and at the New York Public Library. I have been unable to gain access to the archives in the Soviet Union, although I doubt if there would be any new information on Trubetskoi. What the family managed to bring out has been published. I remember with gratitude the people who knew Trubetskoi and shared their recollections with me, especially M. P. Polivanov.

CHAPTER 1

THE YOUTH

Prince Sergei Nikolaevich Trubetskoi was a descendant of an old royal family which traced its origin to the fourteenth-century Lithuanian Prince Dimitrii Kaributas, but had a long and intimate connection with Russia. Kaributas married a sister of Dimitrii Donskoi of Moscow, victor over the Mongols, and the Trubetskois had a distinguished tradition of service to the Russian throne which the cowardly behavior of the would-be leader of the Decembrists in 1825 could not shake. In the nineteenth century most of the Trubetskois were high-ranking military officers, often in high administrative posts. With few exceptions, they staunchly supported the regime, intermarried with Russian and foreign high nobility and lived the lives of grand-seigneurs, peppered with dashing eccentricities. They paid little attention to the dwindling of their wealth and, perhaps because their title was not granted by the Tsar, possessed a greater degree of independence than other Russian nobles.[1] Sergei Nikolaevich, born on July 23, 1862, at the family estate in Akhtirka in the Moscow province, was named for Sergei of the Trinity Monastery, a saint renowned for his love of Russia and the Christian virtue of reconciliation.[2] The choice of name proved to be prophetic.

He was the oldest of nine children of Nikolai Petro--vich and his second wife, Sophia Alexeevna Lopukhin.[3] He was closest to Evgenii, his junior by one year, and to Olga, the fifth child and a cripple. She later collected materials about Sergei, while Evgenii became his brother's confidant and partner. We are indebted to Evgenii for information about Sergei's childhood and early development.

Their childhood was spent at the family estate over which the grandfather, a living incarnation of pre-reform Russia, presided.[4] Evgenii, describing the life on the estate, wrote:

> Two worlds fought at my cradle. Everthing in the atmosphere surrounding my childhood reflected that clash. The forms of our existence were a living reminder of pre-reform Rus', but the whole content of life was new.[5]

The very architecture of Akhtirka — its symmetry, its grand ballrooms and reception halls, its formal gardens and cramped bedrooms — reflected the old world. Although serfdom had been abolished a year before Sergei's birth, elements of the old social order permeated life on the estate. Whenever the grandfather was in Akhtirka, he insisted on a formal style in the family's life. The grandchildren saw him each morning, inspected the same toy, and retired quietly from his presence. They hated the procedure, as well as the elaborate formal weekly dinner in the grandfather's wing. Annually on the feastday of the patron saint of the Akhtirka church, the grandfather met his peasants and gave them gifts. Sometimes the Trubetskoi children stood near him and threw cookies to the village children, watching them scamper for the confections. Once Evgenii threw cookies at the children. He was severely reprimanded by his mother.[6]

For it was Sophia Alexeevna, an intelligent woman with progressive ideas, who had the strongest influence on the children. She reconciled for them the traditions of the Trubetskoi family with the new world outside.[7] In directing the children's moral upbringing, she saw to it that they developed social, political and philosophical interests which characterized progressive Russian gentry.

The Lopukhins, Sophia Alexeevna's family, made a mark for themselves in the reformed courts. They personified the stereotype image of the Russian soul — expansive, hospitable, engrossed in a romantically conceived world, dedicated to ideas, impractical. Sophia, a child of a family which typified the gentry intelligentsia, grew up in the charged atmosphere of service to humanity.[8]

She met Nikolai Petrovich Trubetskoi, fourteen years her senior and a recent widower, at the Moscow Musical Society, to which he directed his energy and his wealth. The neat opposites of the formal Trubetskois and the romantic Lopukhins found a meeting ground in their love of music.[9] The marriage, in 1861, began a happy union in which the woman was the more energetic of the two partners.

Nikolai Petrovich, a kind and malleable man, willingly let his wife control the household while he continued to devote himself to music. "The voluntary exile of father," Evgenii later characterized this interest.[10] Although the father shared his enthusiasm for music with his children, he failed to establish any closeness with them.[11]

Until Sergei and Evgenii entered the gymnasium in Moscow in 1874, the influence of the mother was virtually unrivalled.[12] She chose the tutors,[13] supervised the instruction and instilled in her sons a desire for study and a habit for voracious reading. But education, although important to Sophia Alexeevna, was never her primary concern. She was more interested in developing her children's morality and romantic sensibility. Every evening they confessed the day's offenses and if needed the mother meted out discipline.

She raised her children with the concepts of the brotherhood of mankind and equality of all men before God, although it was a struggle to implement any of her ideas. The children could play with the village children only after the death of the grandfather, but this new-found freedom did not prevent the Trubetskois from making fun of their playmates. On one occasion they even twitted the village priest. They were punished by their mother.[14]

The children were cared for by a loving peasant nanny. She constantly grumbled at the bad inluences of the tutors, "the Frenchmen and the Germans" who came to corrupt her charges.[15]

Their childhood was normal, healthy and happy, spent neither in need nor in overly pampered abundance. Evgenii remembered Sergei as the leader of the childhood games and as an innovator of early creative ventures, such as satirical poems and plays.[16] The latter were appreciated in the family and especially encouraged first by his mother and later by his wife.

Sergei's special place in the family continued all through his life. In his childhood, it gave him full emotional satisfaction; in his adult years it served as a source of strength and faith. Family ties, reinforced by a marriage partner from a family within the Trubetskoi's closely-knit social circle, provided a stable framework for Sergei's development.

Thanks to their mother, the changing social conditions and the normal instincts of childhood, the Trubetskoi children did not grow up intimidated by their surroundings. But they took whatever privileges their position offered for granted and did not develop any feelings of guilt about it. They were not "repentant gentry."

In the fall of 1874 the Trubetskoi brothers, then known as Seryozha and Zhenia, left their childhood world to enter the rather exclusive Moscow Gymnasium of Franz Ivanovich Kreyman. The metamorphosis of Seryozha and Zhenia into "Trubetskoi One" and "Trubetskoi Two,"[17] as the teachers called them, was a painful process. Not only did they find it difficult to view themselves as numbered Trubetskois, but the other children saw an easy mark for their jibes in the title "Prince" that was prefixed to the Trubetskoi name. Although the students at the Kreyman Gymnasium came from rich families, they liked to profess their democratic sympathies loudly. Making fun of the princes was an easy way to manifest one's assumed unity with the common people. Gradually, the innate friendliness of the Trubetskois and their willingness to co-operate in the pranks overcame the problems of that adjustment.

At the time, the Russian gymnasia were classical in the special Tolstoian sense of the term. Although the Kreyman Gymnasium had a higher academic level than other schools, since Kreyman chose his staff well,[18] the establishment could not overcome the dominant atrophied classicism where grammar, not content, was the key. To translate well was a game which lost its challenge after a few years. Sergei, who became a staunch supporter of classical gymnasia, would repeat that he had to fight throughout his life against the bad habits of study he acquired in the gymnasium.[19]

In addition to the weaknesses of Tolstoian classicism, success in the gymnasium depended upon good showmanship. Class time was often spent rehearsing plays in various languages which were presented before the authorities as proof of the efficacy of the school. The students exploited this to miss classes and skip their homework. They knew Kreyman had to have the good will of the government to continue operating his school.

While the two Trubetskoi boys were at school, the financial situation of the family became critical. The father had squandered most of his funds supporting the Moscow Musical Society, and the Lopukhins had never been rich. To put some semblance of order into his financial affairs, Nikolai Petrovich accepted the post of vice-governor of Kaluga.[20] The family moved there at the end of the summer of 1877, and the boys entered the state gymnasium.

The Kaluga gymnasium was a typical provincial school. Classics were stressed, and the moral education of the students was ensured by their writing on such edifying subjects as "Don't complain" and the "Danger of using ready translations."[21] Most of the teachers were well-meaning bureaucrats whose efforts were often frustrated by the stystem. The teachers, more so than the students, were victims of the minute regulations of the Tolstoian gymnasium and the government's fear of sedition. The students knew that the teachers would be punished for any unseemly comments in their notebooks if the government inspector came by unannounced, as he has wont to do, and they delighted in making politically *risqué* comments. Despite the police regime, there was a marked lack of discipline both inside and outside the gymnasium. At times, classes bordered on the ludicrous. Sergei, who enjoyed playing jokes, once argued with the teacher of French, a Swiss, that the existence of Mont Blanc was a direct consequence of the republican system of government. In Russia, he asserted, such a handicap to traffic would be immediately removed by any good governor. The old teacher began to defend his native land and its system of government. Whereupon, a parent, informed of the discussion by his son, made a formal protest accusing the teacher of spreading republican propaganda. The teacher was dismissed.[22]

Although the students at Kaluga treated the Trubetskoi brothers well, and although Evgenii wrote of them with some warmth, Sergei hated the gymnasium and did not develop any lasting friendships. In letters to I. I. Kokurin, a teacher from the Kreyman Gymnasium, he criticized Kaluga mercilessly, hitting the dirt and boredom of the school.[23]

The Russo-Turkish War of 1878 influenced the Trubetskoi brothers more than the gymnasium. The whole country was caught up by an upsurge of patriotic fever in which the national consciousness of the teenage Trubetskois crystallized.[24] The boys became interested in politics and followed the lead of their elders in criticizing the inactivity of the diplomats. They read the newspapers, particularly Konstantin Aksakov's nationalistic articles, and listened to conversations idealizing the uniformed Russian peasant and the motherland's historical mission in the Balkans. All this predisposed the youths to a naive acceptance of the simplified political, ethnological and emotional tenets of Slavophilism, particularly since the family was related to Yuri Samarin, one of the most active original Slavophiles. At the time they had no understanding of the religious and epistemological views of the Slavophiles that later became one of the dominant influences in the philosophical views of both Sergei and Evgenii.

There was little to make the boys happy in Kaluga. The city, although pretty and pleasant, was dull. Its social life was permeated by nostalgia for the grand life of pre-reform Russia. Cultural activity was limited to a few concerts by visiting artists. The students tried to edit a newspaper, but had to stop after two issues because they did not have enough material.

So in this charming city with its picturesque rolling

Russian countryside, even Evgenii, who had originally liked Kaluga, succumbed to boredom.[25] Sergei did not. He limited his social contacts to members of his family, and spent all of his free time reading and thinking.[26] The lack of distractions made Kaluga an excellent place for study, despite the inadequacies of formal education. Both brothers became seriously interested in the problems of life, with Sergei turning to the study of philosophy during the last two years at the gymnasium.

When Sergei's mother gave him the works of Belinsky, she did not foresee the ramifications of her gift. Belinsky supplied the initial impetus in focusing Sergei's attention on the "accursed problems of life" and, very quickly, in making him an example of a youthful Russian nihilist.[27] Under the impact of Belinsky, Sergei became an atheist and a materialist. Further reading turned him into what he considered a positivist. At the age of fifteen he outgrew Russian Orthodoxy and family romanticism to such an extent that once, when reproved by his mother for alleged heartlessness, he coldly informed her that the heart was a physical organ whose primary function was to pump blood, a statement which threw his mother into tears. To stress his progressive views, Sergei, joined soon by Evgenii, would ostentatiously eat sausage on the main street of the city on Good Friday, a day of strict fast and abstinence for the Orthodox.[28] A large dose of childish rebellion against the older generation was evident in this early attitude, as well as a desire by the brothers to rid themselves of the strong influence of their mother. By becoming positivists they became members of the intelligentsia, hence adults.

The first crisis of youth — the acceptance of the creed of the intelligentsia — was not very painful. The Trubetskois felt secure in their conviction of being progressive. Even within the family they found some uncles

who would agree with them, while differences in opinion
could always be credited to the difference in age. As
many young Russians, the boys accepted the new philosophy with the same faith with which they had accepted
childhood Orthodoxy. Evgenii wrote: "We went through
a period of youthful dogmatism in negation."[29] Sur-
prisingly, the Decembrists, despite the fact that one of
their would-be leaders — who, to be sure, failed to lead —
also a Sergei Trubetskoi, was their indirect relative, had
apparently little influence upon them.

Positivism in Russia was not so much a philosophy
as the program of the day, the prevalent worldview of the
intelligentsia, the last word in science. The progressive
gentry embraced it for fear of being left outside the main-
stream of universal progress and of stagnating in provincial
Russia. Somehow, reading Buckle, Spencer, J. S. Mill,
Darwin, some Comte and Spencer's comments on Comte,
or at least knowing about these men and agreeing with
their views, made one progressive, educated and cosmo-
politan. Often, as happened with the Trubetskois, the
acceptance of what might be termed as positivist values
was quite uncritical. K. D. Kavelin once characterized the
process as the result of "laziness of the mind."[30] For the
brothers Trubetskoi, acceptance of positivism was facil-
itated by their recent fever of patriotism, ideals of service
to Russia and her people, and criticism of the government's handling of the Balkan crisis.

Yet the brothers, especially Sergei, differed from the
intelligentsia in one important aspect. Although they
brought into philosophy the spirit of wholehearted dedi-
cation which was characteristic of the Trubetskois and the
intelligentsia, they directed it not at the exposition of the
tenets of positivism, but at the thorough study of it. In a
development similar to that undergone by Vladimir
Soloviev, about which the brothers did not know at the

time, the study of positivism led to a painful questioning of its values.[31]

A year before graduating from high school, Sergei stumbled upon Strakhov's translation of the first four volumes of Kuno Fischer's *Geschichte der neuern Philosophie* in the library of the gymnasium. This work, the first volume of which was published in Mannheim in 1854 and the last and eighth in 1893, proved crucial for the intellectual and spiritual development of many Russian philosophers of Trubetskoi's generation. For Trubetskoi it opened a previously unknown world of German philosophy which went beyond the English and French authors. It made him aware of the limitations of skepticism, of the inadequacies of positivism and materialism, and led him to Soloviev on the intellectual and Dostoevsky on the emotional levels. Evgenii, who followed the same course, graphically described the crisis into which Kuno Fischer threw them:

> I remember what a strong impression the very historical approach of Fischer made upon me. So many truths expounded by Mill and Spencer now suddenly seemed false. I had considered the empiricism of Mill to have been the culmination of knowledge and now I suddenly found out that empiricism had been destroyed by Leibniz in his polemics with Locke; I had been charmed by Spencer's attempt at a purely mechanical presentation of life, and now suddenly found out that the purely mechanical explanation had also been demolished by Leibniz. I realized that it was trivial to characterize schools of thought as progressive or old-fashioned. All evaluations of philosophical systems changed as soon as I began to view them in a historical perspective. When I approached Kant I made the painful discovery that

my beloved English philosophers had known nothing of German philosophy.

Finally, Evgenii lamented,

> . . . all the formulae in which I believed blindly and dogmatically were shattered . . . Childish self-assurance vanished and I humbly realized I had yet to develop a philosophy of life.[32]

The ramifications of this realization were tremendous: horizons of philosophical knowledge seemed limitless. Fischer introduced them to metaphysics, impressed upon them the need for a historical study of philosophy and nudged Sergei to the study of Greek philosophers. Evgenii recalled the last two years of the gymnasium as "the most productive period in my intellectual life,"[33] because of the study done outside the school curriculum.

Schopenhauer's *The World as Will and Idea* precipitated the real crisis. The Trubetskoi brothers were unimpressed by the negativistic elements of his philosophy. Rather, for them, Schopenhauer formulated the ultimate question: either there was a God, in which case there would be reason in existence, or there was no God, and hence no sense in living. They were helped out of this quandary by the works of Vladimir Soloviev and Fedor Dostoevsky.

The writer supplied pithy emotional criticism of the intelligentsia from the vantage point of a former insider. His criticism, unlike that of the conservatives often supported by the government, had to be taken seriously by the intelligentsia. Dostoevsky's awareness of God and search for the good supplied the emotional impetus for the return of the Trubetskois to a belief in the Deity. They hung on every issue of the *Russkii Vestnik* in which the *Brothers Karamazov* appeared.[34]

Soloviev supplied the intellectual base to the emotions awakened by Dostoevsky and showed them that they were not alone in their philosophical tribulations. His influence was crucial on the life and outlook of the Trubetskois.

Vladimir Soloviev, one of the numerous children of the historian, was a decade older than the Trubetskois and had gone through the same development they had: the loss of faith, the acceptance of popular materialism, and under the influence of Kant, Schopenhauer and Spinoza, a complete change of philosophical views. The influence of Schelling, although unacknowledged, was profound.[35]

Soloviev, perhaps the greatest of Russian philosophers, was more than a philosopher. He argued that the task of philosophy was to reconcile knowledge and religion and he acted accordingly.[36] The pervading influence of Christianity, the desire to actualize the good, an ever present sense of morality and a strong mystical streak led Soloviev to publicistic activity. His master's essay in 1874, *The Crisis of Western Philosophy*, subtitled "Against the Positivists," initiated the long trek toward idealism in Russia. His defense of Orthodoxy, his theocratic and modified Slavophile views, necessitated a polemical defense. Even in external appearance Soloviev, with his long hair, emaciated figure, dreamy eyes, recurrent hallucinations and eccentric manner, resembled a prophet. His plea to the Tsar to forgive the assassins of Alexander II in 1881 led to the end of his teaching career, but only heightened his fame within Russian society.

The first work of Soloviev which the Trubetskois read, *The Criticism of Abstract Principles*, made an overwhelming impression upon them. Soloviev's criticism of all one-sided theories, his insistence on both the reality of perceived phenomena and on faith as a valid means of knowledge offered the way out of seemingly insurmountable difficulties created by the study of philosophy. The influence continued, although the two were dismayed by Soloviev's flirtation with Roman Catholicism and his criticism of Slavophilism.[37] Sergei even began writing a study on one of the pet subjects of Soloviev, Sophia as the wisdom of God, although he would not share his views even with Evgenii on that matter.[38]

But the influence of Soloviev was not exclusive.[39] The Trubetskois had been ready for the impact of Soloviev ever since their faith in reason had been severely undermined. In the last year of the gymnasium, Sergei came upon some works of Khomiakov and was impressed by their logic. Khomiakov strengthened most of the views elaborated by Soloviev. The same was true of the works of Kireevski. As Sergei's thought developed, it bore a striking affinity to that of Chaadaev, whose views he could not have known well.[40] Sergei was particularly impressed by the argument that truth can be known only through an organic unity with God, since human reason was limited, one of the basic contentions of the Slavophiles.[41]

This view came as revelation, as actual healing:

It was the joy of *healing* in the literal sense of the term, because I lived through the processes of the restoration of my lately destroyed human *completeness*. Up to this moment there had been discord and internal contradiction, since the soul demanded the fullness of existence as well as an aim . . . while reason considered that aim an *illusion*.[42]

It led to God because

if there is no God, there is no completeness, there is

consequently no sense and no aim. There is, in this negation, an internal contradiction between reason itself, since reason in its very essence is the search for the *meaning* of existence, which is negated in atheistic rationalizing.[43]

Now the limitation of reason was not only known, it was explained. Yet the competence of reason within its sphere was asserted. The balance between faith and reason was restored, as was the emotional equilibrium between the lives of the brothers and their immediate environment. The crisis of youth was over.

The return to faith was a return to a specific form of faith, to Russian Orthodoxy. Deism was inadequate, since under the influence of Dostoevsky, Soloviev and Khomiakov, the Trubetskois needed a people to be the carrier of truth. The return to faith meant not only a belief in God but also a restoration of the faith of their ancestors. It therefore strengthened their nationalism and for a time also their Messianism.[44] It meant a restoration of faith in the Russian traditions and also in the Russian state which Evgenii justified as a necessary step in "the struggle against nihilism."[45] Love of Russia as a state, as an Empire, not a vague attachment to either people or traditions, would be a prime factor in Sergei's views.

Continued study of philosophy prevented both brothers from becoming Slavophile epigones. The initial criticism was again supplied by Soloviev who, by his stress on Western European mysticism, proved the fallacy of the Slavophile contention that the West had atrophied because of a one-sided rationalism. The critical sense of the Trubetskois and the depth and seriousness of their studies saved their emotional natures from getting carried away by any one narrow idea.

Yet in line with the Trubetskoi tradition of dedi-cation, both brothers decided near the time of their graduation from the gymnasium to throw themselves into the study of philosophy. Both entered Moscow University in 1881. From that year on, both dreamt of a university career.[46]

Moscow University had little to offer Sergei. With a thoroughness which was surprising for a youth his age he had read through the classics of positivism and materialism and had discovered their inadequacies. The professors at Moscow University did not share this new enthusiasm for German idealism. Evgenii later complained:

> For me and my brother philosophy at the time was everything and . . . the university made an extremely oppressive impression . . . We felt at once that there was no one . . . who knew Kant, Schopenhauer and Plato better than we freshmen.[47]

The foremost professor of philosophy, Matvei Mikhailovich Troitskii, despite his stature as a scholar, seemed limited with his cheap jokes at the expense of German philosophy.[48] Other professors bored the Trubetskois. Their lectures were often tedious repetitions of a text which had been composed and mimeographed decades ago and which all students had. After a few lectures, the brothers decided that classes were a waste of time, justifiable only for students who could not impress the professor.[49] Henceforth, they came to classes only to take examinations for which they prepared by brief but rigorous cramming. Before the whole family moved back to Moscow, they often spent months at a time in Kaluga.

Both Sergei and Evgenii had originally enrolled in the law faculty since it seemed least demanding. Evgenii remained in law, but Sergei, after a few months, trans-

ferred to the faculty of philology. The university, with its
tradition of youthful turbulence did not push Sergei
towards politics, as it did, for instance, Maklakov. Sergei
was not interested in politics, social theory or the university. His only consuming interest was philosophy, studied
on his own.50

Despite this interest, his social life in Moscow was
much more active than in Kaluga. He still refused to go
to balls and make all the rounds of visits expected of him,
but he was willing to participate in parties of family
friends where he wrote and staged elaborate plays ribbing
the social and political establishment. Throughout his
life Sergei made fun of things which he would also criticize in a serious fashion.51

Trubetskoi's peers liked him for his wit, his direct-
ness, willingness to help and his friendliness, although the
initial impression of him was one of aloofness. The Moscow elders viewed the Trubetskoi brothers as celebrities —
two young men who were educated, bright and convinced
philosophical idealists. This rare combination prompted
as respected a philosopher as Boris N. Chicherin to express
a desire to meet the two young men. Chicherin was impressed by their knowledge, and did not hesitate to say so.
Despite professional disagreements, Chicherin and Sergei
became friends.52

Sergei Trubetskoi was a very emotional person who
could control his emotions with diplomatic skill and
finesse. He enjoyed good company and good wine, witty
conversation and interesting trips. He was an effective
public speaker and relished a good debate. Even his absent-
mindedness was endearing.53

As a student, Sergei took part in an informal social
circle at the Lopatin home. Lev Mikhailovich Lopatin, a
brilliant philosopher later connected with Moscow University, introduced Trubetskoi to Soloviev and offered the

young man both encouragement and criticism. The circle at Lopatin's formed the basis for friendly cooperation in philosophical activity of the young generation of philosophers.[54]

Because of university disturbances, which necessitated a temporary closing of the universities, Sergei graduated from the university in 1885. He was asked to continue his studies on the graduate level, and in 1888 began teaching at Moscow University. He defended his master's essay in 1890 and became an associate professor. After a successful Ph.D. defense in 1900 he received the rank of full professor in philosophy.

In 1887 he married Praskoviia Vladimirovna Obolenskaia, a young woman who shared and supported his interests and came from a family closely associated with the Trubetskois.[55] They had three children.[56] Praskoviia fitted well into the family. She was on good terms with his mother and with his sister Olga, both of whom at times lived with the couple.

Sergei, with his immediate family, took his first trip abroad in 1890/1891, spending the academic year in Berlin. Although neither Europe nor the German universities impressed him much, the stay was profitable professionally.[57] He had fully assimilated not only Western culture but the modern critical approach with which he viewed the whole world, including Western Europe. For Trubetskoi, Russia was European. We do not find in him excessive adulation of Western Europe; on the contrary, he was often as critical of it as of his own country. Contemporary European thinkers who impressed him were Hartman and Kierkegaard, and the philologist Diels.

In the spring of 1893 Sergei went to the south of France, and the following two summers he spent in Norway and Finland. He travelled to Western Europe again in 1903/1904.

Trubetskoi preserved an originality of philosophical approach because he was largely self-taught. Adulation of his mentors was significantly absent in his work, and all philosophical systems disappointed him. Neither empiricism nor rationalism nor mysticism could satisfy his logical, intellectual and emotional needs; nor could any system reconcile scientific findings with religion. Yet the emotional need for religion, he felt, remained incontestable.

For these reasons Trubetskoi began to develop his own philosophical system, and although he did not perfect it, he considered it essentially sound. His inability to finish it did not bother him unduly, for his system took care of such contingencies. The truth would be developed regardless of his efforts, and he felt his theories to be true. His philosophy served him well when the scope of his interests and commitments widened to include academic and political problems.

CHAPTER 2

THE SEARCH FOR UNITY

Trubetskoi made his professional reputation by the publication of his master's dissertation, *Metaphysics in Ancient Greece*, in 1890. This exposition was the first critical step in nineteenth-century Russia in the study of classical philosophical heritage, and its pedagogical importance has been termed "tremendous" by a usually critical commentator.[1] At the same time Trubetskoi serialized his first original philosophical article on consciousness, "About the Nature of Human Consciousness," in *Voprosy Filosofii i Psikhologii*, Russia's scholarly philosophical journal. After two shorter articles, "Psychological Determinism and Moral Freedom" in 1894 and "Ethics and Dogmatics" the following year, he published his major original philosophical work, "The Foundations of Idealism." This was followed by *A Study of the Logos in History*, the first volume of a projected two-volume work. It was first published in parts and in 1900 Trubetskoi presented it as a doctoral dissertation at Moscow University. His last philosophical work was published in 1902-1903 under the title "Belief in Immortality." Interspersed among these were review articles, polemics and smaller expository and bibliographical works, as well as a textbook on the history of Greek philosophy.

Trubetskoi's philosophical output was relatively small, limited in his life by the sacrifice of his energies to what Evgenii called "the interests of the heart" — the struggle for university autonomy and for reform in Russia — and tragically cut off by his untimely death at the age of forty-three from an apoplectic stroke. After Trubetskoi's death, Evgenii complained that his brother had not produced a tenth of what he could have contributed to philosophy.[2] Yet in the brief period of philosophic activity and writing from 1890 to 1903, Trubetskoi succeeded in carving out for himself an important niche among Russian philosophers.

In Trubetskoi we find a mixture of professional competence, scholarly thoroughness and a typically Russian sweep in the philosophical questions posed. Furthermore, his original philosophical theories, in particular that of concrete idealism, assured him mention in any discussion of philosophical development in Russia. The strong influence of Soloviev and, according to Zenkovskii,[3] Trubetskoi's urge for neatness might have detracted from his originality. But to understand Trubetskoi is to accept his unconcern with originality. His own philosophy served him well, and even the realization that it was unfinished and would probably remain so left him only with the trust and belief that others would continue developing similar ideas.[4]

Trubetskoi became interested in philosophy because of the "accursed problems of life." Philosophy was necessary for him as a means of reconciling himself with his environment. The social and political conditions in Russia stimulated him as much as they did the entire Russian intelligentsia. Of particular importance were the split between the educated classes and the peasants and the patent inability of the Orthodox Church to serve as a unifying factor of Russian society. The short-sighted policies of the government politicized all issues by banning legitimate discussion of non-political subjects. Philosophy, because of its inherent connection with all facets of human activity, was particularly prone to a political interpretation. Trubetskoi, despite his scholarly interests and professional approach, provided a variation rather than a refutation of this rule. His political interests flowed directly from his philosophical inquiries. In an early work on Sophia, the Wisdom of God, Trubetskoi openly acknowledged the connection between philosophical problems and the existing conditions in Russia. In his last philosophical article Trubetskoi blamed the political conditions in Russia for her backwardness in philosophy.

Trubetskoi's milieu, his education and his travels, and the very scope and depth of his interests prevented him, however, from providing a simple publicistic solution to the questions posed by every Russian *intelligent* on the meaning of life. No ideology could satisfy Trubetskoi, least of all any of the programs offered by "the most philistine of social groups — the Russian intelligentsia."[5] He was perturbed by the lack of integration of the individual within the society and within the cosmos. Man seemed to him lopsided and incomplete, yet a creature that yearned for unity and harmony. Trubetskoi searched for a system which would unify all elements of the human personality, its individualism and its place within a broader framework, and yet not be exclusive or stifling. He could not find the unity for which he was searching in the Russian tradition or in the peculiarities of the Russian soul. Moreover, other societies and their individual members did not strike him as being either particularly well integrated or harmonious. He concluded that the lack of unity was a general condition of man and not only a result of the drawbacks of the society in which he lived. Further study showed him that the philosophical thought of Western Europe also failed to give adequate answers to "the accursed questions." Dissatisfied with what phil-

osophy and the history of philosophy had to offer, Trubetskoi turned to the fundamentals, to the Greeks.

Trubetskoi realized that self-consciousness lay at
the root of man's conception of his place within the world
and of his relationship to it. Essentially, he faced the same
issue as the most perceptive of his Western European contemporaries. But whereas the Western Europeans, in their
search for disciplines capable of solving the concrete problems with which they grappled, were able to break out of
the shell of traditional philosophy, Russian philosophers,
among them Soloviev and Trubetskoi, back-tracked to
Greek philosophy and to religion. By viewing philosophy
as the rational reworking of the data given us by consciousness, Trubetskoi approached modern psychology.
His notion of consciousness was somewhat similar to that
later developed by Bergson in the latter's theory of intuition. But, unlike Bergson's intuition, Trubetskoi's
consciousness was grounded in a rational world spirit and
was in itself rational.

He soon discovered that the questions he asked
were akin to those posed by the ancient Greeks, by Socrates and Plato, and the solution Trubetskoi finally devised
was based on the Socratic concept of consciousness.[6] In
Socrates, moreover, Trubetskoi found an example he could
emulate in transferring philosophical tenets into everyday
life:

The philosophy of Socrates was not only a teaching,
it was his spiritual activity, his life.[7]

And again in Plato:

Life tears into his philosophy and echoes of passionate
struggle are heard in his works. The older Plato gets
the stronger, the more urgent, becomes his striving to

be the real *lawgiver* of society, to put his ideals into life.[8]

Socrates, Trubetskoi continued, brought philosophy down from heaven to earth at a time of national crisis similar to the one Russia was experiencing.

> In the epoch of general fermentation, of the questioning of all philosophical, moral, religious, and political beliefs and traditions, [Socrates] pointed to human self-awareness as the source and the beginning of all true knowledge and philosophy. Self-awareness is the task of all philosophy in general; the philosophy of every nation is the expression of its self-awareness, the objective consciousness of its ideals. But the time comes when the intuitive clannish consciousness is not enough, when traditional ideals seem to become somewhat limited, when they come into a direct contradiction with reality. What is needed then is exceptional personal self-awareness which would enable the return to the original source, to the deeper positive ideal. In epochs of doubt and destruction, when firm ground slips from under our feet, the need for absolute, authentic and positive knowledge, for a firm belief . . . in absolute principles is felt with particular force. Then it is especially important to *find oneself*, to collect oneself and to understand oneself to the very depths. It is necessary to understand the sense, the aim of our existence and of our activity; to see what we know and what we do not know, what we should know and what we should do, what we can and what we can't, what to believe, what to serve, with what meaning to fill our life, and how to live.[9]

To Trubetskoi, philosophy was the most important

discipline of the human mind since it answered these real, day-to-day, practical and moral questions. The urge to know the truth was inherent in every man and philosophy was

> the living, the higher, the ideal attraction of our inquiring spirit to truth, a striving to enter into the reason of truth.[10]

Various philosophical systems were proposed, modified and rejected down through the ages, and numerous perceptions of truth were at times incorrectly considered to be the truth itself. Yet the search for truth went on. Each solution proposed, much as it differed from the others, was an important step in the world process, since it portrayed an aspect of truth and brought humanity closer to it.

> Each historical philosophy is free as the product of free creativity. The very path to truth, to the absolute positive ideal, is the path of freedom. Even if there is no ungrounded speculation, completely ideal and independent, even if there is no philosophy thoroughly positive or completely rational, the gradual development of thought in the consciousness of this ideal manifests its progressive emancipation.[11]

These basic issues did not change:

> Despite the distance we have travelled from the apocalyptic ideas of the ancients, the issues confronting us are still basically the same — will chaos or reason triumph?[12]

Was there any sense in existence? Were there any solutions

to the accursed problems of life?

These questions, argued Trubetskoi, regardless of the basis for the answers, were metaphysical ones and had to be answered by conscious or unconscious metaphysics. Despite the difficulty of developing a truly scientific metaphysics, the discipline itself was both useful and much needed. Its rejection was impossible because the rejection of philosophy led to unconscious philosophizing, to abstract dogmatism.[13]

The argument that metaphysics itself was not conducive to a scientific approach was wrong, for it was an incorrect metaphysical argument in the first place: "The mind is a born metaphysician and cannot limit itself solely to appearances."[14] The need for metaphysics was particularly strong in the present age of specialization which threatened the underlying unity of knowledge.

Since "the philosophical history of metaphysics is . . . the history of an internal rational process,"[15] a thorough study of the history of philosophy is essential if any progress were to be made by mankind. A critical, objective, and historical study of the past should provide not only the foundation of all philosophy, but also would permit us to reconcile the various systems, to get at the real truth as closely as possible.[16] For truth as such lay beyond reason and "none of the philosophical schools of thought will satisfy the demands of the human mind, for these demands are absolute."[17]

The argument that historicism of any kind would simply lead to repetition was beside the point for Trubetskoi:

Philosophy seeks truth, not originality. The independence of philosophical creativity is established not . . . by the lack of education and positive knowledge, but by the depth, sincerity, and purity of

philosophical interest, as well as by the scope of the
philosophical project.[18]

The study of the history of philosophy, which
should also include the study of the overall development
of man, explained for Trubetskoi the constant disagreements among philosophers and the continued formulation
of philosophically grounded ideologies which were subsequently proven wrong. All philosophical theories, regardless of whether they were correct or not, were for
him but stages in man's search for a perfect philosophical
system and had to be studied by anyone interested in
developing his own concepts.[19] As a result, philosophical
study should begin with Greek metaphysical thought, the
basis of all European philosophy:

> It is the school in which European thought ripened.
> Anyone who wishes to philosophize, to judge, and to
> understand more complex contemporary problems
> and tasks of speculation must also pass [through this
> school] .[20]

In Russia, Trubetskoi continued, the study of the
history of philosophy was of particular importance:

> For [Russians] have never gone through scientific
> training, and random, arbitrary philosophizing is the
> norm. Our philosophical views are often determined
> by chance readings and arguments and by traits of
> the character and the education [of their proponents] .
> What is missing is the regularizing discipline of the
> mind.[21]

This course of events in Russia led not only to lack of
knowledge but to bigotry:

> The few remaining metaphysicians . . . know how
> many old prejudices and misunderstandings are hidden
> in the arguments of [their opponents], who, not
> having gone through the school of historical scepti-
> cism, . . . repeat the trite phrases on the uselessness of
> metaphysics.22

The need for a historical approach permeated Trubetskoi's
writing and teaching, and the repercussions of that approach were evident in his gradualism in political matters.

The analysis of various Greek schools of thought
offered Trubetskoi the possibility of criticizing different
philosophical systems, of stressing their good points and
their weaknesses, and of either elaborating or of adum-
brating his own philosophy. In this real sense Trubetskoi
built his philosophy on his historical studies. For instance,
in analyzing the Sophists, he compared them to philosophical nihilists and to English anti-metaphysicians to explain
the age-long popularity of their teachings.

> The anti-philosophical subjectivism of the Sophists,
> now completely nihilistic, is particularly popular
> today, when Europe is undergoing a critical period
> which is in many respects similar to that of Greece
> during the Peloponnesian wars. For today also the
> basic contradictions of the internal and external
> lives of nations are sharp and clear, and the force of
> contemporary events shakes the moral beliefs of
> humanity.23

The careful study of various philosophical systems
proved to Trubetskoi the inadequacies of all of them.
Following Soloviev and the Slavophile, Ivan Kireevskii,
Trubetskoi criticized the existing philosophical systems for
their one-sidedness which, if logically developed, would

lead to absurdity. Since none of the philosophical systems was free from such shortcomings, doubt was cast not only on the credibility of philosophy, but also on man's very capacity to know.[24]

Trubetskoi found the source of man's capacity to know not in his reason, nor in his sensibility, nor in any innate idea or direct revelation, but rather in what he called his "concrete consciousness." We know because we are conscious of a reality outside of us, he said, because we can really leave ourselves, and because the consciousness of causality is innate in our consciousness.[25] At another point he likened the activity of the individual in grasping the external and internal world to the perception of the artist.[26]

The old question of what came first, the individual or the species, was irrelevant and confusing.

Actually, there is no species without the individual nor is there any individual without the character-istics of the genus . . . their very existence creates an element in *common*.[27]

After analyzing the various philosophical theories of cognition, Trubetskoi reached the conclusion that the basic mistake of modern philosophy was its undue stress on the individual and its contention that individual con-sciousness was solely the function of the individual. That, it was not. Rather, Trubetskoi found the key to his phil-osophy in communality.

Our very capacity to perceive and to give form to our perception was based upon communal elements, such as language, instinct or memory. Consciousness of the in-dividual predicated the existence of consciousness in general. As psychology has proved, argued Trubetskoi, consciousness was not congruent with personality and even the normal individual might possess many personalities, although not the consciousness of these personalities. We have no proof that our present consciousness was fully developed. Just as the senses of sound and smell were inborn but developed much later, so our underdeveloped consciousness, thanks to its generic base, had the capacity to evolve into something higher. Individual consciousness was limited; it presupposed a general, collective consciousness. Consciousness, therefore, was actually the function of the species.[28]

The collectivity, the *sobornost'*, of consciousness was not only possible, it existed. "Whenever I make any decision," ran the celebrated formula of Trubetskoi, "I hold within myself a conference about all with all."[29] The common voice cannot be drowned out in the self; it gives one power and security.

Unfortunately, continued Trubetskoi, although the principle of the collectivity of human consciousness was accepted in several discrete cases, it was never given a scientific basis.

> The task of philosophy lies in understanding the ideal of the full life, i.e., in the assertion of the full possible consciousness of the All in the individual. It cannot be a purely theoretical task.[30]

At present the very fact of collective consciousness had to be established scientifically.

> *Is the individual consciousness of man capable of knowing the truth, and if so, is his consciousness personal?*[31]

Neither the idealists nor the materialists could offer

adequate proof of the personal nature of consciousness, while some of their arguments, as well as data of psychology of humans and animals, proved the exact opposite. The nature of consciousness was of prime importance for metaphysics, for it was through our concrete consciousness that we learned the reality outside of us. The issue should be studied by all available means.

In "The Foundations of Idealism" Trubetskoi took upon himself the difficult and unpopular task of presenting and evaluating the positive discoveries of speculative idealism in the field of metaphysics.[32] He was interested not so much in rehabilitating idealism as in presenting its achievements and his own theory of concrete idealism, which would rectify the drawbacks of the earlier systems, particularly the equation of reality with thought. Although the reaction against Hegelianism was understandable, the rejection of the logical principle was unwarranted. Trubetskoi predicted that metaphysics and philosophical Logos, as the Universal Reason, would again take their rightful places in philosophical study.[33]

Trubetskoi offered an exhaustive analysis on the nature of reality and on the means of knowing it. If it was possible to know reality even partially, he argued, then reality was consistent with the laws of human reason, i.e., with logic. Our capacity to know even a segment of reality would prove an essential similarity between us and reality and would suggest the potential consciousness of general reality, a potential unity of consciousness. The logical principle of our knowledge was at the same time the universal essence of the reality which we perceived.

Reality may be perceived on different levels, and the comment of Plato that one of his opponents did not have eyes to see ideas was fully justified, according to Trubetskoi.

We view both material and spiritual reality, Trubet-

skoi proposed, first and foremost as that which is perceived by the activity of our concrete consciousness, for,
as Kant had demonstrated, we cannot know reality outside
of ourselves. This, however, does not doom us to a self-
contained realm, for if we delve deeply into our consciousness we will find there universal forms which are
independent of our personal experience and consciousness
but which condition *a priori* all possible perception. It is
impossible to think of an absolute non-logical world, for
that would necessitate logic as analogy. No objects could
exist without subjects, no perception without sensibility.
Within universal time-space, reality has an essence common
to our own, a logical beginning. This logical element of
reality permits us to know it, even if only partially. If
reality were something absolutely foreign to us, then our
mind would not be able to perceive it. Hence, reality is
not only perception, it is also an idea.[34]

The view that reality could be reduced to an Idea
had been most consistently developed by Hegel, who
showed that without thought and outside of thought
nothing could be conceivable.[35] German idealism actualized the results of Greek speculation, yet Hegel's system of
pan-logism failed. It failed for the simple reason that
reality could not be reduced to a logical idea.[36]

Reality cannot be deduced from our speculation
. . . It is given us, it is perceived, or supposed as an
*object of faith. The assumption of such a reality is
an essential assumption* (not deduction) *of all our
thought.*[37]

The antinomy between logical idealism and empiricism lay deeper than Hegel's philosophy. It lay in the
unnatural dichotomy between thought and reality which,
according to Trubetskoi, had plagued philosophy from

ancient times. In essence, thought and reality depend upon each other:

> *Our thought is truly positive only in its potential (or actual) relationship to reality, which is given it or which inevitably is supposed by it.*[38]

The realization of the constant relationship of thought to reality suggested to Trubetskoi yet a third manner of knowing reality. For want of a better term, he called it faith.

Among the essential suppositions of our thought is our belief in the existence and reality of subjects other than we. Even our own ego is not limited by the perception of our consciousness, hence the existence of the soul as a separate independent substance. Faith, the same faith which underlies all religious forms, is actually a factor of knowledge. We view the world not as it is actually composed, of atoms, etc., but as the material forms of which we become conscious.[39]

The only reality of which we personally can be definitely certain is the belief in the reality of oneself. All other reality cannot be proven satisfactorily.

> The only reality which is *given* directly to my consciousness is the reality of my subject, and therefore I naturally *understand* all other reality through an analogy with this [reality].[40]

The popularity of spiritualism and of crass mysticism at the turn of the century warranted, for Trubetskoi, a scientific study of mysticism. This undertaking, however, coupled with his empathy for religion and his understanding of mysticism, as well as his friendship with the mystic Soloviev, laid him open to allegations of mysticism from which he defended himself vehemently.[41] In "The Foundations of Idealism" he offered a factual analysis of various mystical teachings, impressed by the fact that all mystics repeated virtually the same ideas although there was no proof of definite historical influence of one mystical trend on another.[42]

On the whole, Trubetskoi found that mystical gnosis, as important as it was for religion and modern pessimism, could not exhaust the study of reality because it demanded the suppression of the self. Yet despite its obvious weaknesses and drawbacks, it did offer a means of studying an aspect of the self and its spiritual development.

> Today, instead of raging against the abuses of mysticism, we would do better to study the basic truth incorporated within it. If the world is a totality of mutually interacting beings, then that mutual interaction presupposes an internal immanent inter-relationship among them. If the world, as perception, is determined by the conscious subject, if the order in it is logical, then the desire to understand the very spiritual essence, the subject which determines the objective existence, seems inevitable. And it is most natural to seek that understanding primarily within ourselves, in the depth of our spirit. In it we become conscious of our relativity in everything that exists. It then ceases, as it were, to be something external and appears immanent to our consciousness.[43]

The source of true knowledge, he concluded, must be sought in concrete consciousness, which is a combination of experience, the universal logical laws of our thought, and faith in reality. This combination provides us with all the necessary means to know reality.

But, argued Trubetskoi, nothing could exist simply in itself but only in relationship to others.

> The existence of objects in time and space is possible only on the condition of their internal relationship to each other, the ideal unity in their real diversity. . . . Everything which exists is in a constant relationship to our conscious subject.[44]

The law of universal relativity of objects, which Trubetskoi characterized as a type of metaphysical socialism, substantiated the physical and spiritual existence and development of reality. Reality is therefore in constant relationship to us and nothing exists which is unrelated to us. This view of the inter-relatedness of the individual and reality formed the basis of Trubetskoi's idealism, which — defined in such terms — he considered to be the result of philosophical development.

The fact that there was a concrete interaction between the I and the non-I, between spirit and nature, subject and object, presupposed a basic unity in their diversity, a universal encompassing of the spirit with its opposite, of thought with reality of existence. The description, or rather proof, of such a unity showed the path to the solution of the problems of cognition and metaphysics.[45]

Trubetskoi said that the being above and outside relativity is the absolute, which is not existence, but the source of all existence. Yet the absolute is pertinent only in its altruism.

> *The absolute exists not only in itself and for itself, but for everything else. It establishes its other.*[46]

What this "other" was to the absolute, Trubetskoi did

not specify. He only hinted at it, without elaborating on what "many would consider to be pure fantasy."[47]

As a youth, Trubetskoi began exploring a problem close to his heart, Sophia, the Wisdom of God, as an intermediary between the absolute and man. He never finished the study, and only a brief segment of it was found.[48] Together with Plato, the Platonists, some Renaissance philosophers, as well as Schelling and Soloviev, Trubetskoi considered the world animated and posited the existence of a world soul, a cosmic being, or the world in its psychic basis. He argued the need for a thorough scientific study of this concept of the world soul, but he himself supplied only an introduction to the subject. The "other" to the absolute, the world soul, would substantiate reality and would serve as the object of universal sensibility, Trubetskoi claimed. It should not be confused with the concept of the rational principle of existence, the Logos.

For Trubetskoi, the issue of the Logos was an even more practical one than that of the world soul for coping with life's "accursed" problems. It would determine whether reason did indeed rule the world and thus make our own lives meaningful.

> Is there any rational meaning and rational aim in human activity, in the history of mankind and in what do we find this meaning? . . . Is there any aim in the world process, is there any sense in existence in general? . . . Natural science cannot answer and does not even try to answer these questions, but this does not mean that they can be solved by faith alone, without recourse to reason. For whenever we inquire about the aim of our activity and about the rational meaning of our existence, there reason has a say.[49]

The problem was important enough for him to become a

Biblical scholar, to turn from the world of ancient Greek philosophy to that of the ancient Jews, to try to trace historically the concept of the rational principle of existence, of the Logos. His dissertation, *Teaching about the Logos*, which he defended and published in 1900, is a case in point. He limited his work to an attempt to establish the origins and the development of the idea of the Logos. This study enabled him to formulate a new theory on the relationship of the Greek Logos with that of the Logos of Christianity. Trubetskoi wanted to follow up this initial study with a further analysis of the Logos in Patristic theology, but his political activity and early death prevented the realization of his plans.[50]

In presenting a historical analysis of the Logos, Trubetskoi ascertained the existence of a pre-Christian Jewish gnosticism from which, more than from the philosophy of the Greeks, the Christian idea of the Logos stemmed.[51] In contrast to the Hellenic Logos, the Christian Logos was not a rational concept but a concrete person. The Logos was Christ, the unique person of Christ, conscious of the genuine character of his own self-consciousness of being God.[52] Christ had come in the period of Judaic ripeness and had poured new content into the idea of the Messiah, making it the central point of the new faith:[53]

> [Christ's] originality lies . . . in the single completely new, purely religious basis which he established for moral life, creating in His person a *new relationship to God and to the World*.[54]

The importance of this claim was tremendous, although its validity could not be proven scientifically. For Trubetskoi himself, one of the most forceful arguments for Christianity being the true religion was its system of morality. Although moral good could not be proven empirically, the demands of morality were precisely to consider the good absolute. Except for Christianity, all other religious systems limited morality. Christianity was the only religion which identified the good with welfare, and true welfare and true goodness with God.

> The Christian concept of morality seems absolute and autonomous in the full sense of the word. Even the opponents of absolute morality can concede that much — Christianity gives them the decisive argument. Christianity shows that the acceptance of an absolute source of morality presupposes belief in the greatest of *miracles*, i.e., belief in the good as God, who is greater than the world and not limited by it.[55]

Christ supplied the justification for man's existence by providing him with a direct link to God. Christianity offered the guideline for the actualization of the good, for the establishment, therefore, of a perfect society.

But the acceptance of this view, he realized, depended, because of the lack of scientific evidence, largely on faith.

Trubetskoi's conception of Christianity was integrally related to both his philosophy and to his politics because it provided the link between the individual and the society, as well as the means for establishing the perfect society. Trubetskoi viewed Christianity in very committed and concrete terms. For him it was not only an organized religion, it was a way, the only way, of solving the very real problems of his philosophy.

The ideal demands of Christianity are for the in-

dividual to act in such fashion that God, in Whom
the individual believes, should appear in his activity
more real than the world and the individual's soul.[56]

Trubetskoi stressed the active elements of Christianity,
its spirit and vigor.[57] The church, as the prototype of
the God-man organism, should incorporate, not subordinate, the individuals constituting it. In this respect
it should serve as a model for all social organization.[58]

Trubetskoi argued that because of the person of
Christ, Christianity could not be reduced to a system of
ethics and morality. The teaching of Christ was first and
foremost Christ Himself — neither dogma, nor morality,
nor theology, nor philosophy, but the word of God made
man in the person of Christ.[59] The religion of Christ,
whatever one's views on Christ may be, must be recognized at least for its psychological truth. Whether Christ's
consciousness of His being the Son of God and God-Man,
genuine as it was, was true, became a matter of faith which
could not be proven by science. What could be questioned
and should be analyzed was whether the religious considerations portrayed by Christ were correctly formulated
by Christian dogma, especially at the Council of Nicea,
to ascertain whether Christianity, as conceived and practiced in modern times, was really Christ's religion.

Christianity portrayed not so much an ideal, as
the potential for the realization of the kingdom of God.
Trubetskoi emphatically rejected the notion of God as
the Absolute actualizing Himself in history, since the
Absolute, by its very nature, could not be in the process
of becoming.[60] God, as manifested in the kingdom of
God, was potentially within us, but the process had to
be actualized externally with the help of our own volition,
as well as with the help of God.[61]

Although reason, science and knowledge in general

offered proof enough that progress of man existed, science in itself could not constitute the final aim of mankind. Science could not transform man, could not fulfill either his spiritual or his material needs.[62] Man could find justification for his existence only in ideal love, which, in turn, could be realized only in an ideal society.[63] Christianity charted the course for that slow painful, but free, process. Of course, one could reject Christianity but that, Trubetskoi felt, could lead only to pessimism, withdrawal from, and denial of, the world.[64]

Individually man's potential and consciousness were limited. The individual became fully aware of himself and of his potential only within a society. Upbringing and education were but a continuation of the process of heredity. Man's very ability to learn was closely tied with the community in which he lived.[65] In the sociological sphere consciousness progressed together with organization and presupposed it. The individual portrayed his epoch and his society, although, by exceptional personal exertion he could, as we shall presently see, transcend both.

Society was, according to Trubetskoi, a higher type of organism.[66] In it,

real, actual reason was formed. . . . Therefore society cannot be viewed as a random total or mechanical aggregate of human personalities. Its members mutually presuppose one another, and if the social whole did not exist, then these members as rational beings would also not exist. There would exist only animals of the human species. At the same time the *society* is not a simple natural organism in which the parts are united by unconscious . . . physical laws: the society is *the product of a supra-organic rational development*. On the one hand it incorporates within itself the organic, generic basis of individual life, and on the other it is a supra-personal, moral whole, the product of collective reason. Whereas on the lower levels of social development unconscious instinct prevails, on the higher [level] social relations are subordinated to conscious rational norms. Therefore, the evolution of both individual personality and of society and their rational progress mutually depend upon one another.[67]

Reason, developing within the community, awakened in us the sense of moral consciousness — which we call conscience. The task and the justification of any society was to preserve and spread higher norms of morality based on conscience, which was also the consciousness of charity.

In order to enable the observance of these norms, the nation realizes the existence of state and religious *power* above itself, a power which would, if possible, be independent and just. The justification of the right to power is found in the objective norms of the *law* of human social life and in the ideal of the universal truth.[68]

Progress, argued Trubetskoi, depended upon the realization of the higher universal ideal of charity, of truth and of goodness. "This ideal cannot be accepted without individual free exertion," he continued, nor can it be known instinctively either by the collective whole or by the rulers of the society. Often individual genius, which in itself was partially the product of society and historical conditions, uncovered an aspect of truth and beauty which had previously remained unknown. Society, therefore, should not hamper the individual in his search for truth, because that might hinder the development of society itself.69 The practical question was very simple:

> Humanity — can it become as real . . . an organism
> as one man, can it become an eternal man? And can
> individuals . . . acquire eternity? Up to now, obviously,
> the contradiction was insoluble. It is obvious also that
> man by himself cannot resolve this contradiction. If
> he ever had sought such a solution, it was always on
> practical-religious grounds, in a kind of ecclesiastical
> God-man organism.70

Although we can neither prove it, nor as yet define such
an organism, the potential for this higher stage of humanity, for which the modern nation-states were only preparatory stages, existed, Trubetskoi maintained. A proper
comprehension of Christianity and the true tasks of
philosophy will provide a closer analysis of the potential
God-man organism.

Neither the authenticity of Christianity, nor the
reality of the good, nor the higher God-man organism
could be proven satisfactorily. What could be proven,
however, was man's capacity to reason, and by force
of that reason, to rise above natural causes and to act
morally. Reason, as Trubetskoi had established was not
a simple abstraction for man; the very concept of thought
was drawn from reason and reality. The concept of physical and spiritual activity was drawn from our consciousness — hence the existence of the will. The existence of
the will was crucial for Trubetskoi, for the rejection of
the will was the best way to finish off freedom.

> The question of the freedom of the will is closely
> connected with the problem of the moral nature
> of man, of his moral consciousness — does he enjoy
> the ability of purely ethical judgment, of the uni-

versal knowledge of the good?[71]

History offered adequate proof for answering that question for Trubetskoi. The force of ideas and the variety of means by which these ideas manifested themselves showed that the individual was capable of asserting his will. The liberation from the physical will by the force of ideas manifested the freedom of the will.[72]

Will could be more rational or less rational, but there could be neither an aimless will nor a will-less intellect. The activity of the will could be explained in terms of either psycho-physical determinism or of motivation by an ideal.

Ideals influenced the individual and worked through the individual, not through the society. The individual's capacity to reason enabled him to judge the moral worth of an ideal and preserved him, hopefully, from fanaticism.[73] But the individual alone was incapable of moral activity. Morality developed only in contact with rational creatures. Trubetskoi maintained that a man living alone, alienated from others, could not be a moral man. Morality was based on love, the guideline of Trubetskoi's system of social organization, and love presupposed the existence of another being. Although both morality and love were inborn, they developed only by stages and with the help of individual exertion within an entity larger than the self.

When man achieves a definite level of self-awareness, when he rejects the all-powerful rule . . . of prejudice and of traditional principles of family morality, he *becomes* conscious of [the moral] law, finds it within himself. This law is not something external to us; it is built into our very consciousness. We do not, how-

ever, want to repeat after Kant that the human will
is a law unto itself (that was Kant's mistake). [The
moral law] is the law of our consciousness, universal
in its real essence but not yet perfect, since it has not
yet reached its ideal aim. The knowledge of this law
is the consciousness of our ideal calling and at the
same time of our guilt and of our failure. For studying
himself, man finds in himself a deep contradiction
with the truth he is not fulfilling, with the truth of
his own consciousness.[74]

Man became conscious of his intellectual and moral
capacity only within the society where his individuality
and individual potential, far from being subsumed by the
collective will, was asserted. In Trubetskoi's system, which
he called "metaphysical socialism" (since it was based on
the recognition of the organic unity of society), the
collectivity of consciousness proved the existence of an
individual and of an individual soul. The value of society
stemmed from the fact that each individual brought into
it his liberty. Since it was the individual who could contribute creatively to the epoch, society could not limit
the potential of the individual without dooming itself to
extinction. True progress occurred only in a society in
which the talents of its members were not hampered.
Restricting the scope of individual activity could block
progress.

Where the national intelligentsia is not organized or
where it is disorganized, the national body may suffer
from want without calling forth a suitable reaction of
the central organs. . . Where there is no organization
of the common consciousness, where this consciousness, as in lower animals, is scattered by incoherent
ties throughout the social body, inaccessible to the

central organs, there only elemental social or state
instincts rule, which, although they create the conditions of strength and moral wholeness of the state,
are not by themselves adequate to solve complex
tasks and problems. Man cannot live without elementary organic tasks, without instincts, but he
would be an animal, not a man [if he lived by these
alone]. The state also cannot satisfy itself with this
. . . spontaneous oneness of consciousness which
becomes evident in the people in moments of great
need or of great enthusiasm. The strength of the
government lies in its living principles on which the
political and cultural life is based. But the will of
the people should not remain unconscious, forever
impulsive, and national wisdom should not manifest
itself [only] in convulsive instincts and wild cries. If
the nation is a living being, then it is an organism of
the higher order, whose members enjoy a rational
nature. That is the reason why the essential task of
every government is the enlightenment of the nation
and the education of its intelligentsia.75

This excerpt shows how naturally Trubetskoi's philosophy
became his political credo, how unified his own life was,
despite his diverse interests. The problems could be posed
on various levels, and only philosophy could offer a satisfactory solution.

For Trubetskoi, the worth of the individual was
incontestable, since it was the individual who was, in the
last analysis, incontestably real. The individual was not
limited to his physical body; his reason and his spirit were
more real than his material manifestations. Although the
existence of the soul could not be substantiated outside
the Church and could not pretend to be scientific, Trubetskoi firmly believed in the existence of the individual soul.

His last philosophical article, "Belief in Immortality," written in 1902-1903 under the impact of the deaths of his intimate friends, was a forceful and bold assertion of the belief in the immortality of the individual soul.

What strikes one most in this work is the stress on the individual, on individual exertion and on individual faith as a means of developing a personal philosophy. In comparison with his earlier works, this study, written after Trubetskoi's period of political disinterestedness, stressed the personal rather than the communal aspects of his philosophy, the need for every individual to face personally the problems of existence. And yet Trubetskoi realized that the personal nature of philosophy was the reason there was no progress in philosophy comparable to that in the field of science, since each philosophy was the product of the individual mind.

The differences among the philosophers, suggested Trubetskoi, might be due to the different levels of understanding. The only philosophical argumentation of eternity offered by the ancients was given by Plato, and he placed it in the mouth of the dying Socrates. The example of Socrates' life and death was essential for the validity of the statements made. For man needed to believe, and Plato recognized this psychological need. The reality of faith justified concepts which could not otherwise be proven.

> One glance at the heaven — the sensory picture of eternity and endlessness — is enough to shake the foundations of "psychological phenomenalism."[76]

The source of faith was within the individual, and it was up to each individual to discover it and to actualize it.

Is not faith in eternity the result of the direct, in-

voluntary consciousness of our spirituality? . . . In our inner consciousness we can rise above various contradictions — relative versus non-relative; temporary versus timeless; . . . limited versus transcendent . . . The root of *faith* in eternal life lies in our personal self-consciousness. Personality . . . is not a simple individuality, but individuality determined by ideal characteristics, both moral and esthetic. . . . Spiritual life is the life of the individuality, and therefore faith in eternity develops and grows along with the growth of the individuality and its inner life.[77]

Faith in the individual or the revelation of the spiritual basis of the individual could both serve as the basis for faith in eternity. We live through these revelations in our moral experiences, in our own self-consciousness, and in our relationships with other individuals. Although our belief could not be based on any empirical facts nor on abstract reasoning of speculative philosophy, this belief could nevertheless be real for us, particularly if we become intimate with Christ.[78] For Trubetskoi the problem of death, hence that of the meaning of life, was solved in Christ.[79] Philosophically, the very existence of the individual soul, not to mention its eternity, remained problematical. But in faith these essential beliefs were justified, and the basic questions of life answered.

For Trubetskoi, his faith and his philosophy were real aspects of one and the same process.[80] They enabled him to survive bitter attacks, difficult experiences and unjustified condemnation by the Orthodox Church and by his own government, the two institutions he supported. He developed his philosophy in the period of overall rebirth of idealism in Europe and shared, rather than followed, the intellectual trends of Western Europe. His exhaustive background in Greek thought qualified him to analyze the further evolution of Western European thought, particularly that of Kant and Hegel. Within the context of Russian philosophy, Trubetskoi illustrated an intellectual trend which stressed the need for an historical approach, an approach that had not been popular.

In determining Trubetskoi's place among Russian philosophers, one may rightly consider him a follower of V. S. Soloviev. His frame of reference, his philosophical constructs, his basic ideas were the same as those of Soloviev.[81] But Trubetskoi arrived at them somewhat independently and in a manner different from that of Soloviev. Whereas Soloviev was given to the formulation of broad schemes and unrealizable theories, Trubetskoi worked on a more modest scale. His methods were scientific ones, based on philological and historical research, which resulted in philosophical formulations. He was a down-to-earth philosopher who drew a distinction between faith, particularly in philosophical constructs, and provable reality. Therefore he did not expound, or even explain fully, his bolder suggestions, such as the Sophia, or the idea of metaphysical socialism or the unity of all in all. He realized the difficulty in the acceptance of such ideas by anyone who was not predisposed to them. Soloviev, on the other hand, did not have these intellectual scruples and the boldness of his thought made him a great and fascinating philosopher. Trubetskoi, the philosopher, exhibited his favorite virtue, moderation, and his originality as a philosopher suffered as the result.

Yet, in no instance did Trubetskoi consider himself intellectually subservient to Soloviev. He felt that Soloviev and all his colleagues were expounding a cosmic process which was one, despite the variety of its manifestations. Trubetskoi's concrete idealism, unity of consciousness, universal relativity, and metaphysical socialism offered explanations of aspects of this process. His philosophy stood independently on its own scientific merits, but it was part of a broader, almost a communal process.

Such were the contributions of Trubetskoi to Russian philosophy, which merit him an incontestable mention in its modern development. Yet the extent of his influence was not limited to the formulation of his theories. His stress on the history of philosophy, on the educative functions of philosophical study, as well as on the limitations of philosophy, had significant repercussions in the outlook of the Russian intelligentsia. His philosophical expositions created a means of overcoming the alienation of the Russian intelligentsia from the people, from the nation and from the Church. His theories offered the means for tackling the overall problems of the alienation of the intellectual from the whole modern world.

CHAPTER 3

"PHILOSOPHICAL PROSELYTIZATION"

Trubetskoi's philosophical theories went against the trend of thinking prevalent among the majority of the Russian intellectuals at the time. Yet, in contrast to the solitude of his study of philosophy, its articulation and development took place within the confines of a closely knit circle of men, who were politically and socially aware without being directly involved in activities which might have been construed as political. The most prominent of this group were Soloviev, N. Ia. Grot, V.P. Preobrazhenskii and Lopatin. Their philosophical views varied, but their conceptions on the functions of philosophy were remarkably similar. For all of them, philosophy constituted much more than a scholarly discipline: it necessitated the acceptance of certain ethical norms and a code of personal behavior compatible with these, an integral part of which was the spread of their ideas, or, in the words of one of their critics, "philosophical proselytization."[1] Soloviev likened his publicistic activity to "monastic obedience in service," and Grot studied philosophy because he felt Russia needed philosophy at the time.[2] They avoided politics as such, yet felt the need for the reconciliation of the intelligentsia with the masses, the traditions of Russia and with purely philosophical interests. They condemned the inadequacies and the reactionary policies of the bureaucracy, the exclusiveness of the theories of the

conservatives and the later Slavophiles, yet they did not
turn their back on the government. Periodically, they
strove for reforms and for a dialogue with the regime
and with the Church, which was subordinate to it.

To a greater or lesser degree, they all had become
disillusioned with a philosophical system they had passion-
ately embraced in their youth. This disillusionment resulted in a healthy scepticism, as in the case of Preobrazhenskii, who chose to make his living working for the
Moscow City Duma rather than in the university, or, as
in the case of Grot, the realization that a final and definite
solution in philosophical issues was impossible:

> Anyone aiming to be objective . . . can never end the
> process of the development of his scientific views and
> come to the naive conclusion that the results achieved
> by him are perfect . . . To consider one's results final,
> if for no other reason than because they are presented
> systematically, can be done only by someone who is
> thinking for the first time.[3]

They were fortunate in that their common goals, shared
intellectual predispositions and personal friendships miti-
gated their technical philosophical disagreements and
fostered concerted action. Philosophy served as an identity
symbol for the group, as can be seen in this letter from
Trubetskoi to Grot:

> I embrace you firmly, become a philosopher at last;
> keep in shape and don't succumb to your temporary
> moods. You'll say that this is not easy. If it were, then
> everyone would be philosopher. And anyway, one
> need but try and then everything difficult seems
> difficult only in the beginning and becomes easy as
> soon as you conquer yourself.

You always imagine that everything depends on external circumstances, on family difficulties, on the journal, on the teaching and the society. But please understand that you cannot escape from these outside circumstances by any other means except activity. [These annoyances] will always exist, one little thing instead of another, life is built that way. . . It's better if trifles are harnessed to beautiful and good things. You're always thinking that editing your own works will be more useful than continuing your present work; . . . you'll have time to publish your works, and if you don't, your children, your students will publish them. So far you are the only *activist* and organizer we have in the sphere of philosophy, and for the spread of philosophy in Russia . . . we need exactly a "sower" like you.[4]

The group, moreover, was closely attached to Moscow and Moscow University. Grot, whose road to a chair in philosophy at the University was long and difficult, was moved to write to his father upon crossing the Kremlin:

With what pleasure do I cross the Kremlin, musing that this is the heart of Russia, that I am also a part of that heart. So far, I have not yet enjoyed Moscow fully. First, I have to work to . . . deserve that.[5]

Perhaps it was a combination of Grot's emotionalism and his friendly and outgoing nature that attracted Trubetskoi to him. Both men not only became intimate friends, but became related in the eyes of the Orthodox Church when Trubetskoi stood God-father to one of Grot's sons. Grot, eight years Trubetskoi's senior, came from a similar closely knit and prominent family as Trubetskoi. His father, a literary scholar, taught for a time at the Uni-

versity of Helsinki before being appointed to the Academy
of Arts and Sciences and as tutor to various members of
the imperial family. One of Grot's uncles, who took an
active part in Grot's education, was a prestigious bureaucrat and a member of the State Soviet. Grot, as a young
scholar at St. Petersburg, Kiev, Nizhyn and Odessa, shared
the intellectual predilections of such progressive thinkers
as the liberal law scholar K. D. Kavelin and M. M. Troitskii,
the foremost positivist scholar in Russia. Grot's polemics
with high churchmen on philosophical matters were
known, as was his friendship with the writer Lev Tolstoi.[6]
Grot was in the process of completely changing his views
and becoming an idealist philosopher when Troitskii's
long attempts to get him appointed to a chair in philosophy at Moscow University in 1886 were finally successful. Troitskii did not like the idealist philosophers hired by
the department, particularly since he was also looking for
someone to take his place as chairman of the Moscow
Psychological Society.

This Society, despite its name, was the largest and
longest lasting philosophical society in the modern Russian
Empire. It was founded in 1885 by a group of largely
liberal scholars who were interested in establishing an
additional forum for the intellectuals, as well as in popular-
izing the study of psychology. They hoped that this new
discipline, untainted with political implications, would be
less mistrusted by the government than philosophy, with
its tradition of alleged collusion with revolutionary doc-
trines.[7]

Grot assumed chairmanship of the Society in 1887.
Under his chairmanship the Society became a haven for
the "philosophical proselytizers." Its membership grew to
over two hundred, and included prominent international
figures and various Russians interested in philosophy,
psychology and the humanities.[8] The Society popularized

metaphysics and idealistic philosophy among the educated classes in Russia, reconciled them with some of the traditions in the country and enabled the cooperation of genuinely moderate forces, although Grot found it difficult to reconcile his impatient nature with the overall lack of interest in philosophy:

> I work on the organization of forces which are completely chaotic and which as yet do not understand each other. They don't believe in themselves and often denounce each other — I alone have to believe in all and in myself. I have to inculcate in all the conviction that we can become a "force" and move masses, lead society forward, that we are capable of inspiring it.

> You can imagine how difficult it is, how much moral energy I spend on it, how often I despair, only to rejuvenate myself and to inject life and faith in others. [It would be simple] if it were only a problem of editorial correction and organization of ready material — but I must create, convince others to write, develop thoughts in print, nudge the lazy, correct the careless, teach the beginners and show the others how to use Russian words correctly.[9]

Trubetskoi was very active in the Society, accepting various elective positions, delivering lectures and working on committees.[10]

The meetings of the Society, held every two weeks, were followed by intimate suppers, at which not only philosophical issues were debated, but the course of work of the Society was planned. Publications constituted an important aspect of the work of Society, and one in which Trubetskoi was particularly interested. The Society published translations of philosophical works not readily available to the educated Russians, such as Kant's *Prolegomena*, Spinoza's *Ethics*, some works of Leibniz and Trubetskoi's translation of Caird's book on Hegel.[11] The Society also published some of the essays delivered at its meetings.

These publishing ventures were successful to warrant the publication of a journal where not only most philosophical points could be debated, but where also a common ground for the general rejuvenation of Russian intellectual life could be found. Grot, in a letter to his father, summed up the aims of the *Voprosy Filosofii i Psikhologii*, as the new journal was to be called:

> I hit upon the idea of the journal to bring Russian society back to its senses, to direct it to higher spiritual ideals, to draw it away from empty political struggle and everyday petty annoyances, to aid in the reconciliation of the intelligentsia with the national foundations of our life, to bring it back to our native religion and to healthy national ideals. Such a reconciliation inevitably flows from the assertion of a philosophical faith in a personal God, in the eternity of the soul, in freedom of the will, in absolute beauty, in goodness and truth.
>
> I could not put this into the program openly, so as to be able to pursue our goals freely and not to intimidate the public.

Publicly he argued in the first issue of the journal:

> The most urgent and the most pressing task of contemporary humanity consists in the establishment on the basis of philosophical criticism of scientific data and with the accompaniment of the creative

work of the mind based upon logic, of a teaching about life which would give men again purer and cleaner bases for our moral activity than that which we have at the present time. This is particularly important for the Russians who have not yet lived their own life in philosophy. . . For this public reason we have embarked upon the publication of a separate *Russian* journal on the problems of philosophy and psychology. Our task is new and most difficult.[12]

Grot attracted a broad range of contributors to the journal — from the grand old spokesman of moderate intellectual liberalism, B. N. Chicherin, to the stormy petrels of intellectual Marxism, P. G. Struve, S. N. Bulgakov and N. A. Berdiaev; from the idealist Soloviev, to the positivist Miliukov; from the psychologist A. A. Tokarskii, with his experimental laboratory and lengthy laborious proceedings, to V. F. Chyz with his psychological analyses of the cultural crisis. The topics in *Voprosy Filosofii i Psikhologii* ranged from the "Kabbala" to criminal anthropology; in 1890 there was even an attempt at psychoanalyzing the poet Lermontov.[13] Philosophical articles in the idealist vein, however, formed the basic fare of the publication. When extremely controversial articles were published, as Bulgakov's extensive review of Rudolf Stammler, the editors prefaced it with a warning note.[14]

The money needed for the publication of *Voprosy Filosofii i Psikhologii* was raised partly from the earlier publications of the Society, partly from membership dues and from subsidies from the university, but the largest contribution came from the financial backing of the wealthy Moscow merchant A. A. Abrikosov. Abrikosov remained the publisher of the journal until 1893, a time he felt necessary to launch the new venture on solid

financial grounds. At that time, four years after the first
issue of the journal appeared, the publication and administration of *Voprosy Filosofii i Psikhologii* was taken over·
by the Society.

For a few years Grot tried to combine the duties of
chairman with those of editor, but that proved too much
and Lopatin and Preobrazhenskii took over the editing of
the journal.[15] Trubetskoi became the editor in 1900, after
the death of Grot necessitated Lopatin to take over the
chairmanship. Trubetskoi remained editor of the journal
until his own death in 1905.[16]

A major problem of the Society and of the journal
was censorship. Its activity and its publications were
subject to religious, academic and governmental censorships, which were often exercised. Grot, to be sure, had
managed to by-pass the time consuming prepublication
censorship which was often required, and was himself
willing to exercise self-censorship over articles which he
felt ought not be published at the time. P. E. Astafiev,
himself a censor, had been invited to participate in the
editorial board of *Voprosy Filosofii i Psikhologii* and at
times contributed articles to the journal.[17]

His participation did not prevent the journal from
having difficulties with publishing all of the desired material. In 1891, for instance, the articles by Tolstoi, Soloviev and Grot on the relationship of the famine to ethics
were banned from publication and no amount of intervention helped. The following year, however, the journal
carried a series of articles on Nietzsche. Its circulation rose
from 1,500 to 2,000.[18]

The journal was attacked by the conservatives and
by the radicals, the former accusing it of lack of patriotic
respect for Russian philosophical achievements, the latter
of short-sighted reactionary idealism. Grot and Soloviev
were good defenders of the journal; Trubetskoi generally

suggested a frontal line of attack which, as shall be seen in a few pages, Grot tried to avoid.

For the moderates, the Society and the journal offered a forum on which to develop alternative philosophies to the ideology of the political intelligentsia and of the conservatives. Its discussions served as an outward sign of the process of the intellectual and political moderation of educated Russians. As late as 1897 Lopatin complained that purely philosophical discussions in the Society were being slighted in favor of publicistic ones.[19] The participation of Berdiaev and Bulgakov, as well as of the flamboyant Merezhkovsky at the staid gatherings of academics, was in itself symptomatic of the changing views of the intelligentsia.[20]

The Moscow Psychological Society served as a model for the founding, in 1898, of the St. Petersburg Philosophical Society. The new group first cooperated with Moscow, but after 1900 outstripped it in flamboyancy, outspokenness and the activities of its members, especially in attempts to institute a closer contact with the Church. But it was Moscow which prepared the ground for the popularization of the ideas of Soloviev and for the Religio-Philosophical meetings of Merezhkovsky in 1903. According to Bulgakov, it was Trubetskoi's philosophy which steered him and some of his colleagues away from religious indifference.[21]

The first stage in the attempts of the Russian intellectuals to come closer to the Orthodox Church and to wrest the custody of Orthodoxy from the reactionaries occurred in Moscow. Trubetskoi, with his philosophical system which reconciled religion and philosophy, was instrumental in this process. This sphere of activity was both difficult and delicate because of the historical subordination of the Orthodox Church to the government. Yet it was not impossible.[22] As Father Georges Florovskii has demonstrated in his *Puti russkogo bogosloviia*, the clergy itself was making attempts to rejuvenate the Orthodox Church. Clerics such as A. M. Ivantsov-Platonov and D. F. Golubinskii met the educated halfway and co-operated with them in trying to reconcile the educated and the Church.

Trubetskoi's major interest was the history of religion. He was too professional a scholar to become thoroughly involved in attempts to bring the intelligentsia closer to the Church. He simply wanted to spread the interest in religion, in general, and in Orthodoxy, in particular. Doing this, however, he was forced to face the obvious causes of the lack of religious interest among the educated. The major reason was neither religious nor emotional, he said. It was political.

In a review of an introductory book on the history of religion, Trubetskoi lashed out at the conditions which made the study of the Scriptures virtually impossible in Russia:

> We can't help but think with deep sorrow [of the conditions which] encourage shameless indifference, superstition, ignorance and dilettantism [in religious matters of the Russian intelligentsia] . . . We would like to know who and what wins from such a course of events. There can be no doubt as to the moral evaluation of the matter. The result is self-evident. Instead of scholarship, instead of critical study, imbued with the higher interest in truth and in historical certitude, which would inevitably lead to the greatest *positive* achievements, [we are faced] with a simple scoffing at sacred things, a general lack of knowledge . . . and not by the persecution of science. The indifference [to religion] can be easily explained by what passes for religio-historical studies [in Russia].

> If we convince mature men that history is [the story of] Sheherezade, and that the tales of Aesop are zoology, they will consider history and zoology a fairy tale.[23]

Trubetskoi realized that there were, within the Orthodox Church, men who, like A. M. Ivantsov-Platonov, "fervently adopted the best interests of the educated Russian society in its attempt to reform our regime, to spread enlightenment, to foster the growth of religious, social and scientific interests."[24]

Trubetskoi hoped his *Metaphysics in Ancient Greece* would become known in clerical circles.[25] Not knowing any clergymen and being in Berlin at the time of the publication, Trubetskoi could do little, but even that little was complicated by a very lengthy, unfavorable and unjust review of the book by the Rev. Sergii Butkevich. Butkevich's review, published in *Vera i razum*, was later quoted by Archbishop Amvrosii of Kharkov, and thus his views became widely known. In the review Butkevich presented Trubetskoi as an enemy of the Church, imputing to him heretical views and questioning his scholarship and capacity to reason. Trubetskoi felt compelled to react.

At the suggestion of Grot, Trubetskoi published a rebuttal in *Pravoslavnoe Obozrenie* in 1891 under the title "So-called Paganism or False Christianity?"[26] Although he argued at length that Butkevich had failed to understand his basic contentions and his belief in the Orthodox Church, the person of Christ, and a system of history which was moving toward God, the relationship between Trubetskoi and the Church administration continued to be strained.

The Trubetskoi-Butkevich polemics took place in the first two months of 1891. In October of that year Soloviev delivered a lecture at the meeting of the Society in which he criticized the Christianity of the Middle Ages. Some months later the government banned the publication of the articles on the famine in *Voprosy Filosofii i Psikhologii*.

Meanwhile, the conservative newspaper, *Moskovskie vedomosti*, attacked the Psychological Society for being a forum for heretical teachings. The newspaper refused to publish Grot's factual account of Soloviev's lecture, nor would the government agree to the publication of the lecture itself.

Trubetskoi, still smarting under the recent attacks of Butkevich, wanted the Society to deny the allegations made by the newspaper, but he was outvoted. Grot's view, that the Society could not dignify the *Vedomosti* with a reply and would have to wait until the government granted permission to publish Soloviev's controversial speech, prevailed. The speech was not published until 1901, after Grot and Soloviev were both dead and while Trubetskoi was editor of *Voprosy Filosofii i Psikhologii*, during a period when attempts at reconciling the educated with the Church were becoming more popular. Trubetskoi, however, did not forget this affair.[27]

The Butkevich and Soloviev incidents were examples of the obstacles Trubetskoi and other members of the Society encountered in their attempts to popularize religious and philosophical interests. The cumulative impact of these frustrations made them realize the need for reform first in the government, and then in the Church, as a prerequisite for the popularization of religion and philosophy among the intelligentsia. By the end of the century the emphasis on reforming the government was strong enough in Trubetskoi to refer to it as a shift in priorities.

The original activity of the Society, however, bore fruit at precisely the time of this shift in Trubetskoi and

some of his colleagues. The outward attempts for a reconciliation between the Church and the Russian educated
classes now centered in St. Petersburg where they made
some headway with the religious-philosophical meetings
held from 1901 to 1903.[28] The meetings spread to other
intellectual centers, including Moscow. Trubetskoi was
invited in the winter of 1900-1901 to participate in one
such discussion. He began writing a speech, never finished
it, and apparently declined the invitation.[29] Subsequently
he started an article on contemporary Orthodoxy but did
not finish it either.[30]

These unfinished articles show Trubetskoi's continuing deep concern with Christianity and its acceptance by
the individual. Trubetskoi believed that religion, particularly Christianity, was an organized cult, but at the same time
he felt that religion could not be forced upon the individual.[31] Religion for him was a voluntary act of the
individual, an individual search for real freedom and the
absolute God. Coercive methods could not propagate any
religion, let alone the true one. Given these views, it was
not surprising that Trubetskoi found himself at odds with
the official Church.

The existing situation in Russia, the lack of free
expression and of modern religious scholarship, and the
minimal influence of the Orthodox Church in Russian
society led Trubetskoi to the conclusion that the country
was in danger of losing its religion altogether. In the unfinished article on the position of the Church he wrote:

> The Church does not even hold the place which the
> clergy, the bureaucracy and the church police begin
> to acquire. . . . Tsar Aleksei Mikhailovich . . . were he
> to come back . . . would find precious little Orthodoxy
> in the [Russian] home, and in Russia's social life he'd
> not find any at all. . . . I am speaking here not of those

Russian people who have broken completely away from the Church, but of those who consider themselves practicing believers.[32]

He found the lack of religious freedom to be at the root of religious indifference. In the same article he wrote:

For every believing Russian the present condition of the Orthodox Church in our country constitutes a joyless and hopeless sight. Atheism and indifference among the educated; *raskol* and sectarianism eating into the people; the depressing position of the clergy; official hypocrisy instead of a living healthy moral force; police instead of the Christian apostolic word of conviction.[33]

But despite his realization of the shortcomings of the Church and his difficulties with the clergy, Trubetskoi remained throughout his life a deeply religious man. Faith, particularly a deep faith in the immortality of the individual soul, gave Trubetskoi strength in his personal trials and in the difficulties he encountered as an academic and later as a political worker. Yet some of the Orthodox hierarchy, even after his death, continued to see Trubetskoi as an atheist, as an enemy of Orthodoxy, the more dangerous in that he masqueraded as a friend.[34]

His involvement in religious matters and his belief in freedom of religious choice brought Trubetskoi closer to the political intelligentsia and its views. This transition was due in equal measure to governmental policies of repression and to the concrete manner in which Russian thinkers envisaged the function of religion. For Soloviev, for instance, the Church was to be an all-encompassing force which would lead Russians to a better life. The religious-philosophical meetings in St. Petersburg tried to find means of bringing the Church into social activity. Conversion, or a return to Orthodoxy, always had political repercussions.[35]

One of the students of the attempts at reconciling the Church and the intelligentsia, Makovskii, has argued that the St. Petersburg discussions failed partly because the intelligentsia was not mature enough to work with the Church.[36] The opposite was true in Moscow. There, it was the Church which rendered cooperation with the Moscow philosophers difficult and often impossible.

Nevertheless, the Moscow philosophers, including Trubetskoi, must be credited with initiating and stimulating widespread philosophical and religious interests in Russia, as well as interests in philosophical idealism. The group realized that public opinion had to be made to see that philosophy and social and political progress were not mutually exclusive. In this process of reconciling the intelligentsia with philosophy, with aspects of Russia's intellectual and spiritual heritage, and with the need for moderation in action, the philosophers became more politicized and the intelligentsia, conversely, became more moderate politically. The process culminated in the unequivocal condemnation of the intelligentsia by members of the intelligentsia in 1909 in the collection of articles entitled *Vekhi*.

A highlight of this process, and the precursor of *Vekhi*, was the appearance of *Problemy idealizma*, a collection of philosophically-oriented articles published in 1903 by the Moscow Psychological Society.

Trubetskoi took an active part in the preparation of this volume, although the initiative for the publication came from P. I. Novgorodtsev, a jurist, who suggested a book in defense of idealism under the auspices of the Society.[37] After some discussion, the Society agreed, provided that the title chosen would not be polemical.

The members insisted that a disclaimer, explaining that the
book did not reflect the views of the Society as such, be
inserted in a prominent place. The chairman L. M. Lopatin
wrote the disclaimer, and the book was edited by Novgorodtsev. The articles in this collection were uneven in
size, content, and even approach. Most of the authors,
however, discussed the problems of intellectual development in Russia and the moral debt facing the intelligentsia.
The articles of the best known and therefore later most
influential contributors, such as Struve, Berdiaev, Bulgakov, and to a degree Frank, were partly auto-biograph-
ical. The fact that these men first emerged in public view
as Marxists made their articles particularly significant.[38]

Novgorodtsev's introduction was clear. After noting
happily that the negative attitude toward philosophy
among the educated in Russia was changing, he argued
that the critical attitude toward positivism was but the
first step toward what should be done.

> The main task is to offer help in grappling with the
> problems . . . of the human spirit, for which science
> is but one sphere of its manifestation. . . The basic
> problem which in the present time leads to the rebirth
> of idealistic philosophy is first and foremost the moral
> problem, . . . and that is why we need to discuss ethical
> issues . . . We are searching for absolute command-
> ments and principles. . . The contemporary return to
> philosophy is not only a product of theoretical in-
> terest, of abstract interests of thought, but more so of
> the complex questions of life. The profound needs of
> moral consciousness raise the problems of what should
> be, the moral problem of the ideal . . . The character-
> istic of this new trend of thought consists in the fact
> that it appears at the same time both as the expression
> of the eternal need of the spirit and as the contem-

porary striving for moral regeneration. . . . These new forms do not appear as simple demands of expediency, but rather as categorical imperatives of a morality which is built on the absolute importance of the individual.[39]

Trubetskoi's contribution to the *Problemy* was on the importance of the study of philosophy and the importance of the historical approach to it. He said that the ideals of life were to be found by faith; the means to find them were to be supplied by science and philosophy, by reasoning and study. His article was clear, straightforward, and tightly written; few reviewers could find fault with it.

Other contributors wrote on Comte, Renan, Lev Tolstoi, Nietzsche, and Mikhailovskii. Struve wrote on a book about Mikhailovskii, and Novgorodtsev, on moral idealism and natural law. Evgenii Trubetskoi discussed the importance of ideas in the views of Marx and Engels. In a vague article, S. A. Askoldov argued that philosophy should first and foremost serve as a practical guide in the search for truth. The maxim was illustrated by the contributions of Bulgakov, Berdiaev and Frank. Their articles marked but a step in the development of their views. *Problemy idealizma*, therefore, was a work as much of religion, practical ideology and practical morality as of abstract philosophy.[40]

A particularly lucid review of *Problemy idealizma* was offered by Iu. Aikhenval'd in *Voprosy Filosofii i Psikhologii*. Two paragraphs from it sum up the importance of the book, an importance which its contemporaries realized.

Problemy idealizma victoriously fights utilitarian morality and . . . subjective methods of Russian sociology. But this morality and this fanatical method are not strong philosophically and victory over them is easy. *Problemy idealizma* shows well that service to progressive civic ideals and a spiritual outlook on life are fully compatible. But he who is acquainted with the history of philosophy never doubted it. . . .

Problemy idealizma is widely read, even by those who are not usually interested in philosophy. The importance of the bulky volume lies not so much in the achievements of its philosophical contents as the social views and sympathies which imbue its authors, for the most part, very new guests in the home of abstract thought. What the book says is not important, but that about which it thinks — that is its primary force of attraction for many. If the book were written only by professional philosophers it would not have caused such a stir.[41]

With the publication of *Problemy idealizma*, the Moscow philosophers admitted openly the need for political or at least public activity. Even those who did not espouse this view, like Lopatin, did not oppose the use of the facilities of the Psychological Society for publications which had political overtones.

And this time the notion of philosophy and its uses underwent a change in emphasis. Whereas for men such as Grot and Trubetskoi philosophy was a preparatory step to a deeper understanding of social and intellectual problems, the younger generation of philosophers, whose initial interest had not been philosophical, looked toward philosophy, particularly idealistic philosophy, as a substitute for religion and also as a buttress for a political credo. The younger generation was more prone—actually more accustomed—to political activity. The older generation, those who survived, were nudged into it.

CHAPTER 4

THE STRUGGLE FOR THE UNIVERSITY

Autonomous education was foreign to both the Russian government and to many segments of Russian society. The government, which introduced higher education, regarded schooling as a legitimate province of state influence: education was valid not as an end in itself, only as a means toward service to the state. The educated did not challenge this outlook as long as the regime pursued a policy of modernization. In the nineteenth century, however, the impact of romanticism, nationalism and various revolutionary and reformist ideas tended to replace the notion of service to the state with that of service to the nation, to the people and to the revolution. The slogan of autonomy of the university was raised when the educated could no longer be satisfied within the framework of service to the state. Some became proponents of autonomy in the firm conviction that it would facilitate learning; others believed autonomy would help bring about new social and political goals.

Thus, the government came to view the universitities with alarm. Yet it was in a quandary: it needed trained men to run a modern state and therefore could not completely curtail academic freedom. Russian universities, although controlled by the government, were closely tied with Russian society and reflected the tenor of life in the Empire. Moscow University, the oldest in Russia,

popularized ideas brought from outside.[1] The interaction
of the faculty and the students with society brought problems of Russia into the university. Political repression,
economic and social backwardness of the country in the
latter part of the nineteenth century encouraged political
activism of the students. During repressive periods in the
Tsarist administration, the university student became the
spokesman and the catalyst of public opinion. The rough
treatment meted out to the students by the government
and the willingness of the students to sacrifice their careers
for freedom, strengthened the image of the students as
heroes. For many adults, their own student years marked
their most active political involvement and this contributed to the glorification of student disturbances. Particularly
in the lull of the 1880's, when the events of the 1860's
were either elevated to legend or downgraded to a tragic
mistake, the students played a role of either liberating
heroes or of revolutionary villains. These considerations,
as well as the repressive Statute of 1884, in force until
1905, predisposed the students to repeated demonstrations
and violence which grew in intensity throughout the nineteenth century.

     This Statute, in effect during Trubetskoi's university
career, was particularly galling to the students and to the
faculty. Under its provisions the university was placed
directly under the control of the Ministry of Education.
The strongest powers were exercised by the appointed
trustee, but the Minister of Education was to be consulted
about many, at times even very minor measures. The
material covered in the classroom had to be approved by
the ministry. The university, moreover, was inundated by
agents of the university inspectorate, who were responsible
for overseeing the compliance with all governmental regulations. Frequently the police helped them out. The in-
spectors and the police subjected the students to petty

annoyances, among them the enforcement of dress-code regulations.

Almost all student organizations were banned, which often meant that the students could not even live together to share the cost of lodging and meals. The poverty of the students — for many even hunger — made them prone to participate in various student demonstrations. The students, moreover, were completely cut off from the faculty, which the government also distrusted as contributing to student unrest.[2]

Trubetskoi's academic career coincided with the most turbulent period in Russia's universities. The student demonstrations could be classified into two categories. Until the turn of the century, student demands were limited to academic liberties. But when the government, as part of its overall political repression, turned on the universities and showed an unwillingness to grant even a semblance of academic freedom, the student aims became political.

Trubetskoi argued for the autonomy of education, to reconcile the interests of the students with those of learning in Russia. He was interested in learning, but he was also interested in a strong Russia.[3] His goal was to create an alert public opinion, the *sine qua non* of the modern state. He urged the spread of education, the abolition of the Statute of 1884, the founding of private universities and free admission of all qualified applicants to higher schools.[4]

As a result of his views, Trubetskoi was pitched into the center of the battle between the university students and the government. While he sympathized with the students, he would not align himself with their radical spokesmen who represented to him the extreme politicized intelligentsia. He felt student demonstrations would bring about the politicization of the universities which would jeopardize the entire system of higher education.

He tried to divert the students from political activity by proposing that the pursuit of education was an end in itself. He became a prominent spokesman of "academism," the contention that knowledge needed no ulterior justification. The academics, the men who shared these views in the early part of the twentieth century, argued that within the university the students should refrain from political activity. They should limit their demands to the reform of the university. These views were not popular, and when the academics argued for independent and autonomous education they had to contend not only with the existing conditions but with the whole tradition of Russian education.

His views on the university were formed early. They changed little although the force with which he articulated them grew. He tried to convince the government, the liberal and the conservative public opinion, and the students of the need for programs which would lead to university autonomy. Since he believed in the efficacy of the printed word even within the limitations imposed by censorship, he wrote articles undaunted by the fact that they were sometimes not published.[5] His articles, however, even if printed, had little impact on the government. Hence, using personal connections and exploiting his reputation as an idealist and therefore, in popular terms, a conservative, he tried on many occasions to pull strings in St. Petersburg.[6]

Reform would come more readily, Trubetskoi felt, if it were lobbied from inside the government. To make his reformist views palatable to the government, he said they were developed "in the spirit of enlightened conservatism." He knew administrative slowness and the attitudes of men in authority, and tailored his arguments to them. He was constantly either drafting notes, talking to officials in St. Petersburg, or trying to convince Evgenii, who was teaching at St. Vladimir's University in Kiev, to get his colleagues to submit notes elucidating the university problems. In an article on the university question published in December, 1896, Trubetskoi stressed the difference between student disturbances in Russia and those which occurred in Europe. The chronic student unrest in Russia made normal academic pursuits difficult even in peaceful times.[7]

University autonomy, argued Trubetskoi, could be achieved only when the students and society realized the function of the university — to produce scholars in all disciplines.[8] As future scholars, the students should prepare themselves for "general service to the native land."[9] But as the intensity of the student unrest grew problems of learning were used as means of broaching social and political issues. Gradually, Trubetskoi leaned toward this approach. The more actively he became involved with the students and with political problems, the more he stressed the contention that the academic goal was at the same time a useful social one. But he kept the distinction between politics and university. In a speech to the students in October, 1903, he said

> The university is not and never will be a school for social indifference. . . If I were to think that, I would be the first to leave [it]. I hope that every student will graduate from the university armed with knowledge and . . . possessed of holy hatred for anything which hinders Russian life; but while you are at the university, remember that Russia needs this bright, cultured social force.[10]

It took courage to express such views, and Trubetskoi drew it from viewing the actions of his life in moral terms:

The moral task of the professor . . . as of every honest man, is the honorable service to his function, without regard to personal profit; that is service to the learning which he teaches.[11]

At the height of the university tension, writing to Evgenii on *"the to be or not to be"* of the university, he argued:

We need the Kantian categorical imperative. "Act as if the maxim of thy action were to become by thy will a universal law of nature."[12]

Doggedly and at times with a note of bitterness, Trubetskoi defended knowledge and knowledge as a factor in social progress. He wanted the Russian community to realize the importance of education which would be free of outside influences. Education, argued Trubetskoi, was necessary as the preparatory stage for any activity, including politics.

Trubetskoi welcomed the reform of the secondary schools in 1901 which freed the schools from direct police control.[13] But he publicly questioned incompetent discussion of educational problems and he did not share the intelligentsia's enthusiasm for the new *real-gymnasium* which stressed modern languages and the sciences.[14] The best type of education for youth was, according to him, classical education, and he argued his case. But classicism was so identified in Russia with D. A. Tolstoi's travesty of the system that Trubetskoi had to defend himself from charges of being a reactionary.[15]

The university was Trubetskoi's primary interest. Unlike his sporadic contributions to the evaluation of classicism, Trubetskoi persisted in expounding his views on the university, repeating them whenever he could. The only valid point of departure for him in any discussion on the university was the welfare of the institution. He resented "the constant impingement of political principles . . . on purely pedagogical issues."[16] He resented the fact that the liberals, as the radicals, stressed the political role of the students. *Osvobozhdenie*, a liberal journal published outside of Russia, for instance, justified the political activities of the students by the passivity of their parents.

In 1894 Trubetskoi, returning from a sojourn at Western European universities, was struck with renewed force by the sad plight of the Russian schools. With P. G. Vinogradoff he organized an informal discussion group of faculty and students. It was officially regarded as continuation of class work.[17] The discussions were considered by many students as an unprecedented liberty, and it was symptomatic of the whole atmosphere that one of the moderate students considered the whole affair illegal. Among the topics discussed by the Trubetskoi-Vinogradoff group were de Maistre's philosophy, the philosophy of history of Vico, the ideas of Konstantin Aksakov, economic materialism and its relationship to historiography, and the criticism of Roman law. Trubetskoi realized the limitations of the group, but he also realized that "we can't get anything more useful for the students." All topics of discussion were subject to prior approval by Trubetskoi, who barred "all political subjects without appeal." This limited venture into student-faculty relations demonstrated the difficulties of the faculty in dealing with students in a university which was not run by them. The group disintegrated under the pressures of the government and of renewed student disturbances.[18] Trubetskoi, who could work under the most trying circumstances, felt depressed. He confided to Evgenii:

A thoroughly wretched time . . . I live a lonely life and see hardly anyone. . . The worst thing is the reali-

zation that should things become better it would
simply be the result of pure chance. Villainy and
stupidity are the natural course of events. . . One can
only hear the triumphal grunts as a reply to the swinish
whine. . . Autocracy is rampant in Moscow.[19]

In a letter to Grot, who had threatened to resign from his
teaching post, Trubetskoi was actually arguing with himself as much as he was trying to convince Grot to stay on:
"Our duty is to serve the university, and to keep serving it
as long as we can."[20]

In 1899 a routine disturbance in St. Petersburg,
caused by the tactlessness of the rector, the unjustified
brutality of the police and the wounded pride of the
students, triggered a student strike which spread to all
higher schools and to some gymnasia and a few grammar
schools as well.[21] It initiated an era of student unrest
which continued, with few interruptions, into 1905.

In Moscow University the strike was run by an *ad
hoc* student committee called the *Ispolnitel'nyi komitet*,
a harking back to the glorious era of the terrorist *narod-
vol'tsy*. The strike in Moscow was proclaimed within a
week of that in St. Petersburg. Immediately, the government expelled more than a hundred students from the
university and warned another two hundred to desist from
demonstrations on pain of expulsion. This provided the
Moscow movement with its own martyrs and added the
demand of freeing the expelled and arrested students to
the original ones drawn up by the *Ispolkom*.[22]

The demands of the Moscow students were similar
to those of the students in the whole Empire --- inviola-
bility of the person, publication of the instructions to the
police, and court review of student cases. Later, they also
demanded a study of the system of university inspection.

But the manner in which the strike was handled in

Moscow was different from the methods used in the rest of the Empire: the students and faculty co-operated in ending the boycott in Moscow. During the height of the strike, the rector permitted open meetings and promised to permit arrested students to return to the university. Because of this conciliatory action the majority of students voted to lift the boycott. By the end of February the Moscow *Ispolkom* dissolved itself.[23] Yet the government did not consider the experience of Moscow University significant. The tactics used there were not followed in other institutions, and the student strike continued. It found its echo in renewed unrest at Moscow.[24]

A few days after the original St. Petersburg strike, the government established a commission, headed by General I. P. Vannovskii, to study the causes of student unrest. The creation of the commission was considered a concession to the students. It issued its report to the government four months later, suggesting the introduction of corporate student organizations in the universities, the reform of the inspectorate and the limitation of the number of students enrolled in the universities to prevent overcrowding. The report was not publicized, and the government did not accept its suggestions.[25] Instead, it stepped up the repression of the students. Minister of Education N. P. Bogolepov increased the inspectorate staff, limited the attendance of students to universities within their own district, and continued the ban on student organizations. Moreover, a law meting out strict punishment to anyone hindering the army or police in the execution of their functions was reaffirmed.[26] A new decree was passed in July to permit the drafting of expelled students into the army, one student to a unit so as to neutralize their influence on the soldiers.[27]

The repressive measures failed to calm the students, although attempts at renewing inter-university student organizations were foiled by the police.[28] In Moscow University these measures precipitated a break with academic demands. A resolution of some of the students, passed in February, 1901, "rejected forever the illusion of the academic struggle and raised the banner of political demands."[29]

Its initiators were naturally arrested and exiled. Trubetskoi vainly tried to prevent their arrest by going to St. Petersburg to plead for them. He argued that treating the students as political criminals created an allure of selfless political activity and made heroes out of them. A more effective rebuke would be a charge of rowdyism.[30]

Trubetskoi sympathized with the students and worked well with them, particularly in seminars which he often held at home. He was popular with the students, and was readily accessible to them.[31] But he refused to idolize them.[32] He was particularly wary of student organizations not under faculty control, and as late as March, 1899, argued against the election by students of their own representatives as being "organized *miliukovshchina*, i.e. agitation and demagogy of the most unpleasant sort."[33] In a letter to Chicherin's wife he expressed a fear of radical take-over of the university,[34] but in a memo to Vannovskii he defended the idealism of the students.[35] His own experiences with the students proved that they were amenable to reason. This was aptly illustrated by the Meshcherskii incident in Moscow University in the fall of 1901.

Prince Meshcherskii, the editor of the reactionary Kievan *Grazhdanin*, published an article discrediting women's higher courses. A student committee in Moscow demanded that V. N. Guerrier [Ger'e], one of the pioneers of women's education in Russia and a man of liberal persuasions, rebut Meshcherskii.[36] Guerrier did not want to get involved for fear of destroying his chances for ex-

panding women's courses. The students threatened a
disturbance.

The rector of Moscow University, in a written note
which circulated to all the faculty, permitted student
meetings to discuss the affair. The Trustee of Moscow, in
turn, said he would be willing to hand a petition of the
students to the Minister of Education, provided they
refrain from public demonstrations. He hinted they could
demonstrate against Guerrier.[37]

Trubetskoi was shocked by what seemed to be the
dictates of the student committee to the faculty:

> Under such circumstances neither an elective nor an
> appointed rector will be able to administer the uni-
> versity . . . How can you discuss the university ques-
> tion? By force of circumstances and to the grief of
> all sensible people [it] becomes a problem of pol-
> itics.[38]

He wanted to prevent the demonstration against Guerrier
on principle. He also felt that Guerrier had nothing to do
with the affair. By addressing the students personally,
Trubetskoi averted the demonstration against Guerrier.[39]

The affair strengthened Trubetskoi's contention
that, given proper guidance, the students would not engage
in unnecessary demonstrations. But a simple change of
the Statute of 1884 — "the administrative re-organization
of the University"[40] — would not solve the university
problem. Radical students would have to be neutralized,
and that could be done only when the proper function of
the university was fully realized:

> Should the university have autonomy, should it have
> a purely academic aim and function? And can this
> function be fulfilled in any other manner than by

orderly student life and by a self-replenishing learned
corporation, enjoying both authority and autonomy
in carrying out its pedagogical function?[41]

There was a vicious circle: the students could not be
pacified before the introduction of autonomy, and autonomy could not work without the good will of the students.
Trubetskoi was active on both fronts at once, with the
government and with the students, both to establish
university autonomy and to encourage conditions conducive to its growth.

His views are conveniently summarized in a note
to the Tsar on the educational problems of Russia.[42] The
major reason for student unrest he considered the Statute
of 1884; as proof of need for drastic reform, he stressed
the fact that no one came out in defense of that Statute.[43]

Since the final aim of the university was the spread
of knowledge, the university should not limit enrollment:
Russia was too poor in intellectuals to permit it. Rather,
expanded technical schools should take care of students
interested in specialized programs. What was needed,
maintained Trubetskoi, was the re-establishment of autonomy for the university, the introduction of collegiate self-
rule for the faculty, and of a corporate organization for
the students.[44] The students should be permitted to take
courses outside of their discipline, and the subject matter
should be handled by the faculties, not the ministry of
education.[45]

Student organizations, according to Trubetskoi, had
a legitimate place in the university. Experience had shown
that students organize themselves spontaneously, and the
effectiveness of a corporate structure of the university
would argue the inclusion of the students.[46] Banning
student organizations drove them underground, as had
happened to the *zemliachestva*.[47] The low standard of

living of the students necessitated speeding up the building of dormitories. The government had already taken the first step; the rest was up to Russian society. But under no circumstances, warned Trubetskoi, should the dormitories have police functions over the students.[48] Less costly than the dormitories, but just as important, were special interest clubs which could increase the academic level of the average students. If the government were to sanction the existence of such clubs, that would prevent their take-over by fanatical political groups.[49]

New student disturbances were triggered on February 14, 1901, when an expelled student, Petr Karpovich, shot and fatally wounded the Minister of Education, Bogolepov.[50] At Moscow University the disturbances were again checked by the creation of a faculty commission and by the opening of lecture halls to student meetings, an event considered of major importance in Russia at the time.[51]

Bogolepov's violent death seemed to prove the inefficacy of his repressive measures and old General Vannovskii was appointed by the Tsar on March 25, 1901, to take the post of Minister of Education. Vannovskii tried to reconcile the students with the government. He sent out a fact-finding questionnaire to all universities, where special commissions debated it. The discussion dealt not only with the immediate problem of student unrest, but also with the broader one of possible university reform.[52]

The majority of the faculty at Moscow felt that the detrimental effects of the Statute of 1884, the distrust of the faculty by the government and the excessive powers of the inspector were the primary causes of student discontent. The power of the university administration was ambiguous: what was necessary was a clear statement whether the rector or the trustee was to supervise the inspector.[53] The faculty wanted self-government in the universities, legalization of student organizations and the amelioration of the deplorable material conditions of the students. They stressed that such reforms would benefit the state. Although there was a minority which argued the opposite, the majority of the faculty throughout the Russian Empire supported university reforms.[54]

This time, the government decided to try some of the measures suggested by the faculty, although it continued the policy of repression outside the universities.[55] In December of 1901, temporary legislation legalized certain student organizations. Lest these get out of hand, the law provided for direct supervision by the faculty and the trustee.[56] Despite these limitations, Trubetskoi immediately realized the vast possibilities the new legislation offered and set to work to establish a student Society at Moscow University. The success of the Historico-Philological Society was unprecedented in Russia.[57]

The Society was Trubetskoi's personal achievement. He fought for it in face of suspicions by the government and criticisms by the radicals. The radical students considered the Society a dangerous deflection of student energies from the primary cause — the struggle for a free Russia. The fact that the conservatives had always argued that giving the students more work would keep them away from politics worked against the Society.[58] The publicized liberalism of Trubetskoi's close helpers, P. I. Novgorodtsev and N. V. Davydov, made relations with the government difficult. Yet Trubetskoi persisted. For him, the Society was an important experiment. On it depended proof of his contention that the students, given some freedom, would not abuse it.[59]

Trubetskoi went to St. Petersburg to prod the government into sanctioning the Society. He also obtained the co-operation of the student Academic Party at Moscow University. Academism — the attempt to limit the activity of the students within the sphere of the university rather than the involvement of students in overall political struggle for freedom in Russia — became an organized movement only when this view declined in popularity. The Academic Party of Moscow University was formally founded at the turn of the century. It was a loose structure composed of student groups which limited their immediate demands to the needs of the students and to the autonomy of the university, freedom of student organizations, and freedom of lecturing. The Party tried to publish bulletins and to prevent student demonstrations. Its members were often indiscriminately arrested with the politically radical students. Although the Party stressed the need to spread scholarship and enlightenment, its members disagreed on the actual degree of involvement in student affairs. Quite often they acted as if student demonstrations were the only way to make their views known — which was often the case. If it were not for the support of the "academics" by the faculty, the difference between them and the "politicals" would have been indistinguishable.[60]

Both Trubetskoi and the "academics" hoped the Society would not only provide a forum for study, but would also weaken the influence of the "politicals," as the activist radicals were known. In February of 1902, at a gathering of some faculty and students at his home, Trubetskoi formally proposed the establishment of the Society. It took some thirty meetings to draft its constitution and the by-laws.[61] But, as Trubetskoi wrote to his brother:

> The most important provision of the constitution of the Society is the unwritten one — no strikes and no disturbances shall have any effect on it. . . In these troubled times the scholarly functions of the Society shall not be suspended. That is the reason it should

become the focal point of academic freedom.[62]

Membership was open to all students and even the radicals who did not join were welcome at meetings.[63] By March 16, 1902, the day of the first formal meeting, the Society numbered over 800 members. In the first year of its existence it grew to some 1,000. Trubetskoi was chosen chairman, Novgorodtsev his associate and the student Anisimov the secretary.[64]

The formal inauguration of the Society took place on October 6, 1902, in the Physics Auditorium of Moscow University, where large illegal student meetings were usually held. The ceremonies were open to the whole student body, but Trubetskoi's fears of the radicals staging compromising demonstrations proved groundless.[65] In his opening remarks, Trubetskoi stressed that the Society should make university autonomy its goal. The student speakers, M. Adzhimov and V. V. Sher, stressed the progress made by the very establishment of the Society. Other speakers went further, and spoke of socialism, which caused Trubetskoi, who was extremely careful that nothing be said which might provide a pretext for dissolving the Society, to stop doodling and scribble in consternation to Anisimov: "Who could have permitted the use of this word? It will be in *Moskovskie vedomosti* tomorrow."[66] It was not.

At the time of the planning of the Society, Trubetskoi wrote to Evgenii that the Society would also launch a publishing program, doing some translations and publishing original works of such scholars as Miliukov, Kareev and Gredeskul, as well as good works written by students.[67] No mention of actual publication, however, appears in the available materials on the Society.

The Society was divided into autonomous sections, each headed by a faculty member. An elastic constitution

permitted the creation of new sections. We know of the
work of the philosophical section headed by Lopatin;
there were sections on history, social studies and an
historico-literary section. Some sections were divided
into special interest groups.68

The subjects discussed were similar to seminar
topics and to those handled by the Vinogradoff-Trubetskoi
study circle. Trubetskoi was particularly pleased when a
topic stimulated debate. General meetings, always well
prepared, were open to all students and drew quite a
number of guests.69 In the spring of 1903, Trubetskoi
asked Chicherin to accept election as honorary chairman
of the Society and in the fall of that year a delegation of
students visited him.70 The Society organized its own
library. It failed in its aim to encourage the founding of
similar societies in other universities.

The most spectacular activity of the Society was its
trip to Greece to study the ancient ruins. The idea was
Trubetskoi's; he spent the winter of 1902/1903 going
from ministry to ministry, first getting permission for
the trip, then raising the necessary funds. In his flamboyant manner, he wrote to Evgenii the arguments with
which he bombarded the ministries:

> fatherly care for the students; an attempt to imbue
> the love of the classics in them; the possible direct
> and indirect moral influences resulting from first-hand
> study of the ruins; proof of the vitality of the legal
> student organization; and, finally, patriotism, return
> from [Greece] through Bulgaria with much ado.

Despite a severe illness in the spring of 1903 and a
depression, Trubetskoi went on with the plans for the
excursion.72 By the beginning of the summer he finished
his arrangements, including cheap meals and a welcome at

each train stop.73 Because of the large number of applicants, students who took part in the trip were chosen by lot. Their preparations included the study of classics and a series of special lectures.74

One hundred and eighteen persons were in the group that left Moscow for Odessa by train; twenty-one joined them at Odessa. For the most part they were well received, except at Konotop, which was subdued after an anti-governmental demonstration. For housekeeping purposes the students were divided into sixteen groups, each headed by a student in charge of finances. All student officers were elected by the students during their train ride through the Empire.75 They spent some time in Odessa, then crossed the Black Sea to Turkey and later went to Greece. In both countries they were first given a hostile reception, being considered agents of the Tsar. Trubetskoi talked to local officials, helped by the fact that his younger brother Grigorii was in Russian diplomatic service in the Balkans and had friends there.76 Closer contacts with the local population helped abate the anti-Russian feeling, and the group was well treated in Greece, feted by archaeological societies and beset by reporters.

Trubetskoi was delighted by the conduct of the students. They were well-mannered, jovial and studious. They even participated in religious services aboard the ship and anticipated the needs of their faculty chaperons.77 The students, in turn, were enchanted with the excursion. For most of them it was their first trip outside Russia. Trubetskoi's arsenal of arguments had paid off. The students grew closer to the faculty, referred to Trubetskoi affectionately as *kniazen'ka* [the little prince], and became fond of the idiosyncrasies of the faculty.78 They returned home elated, only to have cold water poured over their heads by the heightened political tension

In 1904, Zenger was replaced by General V. G. Glazov, whose repressive measures precipitated new outbreaks. Some of the student demonstrations were actively supported by the workers.[85]

Members of the Society tried to prevent their friends from joining the demonstrations — but were arrested in the process. Section chairmen, friends of Trubetskoi, resigned in protest of such arbitrary arrests.[86] The return of Trubetskoi in the spring of 1904 did not save the Society. The government dissolved Trubetskoi's "social school" in the fall of that year as a reprisal for the political activity of some of the students. And during 1905 the universities served as havens for political activists.

CHAPTER 5

THE ENLIGHTENMENT OF TSAR AND SOCIETY

Politics did not constitute Trubetskoi's primary interest. Even during the hey-day of his infatuation with positivism, he did not draw political inferences from his creed. As an educated Russian, he was aware of and interested in various aspects of Russia's political life, but his active involvement in it developed slowly under the impact of philosophical and religious views, as well as family tradition, patriotism, polemics with the Slavophiles, activity in the university and first-hand experience with the limited policies of the government.

Trubetskoi had a dual political background. On the one hand, he shared the views of the typical liberal gentry of nineteenth century Russia. On the other hand, generations of the Trubetskois had served the Tsars in high administrative and military posts. Members of Trubetskoi's immediate family held high administrative positions during his lifetime, and he always had close contact with them. That gave him a glimpse into practical politics not readily available to the liberal gentry.

Love of Russia, both as a nation and as an Empire, was an important sentiment for the Trubetskois and it became an integral part of Sergei Trubetskoi's outlook. But unlike the nearsighted conservatives, the Trubetskois did not adhere to a stereotype patriotism of allegedly traditional rural Russia.

Finally, because differences in views were not suppressed within the family sphere, and clashes between the "progressives" and the "bureaucracy" had always spiked family conversations, Trubetskoi grew up appreciating tolerance for the views of others and relishing a good debate on political subjects.

Charades and home plays satirizing conditions in Russia were held frequently in the Trubetskoi home. As a young man, Trubetskoi took an active part in these amateur productions and often wrote texts. At times the criticism of the government was biting enough for his mother to exercise her censorship over them.[1] As he grew older, Trubetskoi continued writing satires worthy of the most typical representative of the politicized intelligentsia.

His satiric pieces, although biting and sharp, remained rather simple allegories on the exploitation of Russia by a greedy bureaucracy, on Russification, on the collusion of the police with the revolutionaries, and on censorship. Although his friends did not consider Trubetskoi's satires as serious works, Trubetskoi continued writing them, frequently with no hope of publication.[2] That a foremost philosopher whiled away his time and energy in writing second-rate fables is illustrative of the degree of frustration experienced by intellectuals in Russia.

Moreover, Trubetskoi's political interests were re-inforced by the fact that he was a Muscovite. The traditional Moscow nobleman criticized the bureaucracy which surrounded the Tsar and shut him off from the people. Muscovites saw the St. Petersburg bureaucracy as distant, aloof and cold, although, as the Trubetskois, many prominent Moscow families were related to the bureaucrats. Muscovites prided themselves on their informality and saw themselves as the link between the Tsar and the people, between the educated class and Russia's national tradition.[3] Trubetskoi's milieu was interested in reconciling morality with politics, and liberal Western-ism with Russia's traditions. Slavophilism left its imprint on Moscow in philosophical and patriotic constructs, and particularly, in the notion that motivated service on behalf of the people was a moral obligation of the edu-cated Russian.

Although, as will be seen later, Trubetskoi's frame of reference in political affairs was Western, he shared some traits with the early Slavophiles. His publicistic writing was sprinkled with evangelical references, his language and terminology were slightly old-fashioned and the concepts of morality and communality played an important role in his outlook. On the whole, however, by the time of Trubetskoi's activity, labels of Westerner and Slavophile in political life were imprecise and were used in a rather subjective fashion.[4]

The repentant gentry syndrome can be widened to include the repentant intellectual and the repentant student. Liberalism took over the characteristic of dedi-cation to the people from the populist tradition. It was well suited for the period of small deeds, as the period of the 1880's was known, in contrast to the grand terrorist campaign of the earlier decade.

When the famine of 1891, unparalleled in its in-tensity, hit the Russian Empire, many Muscovites, in-cluding Trubetskoi, quite naturally saw their duty to go to the villages to alleviate the needs of the famine-stricken peasants.[5] Trubetskoi, having begun teaching in Moscow University the year before the famine, commuted to the provincial city of Riazan', where his brother-in-law, G. I. Kristi, was the governor and where Trubetskoi helped organize and administer aid programs for the needy.

He was struck by the chronic poverty of Russia

and by the paucity of its human resources, "the stupidity and savageness facing us."[6] First-hand acquaintance with the Russian countryside completed his break with the quasi-Slavophilism of the Moscow tradition and led to the forceful development of liberal political convictions.[7]

Trubetskoi had valued Slavophilism "as the first attempt of formulating our social self-consciousness."[8] He had been impressed by the patriotism of the Slavophiles and by their attempts to restore society's respect for the integrated individual. He had even felt that Soloviev, in the course of formulating his theory of the ideal state, had been too harsh on the early Slavophiles.[9]

A close analysis of Slavophilism, however, convinced Trubetskoi of its inadequacies and prevented his identifying with the political views of such men as F. D. Samarin or even D. N. Shipov. The Slavophiles, Trubetskoi argued, had failed to realize the essence of Christianity, its dogmatic immutability, and had wrongly considered it a religion of social democratic structure and of humanitarian progress. The clash between international humanism and conservative nationalism, built into Slavophilism, could be resolved, Trubetskoi argued, only by accepting either Leontiev's non-Christian solution or Soloviev's non-existing one.[10] Trubetskoi argued that Russia had to accept the totality of Western culture because her own Byzantine heritage had proved inadequate for coping with Russian administrative and economic problems. The contradictions in Slavophilism came about when its proponents accepted certain elements of Western liberalism while failing to realize the integral unity of Western European civilization, particularly the relationship between intellectual progress and political conditions. Moreover, the patriotism of the Slavophiles had led them to consider as Russian all the characteristics of the Western European social and political system which they liked,

without accepting the whole structure of Western civilization.

The Slavophiles had urged the Tsar to meet with
the people, but at the same time they opposed Western
parliamentary institutions on the grounds that these were
inimical to Russia's interests. Trubetskoi, on the contrary, felt that the reasoning of the Slavophiles led precisely to a parliament.

> In what form should we visualize this intimate in-
> formal get-together [envisaged by the Slavophiles] to
> which the government and the people are to be invited
> for an all-encompassing mutual acquaintance? . . .
>
> Obviously, it would be impossible to call the whole
> "people" for a mass meeting, even if one were to limit
> it to Orthodox Great Russians. . . .
>
> Therefore, the people will have to be represented by
> representatives authorized by the people for that
> purpose. This will be, not to use the hated word, a
> national representative assembly, a type of *"sobor"*
> of which the liberal Slavophiles dreamed. But how
> will this *"sobor"* differ from a Western "gabbing
> place?"[11]

Trubetskoi hoped that Slavophilism could still offer a
positive political program without rejecting the Slavophiles' monarchic ideal, its concern for the people, its
Slavism, its arguments for the right of election and freedom of conscience. He worked on an article "which would
show my positive relationship to the Slavophiles," but
could never finish that article. With time, he found it
difficult to remain on friendly terms with the Slavophiles.
By 1904, the Samarins, who were related to the Tru-

betskois, barely spoke to them because of political disagreements.[12]

Trubetskoi's own career proved that once the Slavophiles realized the limitations of their ideology, little would be left to distinguish it from liberalism. In 1900 when Shipov proposed that the *zemstvos* petition the Tsar about a return to an idealized version of the autocracy cooperating with the people, Trubetskoi, who had been invited to participate in the deliberations, disagreed with Shipov. He argued that the very idea of a limited autocracy, propounded by Shipov, was contradictory. It led to the introduction of a constitutional system, therefore to a limitation of the autocracy.[13]

Intellectually, Trubetskoi was both courageous and consistent enough to realize his adherence to moderate constitutional liberalism. His indebtedness to Slavophilism in his philosophy did not stand in the way to his sharing the political views of his philosophical opponent, Boris Chicherin, the leading exponent of moderate liberalism in Russia.[14] Trubetskoi emerged at the start of his publicistic career in the mid-1890's as a rational moderate liberal, defending the rights of the individual but realizing the need for a strong government. He was also aware of justified irrationalism in personal and social life.

Trubetskoi decided to speak up in print when it became obvious that Nicholas II, who ascended the throne in 1894, was not only surrounding himself by reactionary advisers, but was being defended by people of dangerous political views. In an article occasioned by the mortal stampede of hundreds of Muscovites during the coronation ceremonies, Trubetskoi ridiculed the attempts of V. V. Rozanov to formulate a specifically Russian notion of politics and publicism:

Mr. Rozanov . . . has uttered a "new word" in our

literature: he has introduced symbolism into publicistic writing. He has done for publicistic writing the
same thing which the decadents have managed to
achieve in poetry by replacing thought and reason with
a gamut of feelings, which are expressed in strange,
newly created sounds, and unrelated, often totally
inconceivable combinations of words and images. . . .
With all of that, Mr. Rozanov has tried to give his
symbolism a national character, imitating the fools-
for-God and . . . seeing in their [babble] examples of
purely Russian publicism, uncontaminated with that
of the West, which is decaying in its "rationalism."

[His] article is written in a psychic gamut which is
totally incomprehensible to us, and that is probably
why we could not understand it at all. . . . At times it
seemed as if Mr. Rozanov simply spoke with "bell-
clappers" and, forgetting the precepts of the Apostle,
likened himself unto a trumpet giving out "an inde-
finable sound."[15]

In his philosophy, Trubetskoi tried to supply a
workable and acceptable statement on the purpose of life
which could serve the same intellectual and emotional
function as ideologies did, but which would not be subject
to ideological limitations. By his activity in the Moscow
philosophical group and in the university he tried to spread
these views among Russians. But even in so limited a
forum the repressive force of the government could be
felt. This was poignantly illustrated by Trubetskoi in a
speech in the memory of Grot:

Alas, we still cannot fulfill your request [of a discussion on the merits of eternity vs. mortality] . . . .
As long as our opponents cannot express their views
with the same freedom as we, . . . there can be no talk

of such a contest. . . . Since you died, immortality
along with other high and pure ideals still continues
to enjoy the unwanted and embarrassing privilege of
the "custody" of the Pharisees. . . . Russian philosophical thought continues to be subject to the control
of the sanitary police. . . . We still try to can ideals
and . . . to pickle truth.[16]

Trubetskoi's philosophical interests, as well as his
involvement in university affairs, led him to write articles
on contemporary subjects, at times signing them with his
own name but often using rather transparent pseudonyms.
He wrote on topics which interested him personally, for
example, the student question, as well as on any subjects
permitted by the censorship which could serve as a spring-
board for his own views. He wrote with an eye to the
censor, limiting his criticism to what could be published,
or not publishing at all. For instance, he prefaced an article
on Dreyfus, in which the French generals stand for Russian
bureaucrats, with the comment that since the topics on
which Russians could write were limited, he might as well
write on the Dreyfus case.[17]

Yet neither the polemics with the Slavophiles, nor
the famine, which had preceded these polemics, made
Trubetskoi identify himself with the political intelligentsia.
As a youth, he had criticized the intelligentsia for being
"philistine," i.e., interested in its own narrow, personal
world.[18] He continued to consider it shallow and to be
wary of it. Trubetskoi and his milieu, the intellectuals of
Moscow, still considered themselves different from the
so-called positivist intelligentsia, as can be seen from the
following incident. Miliukov had delivered a lecture on
the dissolution of the Slavophile ideology in which he
tried to prove that "Slavophilism was dead and could never
arise from the dead." At the urging of Grot and Soloviev,

this lecture was published in *Voprosy Filosofii i Psikho-logii*.19

In his work Miliukov discussed the dissolution of Slavophilism into the reactionary (Leontiev) and the liberal (Soloviev) trends. Soloviev took Miliukov to task:

> The author of *Metaphysics in Ancient Greece* [Tru-betskoi] had a right to call Leontiev "a disillusioned Slavophile," but the author of *Russia under Peter the Great* [Miliukov] cannot have this right. Leontiev had never been an enraptured Slavophile.20

Miliukov was naturally incensed at this double standard. He did not see why Soloviev "limited the horizon of study of the positivists to facts and kept relationships to his own group."21 The double standard, however, remained, at least in the minds of the Moscow intellectuals, and prevented their contact with the political intelligentsia.

There were several reasons for this. Lack of contact was certainly one of them.22 Another was the failure of the radical intelligentsia to stress, and often even to realize, their patriotism. The religious and philosophical interests of Trubetskoi also hampered his contacts with the intelligentsia, which still often identified religion with reaction. Nor did Trubetskoi use the vocabularly of the intelligentsia. His style of writing was often old-fashioned and cumbersome. He had a penchant for archaic expressions and Biblical references. He did not flinch from using a word which was taboo to all progressives — *kra-mola* — meaning sedition, revolt, or political crime — to characterize some of the disturbances in Russia. He continued to use the term even after coming closer to the liberals in 1905, for as much as his basic political goals were similar to the liberals', he could not identify himself with them until events forced him into closer co-operation with such alleged radicals as Petrunkevich.[23]

Another important factor in this respect was Trubetskoi's refusal to admit the primacy of political considerations. He belittled attempts at analyzing the crisis in Russia at the turn of the century solely in terms of the absence of political freedom. Yet he himself, after examining the underlying causes of the discontent, saw the importance of political freedom and the need for an organized, constitutional system.

For Trubetskoi, the crisis in Russia, as indeed in Western Europe, was first and foremost a spiritual one. He found the popularity of Chekhov and Gorkii indicative of a deep moral malaise of modern man. This condition was due not to any limitations on liberty, but to the loss of the purpose of life.[24] The emptiness, Trubetskoi reasoned, was felt most acutely by the masses, since the educated could find a surrogate for the lost religion in a political ideology, while the masses could not. Trubetskoi criticized Russian society just as he criticized its government. "Society," in Russia, as in Eastern Europe in general, was a vague term. It connoted the people, usually the articulate segment, as contrasted with the government. Work with society, in an organized or private fashion, was referred to as "social" or "public work" — *obshchestvennaia deiatel'nost'* — and those who did it were referred to as "social workers." The term could probably be also translated as "civic work," but that would come too close to governmental functions. The social worker worked with the people, prompted only by a sense of duty and for no or very nominal compensation. Very often this type of work was not organized, although such people as teachers, *zemstvo* staff, and doctors were considered social workers, or workers on behalf of society. This society, Trubetskoi feared, was falling under the influence of the narrow-minded intelligentsia. Trubetskoi was

particularly perturbed by the prevalence of narrow ideological views which precluded independent thinking and
by "the spontaneous attraction to illiteracy and lack of
knowledge which is growing in our society not by days,
but by minutes, and which appears as a dangerous fore-
runner of impending barbarism."[25] But he never considered himself alienated from Russian society, much as
he criticized it for its shallowness, its willingness to espouse ideologies, and its failure to appreciate the comforts
of religion.

Naturally, for Trubetskoi the most obvious source
of faith for the individual would be the Russian Orthodox
Church, understood in its fullness and in its personal
freedom. This conception of Orthodoxy brought Trubetskoi, as we have seen, into a direct conflict with the
Church and with the government.

For a believer, the encroachments of the government on matters of conscience, particularly when the
government acted as the agent of the true universal church,
was painful. Publicly he criticized the Russian government
for its policies of religious intolerance; in private he often
gave vent to his indignation, saying that the autocracy
"changed the Liturgy into a royal service," and destroyed
the Orthodox faith.[26] He argued for religious toleration
in Russia under the transparent guise of condemning the
Vatican.[27] By the winter of 1904, which he spent in
Dresden, he could not mince words:

> Not the Church, but the department of the police
> [is one of the] foundations of the state and society
> in contemporary Russia. . . . The Orthodox Church
> becomes the church of bureaucratic caesaro-papism.[28]

But by refusing to publish this scathing attack, he differentiated himself from the intelligentsia, which used illegal

means to make its views known.

Trubetskoi saw his role as a double one. He had to prod and enlighten Russia's conservative groups and through them, the Tsar, on the necessity of fashioning Russia into a modern constitutional state. He also had to check the growing popularity of revolutionary trends which to him presaged a bloody upheaval. Unlike the intelligentsia, Trubetskoi was afraid that social unrest of any kind would lead to a violent revolution. He argued for reforms not for the sake of change, or even for the welfare of the people, but to strengthen the government. In an article in *Sanktpeterburgskia vedomosti* in 1899, Trubetskoi defended the position that the needs of the state necessitated the active participation of society in its affairs.

> Contemporary government, whatever its political system, needs a highly developed society to cope with the increasingly complex tasks of cultured life. In our days a purely spontaneous patriotism is not enough. . . . Individual enlightened functionaries . . . and workers [are also inadequate]. What we need is an enlightened, developed society, which is essential to contemporary government. Where this need is not adequately fulfilled, the government inevitably declines.[29]

He argued that Russian society was loyal to the Tsar and that the Tsar should entrust it with the administration of the country. The bureaucracy, on the contrary, was mismanaging the state, misappropriating funds and leading Russia to ruin. It had cut off the Throne from the people and brought the nation to ruin.[30] St. Petersburg, the heart of the bureaucracy, revolted Trubetskoi. In private he referred to Delianov, at one time minister of

education, and to Pobedonostsev, the powerful procurator
of the Synod, as "riff-raff," and to St. Petersburg as "a
pigsty of lies, embezzlement, and slavery" which filled
him with "moral nausea."[31]

In an attempt to focus the Tsar's attention on the
deplorable conditions in Russia, Trubetskoi argued that
the bureaucracy had dislodged the Tsar as the ruler of
Russia and made him blind to the real functions of central
authority, "as in ancient Egypt where Pharaohs sacrificed
to their own images and instead of being kings became the
priests of autocracy."[32] It was the bureaucracy and its
police regime, which Trubetskoi saw daily at Moscow
University and in the person of the censor, which even
destroyed autocracy:

> Not only does autocracy not exist in Russia, but it
> cannot exist. It exists only nominally and is the
> greatest delusion. . . . It becomes the object of a false
> faith, of an actual cult, as in ancient Egypt where the
> Pharaohs sacrificed to their own images and instead of
> being kings became the priests of autocracy. In actual-
> ity, however, this whole cult, this whole mythology
> conceals a hoax — autocracy . . . is but a *form of
> bureaucratic rule, guaranteeing impunity, irresponsi-
> bility, and unlimited arbitrariness for the partakers of
> the enterprise.* . . .
>
> Autocracy is a large charter of freedoms of the ir-
> responsible and uncontrollable bureaucracy. . . . There
> exists autocracy of the police, of the *zemstvo nachal-
> niki*, of governors, . . . and even of ministers.[33]

But much as he would heap scorn upon official St.
Petersburg, he was closer to it than were many of the
bureaucrats. He was aware of the existence, within the

bureaucracy, of men who were favorably inclined to the idea of moderate reform. Members of Trubetskoi's own family — father, brothers-in-law, close uncles — had high positions within the administrative structure of the government. He was also close to his distant relatives, A. D. Obolenskii, who in 1905 succeeded Pobedonostsev as the Over-Procurator of the Synod,[34] and to A. A. Lopukhin, who headed the Department of the Police from 1902 to 1907.[35] Trubetskoi met them often, corresponded with them, discussed views and policy, and at times depended upon them for news. Because of his acquaintance with some of the liberal bureaucrats, he was willing to credit the government with more good will than the political intelligentsia ever could; he was also willing to co-operate with the government and to be quite flexible in his relations with it. These were precisely the tendencies in Trubetskoi which jarred his colleagues of the political intelligentsia. Yet it was for these reasons that he could act as a mediator between the state and the representatives of society in 1905.

Trubetskoi considered false the conservatism which defended unlimited bureaucratic power. It was even more dangerous than bureaucratic caprice itself.[36] Reactionary policies, he argued, created an atmosphere conducive to the growth of revolutionary activity which in its crudeness, its lack of discipline, and of constructive thought was even more revolting than the despotism which bore it.

> In this social rottenness there sprang up and blossomed Russian radicalism, a by-product of political servitude and police despotism. It shows clearly the other side of reaction. It is a suitable child of the age, uneducated, crude, and perhaps even more anti-cultural than the despotism which bore it. . . It naturally deteriorates into revolutionary anarchy and, con-

tinuing the activities of the fathers, it is capable only
of serving sedition and destruction. A glance at the
present condition of Russian society proves that
nowhere else is there found anything else more conducive to the growth of this product of social rotten-
ness than in our midst. . . . In the damp atmosphere
where neither enlightened, essentially defensive liberalism, nor true patriotism, nor wise conservatism can
flourish, there, without air or light, this destructive
mold grows and multiplies.[37]

Trubetskoi argued that not only the limited, local
self-government, the *zemstvo*, but all the institutions
which were attributes of a modern state, such as local and
municipal self-administration, trial by jury, and the universities themselves, were incompatible with bureaucratic
absolutism. The failure of a clear cut decision either for
or against bureaucratic absolutism resulted in the "Sis-
yphus-like labors of Russian administration and law-
making."[38] The only way Russia could have an effective
government and survive as a great power would be by
giving up the ghost of autocracy. Palliative measures,
temporary expedients, and piecemeal reforms would be of
no use. The central issue of political reform would have
to be tackled — the unity of the Tsar and the people
manifested by the trust shown by the government to the
society in sharing with it some of its powers.
Trubetskoi was at pains to demonstrate that reform,
even a vigorous pursuit of reform, was a tradition for
Russian tsars. He thus tried to wrest patriotism from
those who opposed reform as being contrary to Russian
traditions:

We do not break with the historical past. . . . We do
not rise against the Church when we want its emanci-

pation from the custody of the pharasees who buried the living word. . . . We do not raise our hands against the Throne when we want it to be upheld not by general lawlessness and the caprice of the *oprichniki* but by the lawful order [prevailing in the state] and by the love of the subjects [of their Tsar] . . . . Tsarist authority itself should culminate as the final stage in the organization of the country; should grant it freedom and law, for without these there can be no power, no order, no enlightenment, no internal or external peace. [Reform] will not weaken but immeasurably strengthen power [in the state] .39

In 1904 he argued that the first step of reform was a representative assembly, elected by individual subjects, not on the basis of class suffrage. The assembly should not be limited to ethnic Russians, for the Tsar should realize that Russia was more than a national kingdom, that it was an "Empire, i.e., a world government capable of uniting nations under its peaceful reign."40 Trubetskoi considered the persecution of minorities not only morally wrong, but also politically dangerous. He was particularly offended by the policies of Russification in Finland. In the fall of 1899 he urged Chicherin to use his authority and write an article condemning the Russification of Finland; a few years earlier Trubetskoi had written, but did not publish, a satire ridiculing Russification carried out by neophyte Russians of non-Russian origin who might even be connected with the revolutionary movement.41

Trubetskoi supported a representative assembly for practical considerations: only a representative assembly could inform the Tsar adequately of the needs of the people. The failure to convene such a body could result in ruin for Tsar and Russia.42 The possibility of an assembly

being called and then dispersed also occurred to Trubetskoi. He felt that such action would prove disastrous.
Calling on the authority of Chicherin,[43] Trubetskoi
warned that

> to call the people together without giving them rights
> would mean inviting trouble, for the representative
> assembly in itself is a political force which could not
> remain without rights.[44]

By the summer of 1905 a new argument had occurred to
him for granting genuine powers to the assembly: to
prevent it from engaging in flowery irresponsible rhetoric
which characterized so many impotent gatherings in
Russia.[45] The representative assembly should work out
all the particulars of reform in Russia. As a palliative
temporary measure, *zemstvo* representatives could be
called upon to deliberate on the projected reform, but
neither the discussions nor the assembly should be limited
to the *zemstvos*.

He never clarified to himself his views on power
politics. With Soloviev, he maintained that the same
ethical norms which guide personal lives ought to be valid
in international affairs, yet his notion of the historical
tasks of Russia and the scope of its international affairs
would seem to necessitate the full use of power, rather
than considerations of morality.

A major reason Trubetskoi gave for the necessity of
reforms was that of foreign policy, which should be
worthy of a great state. Its primary aim should not be
annexation, but it should not shun annexations beneficial
to the state. Trubetskoi feared the possible outbreak of a
European war and the danger it presented to an unre-
formed and therefore a weak Russia.[46] He shared the
predilections of central European conservatives in his views

on diplomacy. A note of hostility to England, for her imperialist tendencies and anti-Russian policies was a constant factor in Trubetskoi's views on foreign policy. He considered England, particularly her policy of frustrating German interests in Africa and the Far East, as the threat to peace. His suggestion for peace in Europe was an alliance of Russia, Germany, and France as the only means of ensuring the peaceful progress of the three countries by freeing them from unnecessary and costly militarism.

During a trip to Greece, Trubetskoi, despite the fact that he had buried his adolescent dreams of the expansion of the Russian Empire into the Balkans, realized that Russia had a role to play in the Balkan countries. He justified that role not so much by considerations of power, as by the fact that Russia was idealized by the Balkan nations. The attraction of Russia for the Balkan states could justify Russia's involvement in the area without precipitating an international crisis.[47]

A strong Russia would counteract the national awakening in the Far East. Trubetskoi worried about what would happen when China would modernize and turn against Europe. In language reminiscent of the trite discussions on the Russian "soul," Trubetskoi wrote that "the yellow soul is more inscrutable to us than any other foreign soul."[48] Unless China were divided, the West would be forced to increasing militarism, which, because of the greater number of Chinese, would not protect the West at all, but would rather contribute towards its disintegration. He was obsessed by the population growth of the Chinese, he had nightmares of the yellow deluge engulfing Russia, and he worried, in 1903, about the strength of the Russian fleet in the Far East.[49]

When the Russo-Japanese War broke out, Trubetskoi, in a very panicky article in *Sanktpeterburgskia vedomosti*, published on January 24, 1904, under the title

"Russia at the Crossroads,"[50] explained that Japan was the first wave of the Mongol force. Russia should move in forcefully despite the opposition of England, for not only was Russia herself threatened by Asia, but Russia had to defend all of Europe. The article was probably one of the best known of Trubetskoi's articles in his lifetime. As the war continued Trubetskoi argued that Russia must reform herself or succumb to the yellow danger, the new "hordes of Mongols, armed by modern European technology."[51]

Trubetskoi's interest in foreign affairs was stimulated by the fact that the topic was less subject to censorship than domestic issues. His point was that Russia could hardly play a role commensurate with her historical mission unless she shook off her bureaucratic crust and enacted social reforms.

Trubetskoi also argued that internal reform would strengthen Russia's finances. He predicted that the increased cultivation of wheat in the world would reduce the demand for Russian wheat. An industrialized Russia would then be a necessity. He wrote some letters to his brother discussing aspects of Russia's finances, particularly the tariff, and complained that lack of time prevented him from studying economic problems adequately. The relationship of the industrialization of Asia to European fiscal stability and the silver standard intrigued him.[52] In 1905 he lashed out at the secrecy surrounding the financial dealings of the State as a contributing factor to the lack of confidence in the ruble both at home and abroad.[53]

Trubetskoi's interests and academic bias were very evident in his discussion of policies of social welfare. He felt that Russia should assume responsibility for the welfare of its citizens, but this was also dependent upon political reform.[54] He never could work out an adequate welfare program, although his discussion of the peasant and labor problems demonstrated a grasp of the difficulties.

Trubetskoi realized that the agrarian and the labor questions in Russia were closely related to Russia's poverty. But again, he returned to his original thesis that Russia's backwardness could be overcome only by political reform. Hence, the social problem was secondary to the political one.

Trubetskoi accused the government of failing the peasant in all respects since 1861. While the *zemstvos* had criticized the inequitable agrarian and fiscal conditions in Russia as early as 1862, the government failed to realize them even in 1905. The *Ukaz* of May 6, 1905, on the reform of the ministry of agriculture, showed that "the bureaucratic regime was incapable of solving the agrarian problem."[55] Problems of land shortage, small credit, rent legislation and of the system of taxation had not even been tackled, although they demanded immediate attention, before political reorganization.

Trubetskoi defended private property, yet he realized that the propertied classes and the government would have to sacrifice their interests not only for reasons of social justice but of tranquility as well. How this was to be done he did not know. He simply urged a full-scale study of the problems and the immediate amelioration of the most pressing wants of the peasantry.

Trubetskoi also urged a far-reaching program of labor legislation. He suggested a system of social security by means of governmental insurance, disability, old age and illness pensions, as well as a government-sponsored health insurance. He suggested an expansion of the system of factory inspectorate and its removal from bureaucratic control. He proposed the compulsory education of the children of workers at the cost of the employers.[56]

But the passage of any social legislation was dependent first and foremost on political reform, and that in turn depended upon the willingness of the Tsar to accept

reform. Trubetskoi had begun his campaign for the enlightenment of the Tsar by writing on the wretched state
of Russian journalism. He pleaded for change.

> I am not speaking of a free press (how can one speak
> of freedom!), but of a press which would be inde-
> pendent enough that its rights and duties would not
> only be the *rights and duties of silence*.[57]

He came back to this issue time and time again, for
it was integrally connected with his philosophical outlook.
He felt that the people would strive for the good once it
was known. The power of reason, the power of the rational word as manifested in the responsible press was, for
Trubetskoi, one of the most important prerequisites of a
developed state, for without a free press society itself
could not develop and thus the state would be stunted.
The press was also a condition for law-abiding order in
society.[58] He used strong language and, in order to pass
the censor, vague references to characterize the state of
Russian publications where

> only the wild beast of the desert may discuss im-
> portant subjects . . . and publicists who preserved their
> human likeness may only discuss the Dreyfus affair,
> the intrigues of Albion, the foreign policy and the
> general peace, as well as selected topics of economics
> and trade. . . .
>
> Katkov had said that the constitution of a Russian
> consists of the right and duty to scream "thief," and
> you want to deprive us even of this right.[59]

The Russian publicist-bureaucrats should, argued
Trubetskoi, take a broader view of things and realize "that

a strong government does not fear the printed expression of opinion, even where it does not share it."[60] The argument that a free press was subject to all sorts of abuses was premature in Russia, while the other argument often mustered against a free press, that much organization was necessary to have a good press, was nonsensical.[61] In 1904 Trubetskoi declined an offer of the editorship of *Sanktpeterburgskiia vedomosti* made by A. D. Obolenskii. The editor, A. A. Stolypin, a relative of Peter Stolypin, the later Prime Minister, was under pressure from Plehve to resign. The job brought a substantial salary which Trubetskoi could well have used. But Trubetskoi realized he would not be able to work within the confines of the existing censorship:

> Much as I would enjoy the opportunity of talking with the Russian citizens by means of my own organ, I unfortunately do not see any possibility of talking with them about anything but the usefulness of glass, while at times the actual breaking of glassware is less reprehensible than such chatter.[62]

Censorship, as we have seen, prevented Trubetskoi from publishing articles on topics which really interested him — local administration, Finland, Kishinev, even Mechnikov's book, and controversies dealing with Church history. In a pathetic satire, Trubetskoi likened censorship to a governess who refused to let go of her charges. The children, meanwhile, had learned to read from Marx under her nose. He returned to the issue of censorship in his letters and in a satire of 1905 which was published only posthumously.[63] It was the censor who stood between Trubetskoi and the Tsar (and edited what the Tsar said to Trubetskoi) and between Trubetskoi and Russia. For Trubetskoi, the censor personified the stupidity of the

St. Petersburg bureaucracy.

Trubetskoi's tremendous concern for the individual's freedom from ideological tyrannies was illustrated by an incident at the Pedagogical Society in March, 1905. The Society drafted a set of principles which were to be considered morally binding on all members. A minority of twenty members, among them Trubetskoi, disagreed not so much with the principles accepted, as with the notion of a group formulating any principles on issues which should remain within the realm of individual conscience. Trubetskoi drafted a memorandum to that effect and resigned from the Society, much as he abhorred the exploitation of the affair by the conservatives. The result was the dissolution of the Society. Yet Trubetskoi felt he had no choice but to sever himself from a group which continued, in his words in a letter to the editor of *Russkiia vedomosti*, to "reserve the right to institute certain moral norms." The letter was not published for fear it would aid the conservatives.[64]

Trubetskoi steadfastly refused to subscribe to a political ideology or to draw up a firm hierarchy of enemies. Repelled as he was by the tyranny of the bureaucracy and by the reactionary measures of the government, he nevertheless refused to view them as implacable enemies of reform. He was repelled by all tyranny, and he feared the masses, for he saw in them a threat to the stability of Russia.

> The old order has as yet not received any replacement, and the cornerstone of the new order has not yet been placed. The old order is disintegrating quickly and helplessly before our very eyes, and in its place anarchy, which is acquiring dangerous proportions, moves in both from above and below. Yesterday we were told about revolutionaries calling the national

masses to looting and arson; today the defenders of
"tradition," the supporters of reaction, show their
true faces by preaching civil war, lynch-law, and mass
beatings of the intelligentsia. . . .

We can rejoice at the breakdown of the old order, at
its bankruptcy, but we should not rejoice at the
collapse of order in the country, and yet this is precisely what is happening openly and quickly.[65]

In 1904, when the liberals greeted revolutionary
outbreaks as a prelude to political reform, Trubetskoi
warned of the revolutionary violence destroying the hopes
of reform. He maintained that that had already happened
in Russia's past:

It is no secret to anyone: the hideous crime of
March 1 [1881, the assassination of Alexander II]
prevented the [otherwise] inevitable political reform
of our days.[66]

He condemned the views of the radicals, and the policies
justified by these views, as being immoral and crude.

Trubetskoi's liberalism differed from that of the
later liberal parties in the degree of his moderation, in his
gradualism, in his conviction of the need to co-operate
rather than fight with the government, and in his willingness to accept and to use even the modest reforms of the
government. He also refused to subscribe to certain ideological preconceptions generally connected with liberalism
in Russia. His stress on legality and his unwillingness to
transgress the bounds of permitted political activity
precluded any identification with the politically active
liberals before 1904 and 1905.

Except for the philosophical and academic community, there was no specific group to which Trubetskoi really belonged. He differentiated himself from the political intelligentsia; he did not identify himself fully with the government, but he did not share the anti-statist views of the apolitical Russians. He stressed the need for law, for an established legal order and for the use of lawful, moderate means in trying to achieve the political aims. He insisted that reform would benefit Russia, strengthen its government, and would be true to its historical traditions. He feared the collapse of authority. He wanted to modernize, not destroy, the central governmental structure.

Trubetskoi envisaged a reformed Russia as somewhat similar to the German Empire. What appealed to him most in that country was its internal order, its international strength, the stability of its government and the freedom of expression of its citizens. Trubetskoi was mostly familiar with the German academic community, its academic freedom, and its high intellectual achievements. He liked Germany's social legislation also. He used Germany and Japan as proof of his contention that modernizing reforms strengthened states.

He characterized himself "not only as a faithful son of my motherland, but also as a loyal subject of the Throne and a convinced supporter of Tsarist power in Russia."[67] As such, he argued that lasting reform in Russia could emanate only from the Tsar.

> Whether we like it or not, that is the case, and those relatively small groups of radicals who dream of "liberation" of Russia by means of revolutionary agitation, do not realize fully the strength of the historical foundations of governmental power and the spontaneous force of the loyal historical instinct which united and continues to unite Russia around the

Throne as the only Russian banner. That is the reason our radicalism clashes with patriotism of the Russians, who cannot renounce the covenant with Russia's past without renouncing themselves.[68]

The quotation is taken from the article which remained unpublished because of censorship.

Trubetskoi explained the popularity of decadence and anarchism, which he saw as dangerous signals of an impending, but not necessarily inevitable, catastrophe, as a surrogate for the unfulfilled desire for asceticism in the modern man. But he was certain that "neither communism nor militarism . . . would ever become ideals of rational humanity."[69] Humanity, particularly Russia, could be saved from catastrophe by healthy social organization. His own activity would contribute to this task.

Within the framework of the 1890's, Trubetskoi defended society, individual freedom and the right of free speech. By 1902 he was discussing "the awakening of Russian society from its twenty-year slumber" to face the same old problems which had simply grown more acute.[70] The lack of any open organizations capable of aiding the government in instituting the necessary reforms exacerbated the situation.[71] But Trubetskoi found the illegal organization of Russian liberals, "The Union of Liberation," founded in 1903, and its journal, *Osvobozh-denie*, too radical, if not in its aims then in the means employed by the group. He had always argued against any illegality and felt that most restrictions could some-how be either modified or by-passed.[72]

In 1904, and even as late as the first months of 1905, Trubetskoi was unwilling to identify himself with Struve and *Osvobozhdenie*, the core of the later Kadet Party. His personal aversion to the politicized *intelligent*, of the type of Miliukov, contributed to his hesitancy in joining the group. Trubetskoi first identified himself with "the Party to which I have the honor of belonging," presumably the *zemstvo*-constitutionalists, in a speech to the Moscow University students in September, 1905.[73]

Trubetskoi's political ideal was slightly more conservative than that of the liberal *zemtsy* and of the later Kadets. The difference was quite vague; it can be illustrated better by attitudes than by actual political views. Trubetskoi, for instance, admired the German State; Petrunkevich, a liberal *zemets*, used the adjective "Germanic" to deride the most hated qualities of the Romanov dynasty and of the Russian bureaucracy.

On the whole it was the question of means rather than of ends which differentiated Trubetskoi from the political intelligentsia of liberal persuasions. Trubetskoi thought that the Tsar could be convinced to pursue a policy of reform, while the intelligentsia maintained that the Tsar would have to be prodded into it by a show of force on the part of society.

Trubetskoi differed with the liberals on the assessment of forces in Russia. He considered moderate forces in the country weak and was convinced that reforms were possible only with the support of the Tsar. The radical intelligentsia, on the contrary, saw society as being capable of controlling revolutionary excesses.

Yet, as peaceful measures brought few results, Trubetskoi became more and more outspoken in his criticism of the government. The censoring of his own articles, particularly his *"Na rubezhe,"* pushed him into even more open opposition. He saw Russia threatened. "The time has come when that which had been demanded in the name of the ideals of justice and freedom must now be demanded in the name of direct and self-evident needs of the preservation of order and social security."[74] This realization was crucial for Trubetskoi's career; it justified to him his co-operation with the politically oriented liberals. For what was at stake were not political theories or ideological predilections, but the greatness of Russia, its very existence as a major power, the viability of the state and the preservation of an educated, cultured and moderate society.

His language reflected his impatience with the government. The defeats inflicted upon Russia by the Japanese made the weaknesses of the Tsarist administration blindingly glaring. The explanations of the government were inadequate.

> We were told that we really did not have any concrete interests in Manchuria worth struggling for and dying. But we do have an interest here, in Russia — our very Russia, our Motherland, for which we here can and should be ready to die to a man, to free it from this shameful yoke, to re-establish its greatness and power and to give her that system without which she will be only a corpse. We cannot, we should not, we will not live as we have lived heretofore. Now all procrastination in the calling of the national representatives would be not a mistake, but a crime.[75]

By 1905, Trubetskoi was speaking of the liberation of Russia.[76] He, the scholar who had protested against any calls to society which might be considered in any way inflammatory, turned to public opinion to justify himself when his actions were frustrated by the government.[77] Although he refrained from taking measures to publicize his plight, he was by that time a political figure.

CHAPTER 6

TSAR AND SOCIETY: 1905

Briefly and spectacularly Trubetskoi emerged in 1905 as a symbol of hope for a reformed Russia and a political link between the Throne and the Russian people. This was due in equal measure to the stormy events of 1904 and 1905 and to Trubetskoi's person — his heritage, his personality, his moderation, his patriotism. He was in Dresden when the Russo-Japanese War broke out. Its disastrous course convinced him that Russia could survive only if her government agreed to reforms. He came home that spring, spurred on by hope and anger, fighting severe fits of depression and throwing himself into public activity.[1]

The police regime had always irked him. In 1904, he lashed out against "wretches of the type of Plehve" under whom the police could not even keep order.[2] The more critical the situation at the front became, the more Trubetskoi was convinced that "the [same] irrational policies of the government [which] drew us into the war" made haste in reform imperative.[3]

A quarter of a century of organized, systematic provocation, of systematic derision of Russian society has left its mark. . . . The notion of the state as a lawful union not only disappears but is systematically rejected; political unity is replaced by police unity, and the Russian Tsar becomes . . . a chief of gendarmes of the Empire. Moral and legal ties are shaken . . . [what] remains is a spontaneous, deeply disorganized mass, bereft of all lawful norms and of civic rights, left completely to the mercy of internal anarchy and police arbitrariness, repressed, exploited, abused, constantly hungry, and powerless, [yet] surrounded by limitless natural resources.

It became a matter of reform or revolution:

There is no other choice — either lawful order or unlimited *zhandarmocracy*, with its inevitable consequences, with the anarchy to which it leads.[4]

The sense of urgency spurred Trubetskoi to increase the pace of his publicistic articles, and that in turn gave him a greater national exposure. Trubetskoi considered his popularity as a reflection of the popularity of his views.[5] To him it signified that society was willing to co-operate with the government to institute the necessary reforms to prevent a revolution. The policies of the liberal intelligentsia, he maintained, lacked a constructive side and were based, wrongly, on criticizing the government. The revolutionaries, on the other hand, wanted to exacerbate legitimate unrest for their own purposes. Society was thus left without leadership.[6]

Trubetskoi felt it was his duty to help organize the reform-minded moderates. That is why he agreed to co-operate with the *zemstvos*, the limited local organizations established in the 1860's which came to stand for community interests. Trubetskoi's whole plan depended on the co-operation of the government and society. He knew that there were enough moderates within society who were willing to work with the government, provided the regime evidenced a genuine interest in reform. What was needed now was for the Tsar to identify his cause with that of society, with the program of reform.7

Stimulated by patriotism, Trubetskoi asked for a joint effort by all Russians in the task of peaceful reform of the Empire. He felt that criticism alone was not enough.

> A few months ago people spoke of the defeats as being suffered by others, not by us. Are then we not Russia? Is not the army Russian? And finally the very bureaucracy, the very system of government which [we] all condemn, is it wholly independent of us? And if the government is responsible [for our defeats], does that remove the stigma of our shame, of our guilt, of our sorrow, of our debt and our responsibility?8

Trubetskoi felt that the times not only justified political involvement, but demanded it. The welfare of Russia, threatened equally by reaction and revolution, required the direct political involvement which he had previously criticized in the intelligentsia. Trubetskoi became willing to co-operate with anyone who vaguely shared his views. Moreover, he became willing to play an active role as a moderating factor in the attempt to bring together the government and society.

During 1904 and 1905 Trubetskoi directed his activity toward the university with its intensified struggle for autonomy, toward publicistic work, including an attempt to edit his own newspaper, and toward, what proved to be most spectacular, involvement in the *zemstvo*.

Trubetskoi was considered a member of the *Beseda*, an informal discussion group organized in Moscow by the Princes Petr and Pavel Dolgorukov which was composed largely of *zemstvo* members.9 Most of his friends, and particularly his brother Evgenii, with whom he discussed political matters most openly, were active in the *zemstvo* and in the unofficial group of *zemstvo* constitutionalists which met at the home of Iu. A. Novosiltsev. Trubetskoi frequently attended these meetings. Whether he realized, in 1904, that it was manipulated by *Osvobozhdenie* is not clear, since he refused to be drawn into an open relationship with Struve's group until the very end of 1904, or even early 1905.[10]

It seems that such an open commitment of Trubetskoi to the liberals was undesirable from the standpoint of the liberals themselves. When they chose him to act as a spokesman for the *zemstvo*, or to draft its various petitions or memoranda, they needed the type of man Trubetskoi personified — a moderate liberal with enlightened views, a scion of an old noble family who was an outspoken foe of any class distinctions, a serious scholar untainted by political squabbles, a member of a prominent family with ties to official St. Petersburg, and above all, a man who realized the gravity of the situation. His support of the war and criticism of revolutionary activity could make him acceptable to the Tsar and would be more influential in persuading the Tsar to modify his policies toward the *zemstvo*.[11] He emerged into the limelight as a man acceptable to both the government and the *zemstvo* to present, unofficially, the views of the November, 1904, *zemstvo* congress. His moderation and previous political non-involvement was an asset for the group. It conveyed the impression of its own political and social moderation.

The *zemstvos* had periodically tried to co-ordinate their activity, or even to establish a central organization for that purpose. Often, they tried to hold meetings of several *zemstvos*. After 1895 attempts were made to hold congresses of the *zemstvos*.[12] In the eyes of the government this *zemstvo* activity teetered on the verge of illegality. Therefore, although the *zemtsy* supported the participation of Russia in the Russo-Japanese War, the Minister of Interior, Plehve, forbade all non-authorized *zemstvo* meetings. He also refused to confirm the re-election of D. N. Shipov, the long-time board chairman of the Moscow *zemstvo* who, although politically rather conservative, was very instrumental in attempts to co-ordinate the work of the *zemstvos* and in holding an un-official *zemstvo* congress in 1902.13 Shipov's place was taken by A. F. Golovin who, as a convinced constitution-alist, was willing to follow a policy bolder than Shipov's.

After Plehve was assassinated on July 15, the *zemtsy*, bolstered by the liberal reputation of Prince Sviatopolk Mirskii, Plehve's successor, speeded up their plans for holding a second *zemstvo* congress.14 Originally, they envisaged it as a discussion of *zemstvo* affairs, and as such Mirskii had agreed to its convocation.

Yet the Organizational Bureau of the *zemstvo* could not, in view of the critical situation, avoid political questions. The original program was replaced by the so-called eleven theses, which dealt with issues not specifi-cally within the *zemstvo* sphere of competence.15 Mirskii rescinded governmental authorization of the congress.

The *zemtsy* met nevertheless at various private homes in St. Petersburg at a *de facto* congress which was ostensibly a private gathering. The government did not prevent the meeting from taking place. The participants were not limited to *zemstvo* chairmen. Over a hundred persons, some of them non-*zemtsy*, were invited to the congress which lasted from November 6 to 9. It was chaired, except for the last day, by Shipov.16 The partici-pants felt themselves to be the voice of the people, and perhaps, as Fischer has suggested, remembered Shakhov-skoi's dictum that the impetus for reform should be a *zemstvo* meeting. The November congress marked the apogee of *zemstvo* influence.17

The eleven theses, without actually using the word constitution, placed the *zemstvo* on the side of a parliamentary government in Russia. The first ten theses dealt with the abnormality of the existing bureaucratic regime and with the need for close co-operation between the government and society. The congress urged implementation of basic human rights, of freedoms of conscience and assembly, of equality of all citizens of the Empire, of reform of agriculture, of the *zemstvo*, and of the local administration. The final resolution, passed after lengthy debate, expressed the hope that

> the supreme authority [will] call together freely elected representatives of the people, in order to lead our Fatherland with their collaboration on a new path of state development, of establishing principles of law and interaction between state and people.

This resolution precipitated a break between the constitutionalists, who insisted on spelling out certain functions of the proposed assembly, and the Shipov faction, which envisaged a more modestly conceived assembly. Shipov's faction was defeated by a vote of 71 to 27, but the *zemtsy* refrained from using the word constitution so as not to alienate the Shipov faction completely.18 Both factions co-operated with each other.19 The eleven theses, despite a ban on their publication, became widely known and served as a basis for the program of the banquets which *Osvobozhdenie* initiated.20

Although his faction was defeated, Shipov headed the unofficial delegation of the congress which presented the theses to Mirskii. Mirskii could not accept them, for that would have been tantamount to recognizing officially a meeting which had had no official sanction. But he did suggest to Shipov that a special committee, composed of participants of the congress who would also be acceptable to the Tsar, prepare a petition which Mirskii could use in discussions with the Tsar.

Despite the fact that Trubetskoi could not participate in the November congress, he followed the proceedings closely. He sided with the majority.[21]

After the return of the Shipov delegation from St. Petersburg, the *zemtsy* organized a group for the drafting of the petition. Trubetskoi was asked to formulate the petition which would incorporate the *zemstvo* demands. Trubetskoi, enjoying the "unqualified moral authority" of many of the *zemtsy*, was acceptable to the minority and the majority alike. Spurred by the general excitement, he accepted the offer immediately and agreed in advance to incorporate any changes in his draft that the group would see fit to make. Trubetskoi's acceptance was prompted partly by the serious, solid and non-revolutionary impression that Petrunkevich had made on him. He got along better with Petrunkevich than with Shipov.[22] The impression Petrunkevich made on Trubetskoi had important repercussions for his political involvement. Heretofore, Trubetskoi had known of Petrunkevich as of an incorrigible radical. Now he realized the extent of the mistaken views the government held about the radicalism of the political intelligentsia, personified by Petrunkevich, even within the sphere he himself had considered radical.[23]

By November 23, 1904, Trubetskoi's note was accepted by the *zemstvo* group. Shipov and Petrunkevich, representing opposing factions, were satisfied with the document. On November 28, Shipov and Trubetskoi presented the note to Mirskii. To what extent Mirskii used it in his talks with the Tsar remains unknown.[24] For Trubetskoi the drafting of the note was an important political act. He became one of the constitutionalists.

In the note, Trubetskoi tried to impress upon the Tsar the urgency of the situation in the Empire. The disastrous course of the Japanese war, the social and economic crisis of Russia, and the realization of the crisis not only by the educated but by the masses, the equanimity with which the assassination of Plehve had been met, all showed that the era of bureaucratic absolutism had lived out its span. The Tsar was urged to disassociate himself from the old order. He should take a decisive step, as Peter I and Alexander II had done, supporting both a strong government and an organized society. The Tsar should realize that nothing limited his power as much as indecision, that the most solid foundation of power was freedom, law and national trust. The Tsar, urged Trubetskoi in the petition, should place himself in the vanguard of the reforming party.

> Let the Supreme Authority justify . . . that deep and faithful national instinct which drew Russia around the throne of its sovereigns. And let not the impending liberation of Russia happen without the Supreme Authority and despite its will. [25]

Trubetskoi urged immediate implementation of these specific reforms: the repeal of the martial law of 1881 and of all laws inimical to the spirit of the court reform of Alexander II; the guarantee of religious freedom and of the rights of personal liberty; the guarantee of the freedoms of the press and of assembly; the curtailment of undue bureaucratic power; the introduction of the principle of responsibility of administrative and bureaucratic organs; reform of the local government and of the *zemstvos*, and re-organization of education and agriculture.

But all of these reforms either presuppose political

freedoms, lawful order of governmental life, and
properly organized governmental representation, or
they cannot be adequately worked out and imple-
*mented.*26

Trubetskoi wanted the government to announce
the end of the bureaucratic regime and to set the date for
the convocation of a representative body. The legislative
assembly, to be able to run a modern state, was to be
invested with real powers, including the control of the
budget and of the administration. As a preparatory measure, widely publicized commissions should prepare the
minutiae of elections. The government was to develop a
detailed plan of reform, since nothing would be as disastrous for the government as to face the assembly empty-
handed. To demonstrate his good-will, the Tsar was to
proclaim at once amnesty for political prisoners and
religious tolerance to all. The arguments were couched
in terms of patriotism for both Russia and the Tsar.

The Tsar, however, could not make up his mind
whether to introduce reforms or not. The men he trusted
most, particularly Pobedonostsev, cautioned him against
any radical modification of the existing state structure,
while the moderates, both within and outside of the
government, failed to convince him. Obolenskii could not
get the Tsar to receive the *zemtsy* in person; Mirskii was
not definite enough in his program; Witte, as Chairman of
the Council of Ministers, had concrete suggestions, but the
Tsar did not trust him. The Tsar, confused, turned to
Pobedonostsev and to the age-long expedient of calling a
special conference. The result of all of these discussions
was the drafting, quite in secret, of two documents, an
Ukaz and an ordinance.

The *Ukaz* of December 12, promulgated on December 14, seemed to convey hopes of liberalization. In it,

the Tsar stated that he would do everything in his power
to better the lot of the Russians, particularly of the
peasants. He promised to uphold the law, to grant the
zemstvos the added powers, to guarantee the equality of
all citizens before the law, and to ameliorate the conditions of the workers. There was some indication that the
Tsar might even modify the strictures of martial law and
of censorship. Religious toleration was also promised.[27]
The Committee of Ministers was charged with the task
of reform. No mention was made not only of a legislative
assembly, but even of a possible inclusion of elected representatives (or even appointed non-bureaucrats representing
society) in the already existing bodies. To the average
Russian, this cast doubt on the Tsar's intentions.

Any favorable impression of the *Ukaz*, moreover,
was precluded by the promulgation, on the same evening,
of a separate ordinance directed against the unauthorized
meetings of the *zemstvos*. For Trubetskoi, the ordinance,
which made Witte "a modern Simeon Bekbulatovich"[28]
by placing him in charge of the study of possible reform,
was "a challenge thrown by the hand of a provocateur."
Yet, Trubetskoi still believed that it was not the imperial
hand which did it. What bothered him most was the
complete lack of credibility in the government. "No one
believes the government, neither when it threatens nor
when it promises."[29] This, Trubetskoi realized, was the
real crisis, for it ruined the chances of reform even should
the government decide upon it.

Chances for a peaceful implementation of reform
suffered a dramatic setback on Bloody Sunday, a highlight of the Revolution of 1905. On January 9, workers
marching in orderly procession to the palace were fired
upon. Trubetskoi was informed of the massacres — albeit
in an extremely doctored version — that very evening by
the director of the police, A. A. Lopukhin, a distant rela-

tive. The tragedy, in which about one hundred fifty people died, made Trubetskoi redouble his efforts to make the Tsar realize the dangerous situation in the country.[30]

A few days after Bloody Sunday, Trubetskoi attended a meeting of the Moscow Assembly of the Nobility, chaired by his half-brother, Petr. The majority at this meeting, by a vote of 219 to 147, sided with the soldiers who fired upon the workers and condemned the workers for organizing the march in the first place. Trubetskoi joined the minority in its decision to send a separate address to the Tsar, lest the Tsar think mistakenly that the entire nobility of Moscow supported the policies of repression. Meeting at the home of Novosiltsev, the minority of the members of the Moscow Assembly of the Nobility commissioned Trubetskoi to draft a note countering the support of the autocracy expressed in the majority position.

Supported most actively by Novosiltsev, the Dolgorukov brothers and N. A. Khomiakov — the men who were his closest associates within his activity in the *zemstvo* — Trubetskoi in his draft argued that the petition of the majority misinformed the Tsar about the real situation in Russia.

> We all understand the real gravity of the present war. . . . We are all equally overwhelmed by the rebellion agitating society in this terrible time of national trial. But we are not afraid of the revolutionary movement, which in itself . . . is absolutely powerless; we are afraid [however] of the spontaneous disaffection which is caused by the inadequacies of the existing political, social and national structure. We do not identify rebellion with the mature social consciousness of these needs.[31]

Again Trubetskoi suggested to the Tsar that the only

solution was to call together freely elected representatives of the land who would make the reconciliation of the Tsar with the people possible.

The policies of the government were still not clear. A few days after Bloody Sunday, A. G. Bulygin succeeded Mirskii as Minister of Interior. On February 18, the Tsar issued a Rescript in Bulygin's name promising a limited representative assembly. Concurrently, the Tsar also issued a Manifesto and an *Ukaz*, in one asking the support of autocracy and in the other enabling the entire population to present projects of reform to the Council of Ministers.[32] Trubetskoi disregarded these documents and decided to concentrate on the Bulygin Rescript, which seemed to have the support of most members of the government. He chose to interpret it as a dramatic and definitive Rubicon: "The Tsar, following the example of his ancestors, has decided to call together representatives."[33]

He was supported in this view by Obolenskii, who urged him to make full use of the Rescript and who suggested that Bulygin and Witte would be amenable to a delegation of moderates.

At the end of February, the *zemstvo* central board held a meeting at the home of Novosiltsev in preparation for the projected *zemstvo* conference. Trubetskoi argued for the support of Bulygin and the board accepted the idea.[34] A delegation comprising Shipov, Petr Dolgorukov and a few other *zemstvo* activists was sent to St. Petersburg on March 9, 1905. The minister, however, would not see them except at a general audience and they returned ignominiously.[35] This episode served to radicalize the *zemstvo* further.

The general climate of opinion had become more inflammatory. *Zemstvo* meetings were inundated by radical non-*zemtsy*; strikes, terror, and peasant unrest, although at times overrated by public opinion, fed the spirit of revolution.[36] There were intimations of the creation of rightist organizations.[37] The February documents led to the quickening of organized opposition. The *zemstvo*-constitutionalists joined the Union of Unions, an organization of professionals whose views were outspokenly liberal, thereby creating a stronger and more articulate liberal organization.

Faced with the radicalization of the *zemtsy* and the ambivalence of the government, Trubetskoi tried to create a rallying point for as broad a group as possible, based on a positive program of reform rather than the popular one of opposition. He confided to Evgenii:

> I have the impudent and bold idea to found in Moscow a weekly newspaper, whose aim would be the *crystallization of forces* . . . and not the pleasant tickling of the heels of the liberals. . . . It is not enough to spit on the past, it is necessary to think of a real program for the immediate future, of founding "a governmental party of the future," which is necessary for the preservation of order and for well-thought out reforms.[38]

In the early months of 1905 Trubetskoi spent much energy trying to organize a newspaper. He had the support of such men as Petrunkevich, Prince D. I. Shakhovskoi, F. F. Kokoshkin, A. A. Manuilov, N. N. L'vov, Iu. Ia. Novosiltsev, Princes Petr and Pavel Dolgorukov, V. I. Vernadskii, P. I. Novgorodtsev, S. A. Kotliarevskii, Rakhmanov, M. Ia. Gertsenshtein, V. E. Iakushkin, and naturally his brother Evgenii. Although they could not agree on specifics, such as indirect or direct elections and a one or two house legislature, they were willing to work together. Trubetskoi did not insist on a specific program. He wanted to open the newspaper to conflicting opinions, although he feared that its pages would be inundated with leftist articles.[39]

Yet the main threat to the newspaper came not from the left but from the government, which refused to approve its publication. Petrunkevich, who co-operated closely with Trubetskoi, discussed the venture on a trip to the capital. There he reported,

> the new organ is greatly feared, not for the would-be leftist persuasions of the editor, but precisely because he does not belong to the left. The voice of reason, with its sobering effect, might have greater influence [on the general public] than the statements of the extremists.[40]

Trubetskoi's newspaper was to be called *Moskovskaia nedelia*. The first issue was to appear on May 1, 1905. For technical reasons it was delayed until the twelfth. Two days before the paper came out, the government inspector called on Trubetskoi. The inspector wanted to leave for his vacation, but his instructions were to confiscate the newspaper upon publication. The man had already postponed his vacation once, and he wondered if Trubetskoi could speed up the publication so he could leave soon.[41]

The newspaper was suspended forty-five minutes after the censor received the texts. Court proceedings could not be instituted, for the paper had been suspended before publication. Undaunted, Trubetskoi prepared the second and third issues. These also were confiscated. He tried to press the government into legal action against *Moskovskaia nedelia*, but to no avail.[42] He himself was willing to differentiate between the government and the organs which barred his newspaper, and he wanted the distinction brought out into the open.

Under the circumstances, however, he saw the
futility of continued attempts at publication:

The banning of *Moskovskaia nedelia* forces us to
refrain from publication until a change of course.
There was nothing objectionable in these issues: the
whole affair can be explained by a denunciation . . .
which caused St. Petersburg to suspend the paper.
Obviously, we must wait.[43]

The unrest in the country, particularly the threat of
serious agrarian disturbances, seemed to justify that course
of action.

Trubetskoi, like all other educated Russians, had to
face the peasant problem, and, like many Russians, he
could not make up his mind about it. The *zemstvo* conference meeting in Moscow on April 22-26, 1905, which
accepted a slightly modified version of the Union of Liberation demands for universal, direct, secret, and equal
suffrage to a two-house representative assembly, had
dealt mainly with the agrarian problem.[44] M. Ia. Gertsenshtein and A. A. Manuilov, the latter a colleague of Trubetskoi at the University, were the main speakers at the
conference. The resolution passed at the conference proposed the compulsory transfer of land from the large
estates to the peasants. Trubetskoi disagreed on principle
with it, since it would violate private property. He further
argued that an increase in peasant holdings would not
guarantee an increase in the income of the peasants. He
did agree with the conference, however, to give priority
to the political problems as a prerequisite to a satisfactory
agrarian solution.[45]

Trubetskoi had touched upon the agrarian issue in
the winter of 1904 in the unpublished article, "*Na rubezhe*." There he had argued that the peasant economic

crisis (which, he maintained, stemmed partially from the lack of a clear concept of law governing the private lives and properties of the peasants) was exacerbated by the bureaucratic regime. The government, argued Trubetskoi, did nothing but collect materials which could be used only for doctoral dissertations and for propaganda purposes against itself.[46]

He followed up that line of reasoning in May in his still-born newspaper. Here he argued that only an all-encompassing, carefully planned program of agrarian reform would better the lot of the peasants. Piecemeal measures, however enlightened, would not help. He proposed increases in peasant landholding by grants of state land, which the government would acquire by direct purchase. The system of taxation should be reformed and peasant re-settlement should be permitted and encouraged. Small credit and aid in the establishment of co-operatives and handicraft industries should be instituted, and measures which would increase the yield per acre should be devised. Above all, stressed Trubetskoi, the government should do everything in its power to spread education in the villages and to develop a clearer understanding of law among the peasants. Obviously, added Trubetskoi — now as a matter of course — the government would have to reform itself politically before it could embark on these reforms.[47]

Although the political issue was of primary importance for Trubetskoi, he was still wary of the tactics of the Union of Liberation and other outspoken liberals. When his newspaper was banned, he impetuously turned to public opinion for justification; upon reflection, he shelved the article and was willing to wait for a chance to inform public opinion of what happened when he could legally do so.[48] The liberals used illegal means to make their views known on such occasions.

The third *zemstvo* congress met in Moscow from
May 24 to May 27, 1905, in the atmosphere critical of the
government after the defeat at Tsushima and the nomin-
ation of Trepov as the Assistant Minister of Interior.[49]
Trubetskoi did not want to participate in the congress.
He was not used to the hurly-burly of political life, and he
found confrontations with the intelligentsia draining. He
began to realize, but was unwilling to admit openly even
to himself, the inability of the government to reform. He
was already ill with sclerosis and a serious heart condition,
although the illness was diagnosed as a nervous ailment.[50]
He succumbed to periods of depression and to fits of
nervousness. Only the support of his family and friends
could tide him over these rough times. It was only the
persuasion of Petrunkevich and some *zemtsy* which convinced him to attend the May congress.[51]

The congress represented various shades of *zemstvo*
groupings, as well as townsmen and non-*zemtsy* invited
by the bureau. It therefore became known as the "coalition congress." There was even some opposition to the
convocation of such a broadly based gathering; the Second
Congress of the Union of Unions, also meeting in May in
Moscow, argued for a constitutional assembly.[52]

From the beginning, a serious split threatened the
Congress. Geiden, as chairman, had asked the two strongest *zemstvo* factions, the constitutionalists and the Shipov
group, to prepare a draft of an address to the Tsar. Many
participants, however, opposed the idea. Tugan-Baranovskii suggested a general petition of the entire population
rather than a petition of the congress and Rodichev argued
that if it were deemed necessary to address the Tsar, this
should be the very last time. After a heated discussion,
the congress agreed to draft a petition with Petrunkevich's
arguments in support of this action playing an important
role in swaying opinions. But the congress could not

agree on the wording of the petition.[53]

A committee, consisting of Iakushkin, Petrunkevich, N. N. Bazhenov, Shakhovskoi and Trubetskoi was formed to devise the draft. Trubetskoi was the chief author. His first draft, which is not available, was not considered radical enough and was accepted only by a small majority vote. Since the *zemtsy* wanted the petition passed unanimously, Trubetskoi was asked to re-work his proposal. Petulantly, he at first refused to modify his draft, but eventually he gave in. "It was hell," he later told his sister, "two days of heat, noise, cries."

The new draft was passed only after vehement debate and did not receive unanimous support. Shipov, considering the tone of the draft too risqué, resigned. Two other members of the congress did not sign the petition either.[54]

The petition, written in the emotional style which was clearly indicative of Trubetskoi's authorship, was directed to the Tsar and called the abuses of the bureaucracy to his attention.

> In the moment of the greatest need of the nation and of great danger for Russia and your very Throne, we decided to turn to you, laying aside all our disagreements and differences, impelled solely by a fervent love for the motherland. . . You have seen, as has Your whole nation, all the vices of our hated and destructive *prikaz* system, and you have decided to change it. . . . But your directives were . . . not carried out. Subjection of the individual and society . . . continues.[55]

The petition urged the Sovereign Tsar to fulfill now the promise of calling an assembly comprised of national representatives:

Sovereign! In your hands lie the honor and the
power of Russia, her internal peace on which her
external peace depends; in your hands lie your country, your throne. . . . Do not delay, Sire! In the awe-
some time of national trial, great is your responsibility
before God and Russia.[56]

The resolutions were brief and clear.[57] The Tsar was
asked to convene immediately a representative assembly,
to rescind all laws contrary to basic human rights, and to
reform the bureaucracy. By-passing bureaucratic channels,
the congress resolved to send a delegation to the Tsar
which would personally present him with the petition of
the *zemtsy*. The delegates were chosen by votes from
among the *zemstvo* members.[58] Trubetskoi, not being a
zemets, was co-opted.

He did not want to go to St. Petersburg. After the
congress, he had gone to Menshovo, his country estate, to
rest. There he received Golovin's telegram informing him
that the Tsar wished to see Trubetskoi, as a representative
of the congress. Golovin urged Trubetskoi to go directly
to the capital, but Trubetskoi hesitated. He complained
that he was tired and that not being a *zemets*, he could
not very well represent the *zemstvo*. He was suffering
from nervous exhaustion and was distraught by even the
smallest incidents.[59] It appears, however, that his reluctance was due mostly to the fact that he found it
difficult to believe that the Tsar would agree to see the
zemtsy.

Finally, he agreed to go to St. Petersburg. He arrived
on June 3 and the wave of general excitement gripped him,
so that he forgot even his illness. "You cannot imagine
what a tremendous importance is ascribed to all of this,
both here and in Europe," he wrote to his wife. But his
scepticism would not leave him, and he concluded his

letter with a cryptic — "How all this will end, I do not know."[60] The *zemtsy* convinced him to act as the spokesman before the Tsar and he hoped "that the choir would at least chip in."[61]

For a few days it was not clear if the Tsar would receive the whole delegation, as it insisted, or only a few members of the delegation, as the Tsar preferred. One of the reasons for the reluctance of the Tsar to meet with the entire group was the presence of both Petrunkevich and Rodichev.[62]

The Tsar finally gave his consent on June 5 to see the delegation. He set the audience for the next day. The night before the audience Trubetskoi rehearsed his speech in Petrunkevich's hotel room before the members of the delegation and a few outsiders, such as Petrunkevich's wife and Miliukov. A correspondent, who had somehow managed to get in, was asked to leave.[63]

In the morning the *zemstvo* deputies travelled by train to Peterhof, whence they were transported by private coach to the Tsar's residence. The court greeted them coldly, some courtiers even warning them that they were "playing a dangerous game." Despite this attitude, the courtiers told the *zemtsy* that the Tsar disliked official speeches and that the best way to approach him was to speak in a conversational manner. The deputies, some of whom had been treated as political offenders, were quite agitated.

The Tsar walked into the room at 12:40, looking as afraid as a school-boy at an examination.[64] Eyewitnesses said later that they were immediately struck by the chasm which seemed to separate the Tsar from the *zemtsy* and that that chasm was bridged only when Trubetskoi spoke. Inadvertently, Trubetskoi fell into a soothing professorial tone and, pacing up and down the room, spoke to the Tsar. The Tsar turned his head to follow

Trubetskoi and nodded every once in a while, particularly when Trubetskoi argued against a class representative body. The *zemtsy* were visibly moved — Korff cried and Novosiltsev and Prince L'vov had a hard time holding back their tears. The Tsar apparently had expected a bitter attack from representatives of "society" and was comforted by Trubetskoi's soothing tone and moderate words.

Trubetskoi did not have notes and wrote down his speech only after the audience. No one took notes during the audience and Trubetskoi kept remembering snatches of the speech after he had given his written version to Baron V. B. Fredericks, the Minister of the Imperial Court and a close friend of the Tsar.[65]

This is the full text of the speech. The words in brackets refer to the phrases which Trubetskoi remembered later and which were not included in the official transcript.[66]

Sire!

Permit us to thank You for agreeing to see us. You understood the feelings which prompted us, and You did not believe those who presented us, social and *zemstvo* workers, as traitors to the Throne and as enemies of Russia. Love of the motherland and the consciousness of our debt to You have led us here.

[You see before Yourself persons convinced in the inevitability of a thorough reform of the state along constitutional lines.]

We know, Sovereign, that this minute You are suffering more than all of us. We would like to be able to comfort You, and when we turn to Your Majesty in this unusual manner it is only, believe us, because we realized our debt and the general danger, which is great, Sire.

By the disturbances [*smuta*] gripping the whole land we do not mean sedition [*kramola*] which in itself, during normal times, would not be dangerous, but the general dissension and complete disorganization which dooms authority to weakness.

The Russian people have not lost their patriotism, have not lost their faith in the Tsar, in the invincible greatness of Russia; this is precisely the reason they cannot understand our defeats, our internal disorders. [The nation] feels itself cheated and thinks that the Tsar is being cheated also. And when the people see that the Tsar wants good, and evil is committed; that the Tsar orders one thing, and a completely different one is done; when the directives of Your Majesty are often curtailed and put into effect by people who are known to be against all reforms; then the feeling that they have been cheated only grows among the people. The terrible word "treason" has been uttered, and people look for traitors in everyone — in generals, in Your counselors, in us, in all "gentlemen" in general. This feeling is exploited from all sides. Some direct the people against the landowners, others against the teachers, the *zemstvo* physicians, against the educated classes. Various groups of the population are aroused against other groups.

Relentless and harsh hatred, incrusted by ages of constrictions and outrages, sharpened by need and sorrow, lawlessness and the difficult economic conditions, rises and grows and it is even more dangerous, more contagious, more prone to enflame the masses in that it, at first, robes itself in patriotic forms. That is the terrible danger, Sire, which we, living in the land, have fully experienced and which we consider our duty to report to Your Imperial Majesty.

[We are not lying, Sire!]

The only solution to these internal needs lies in the path You have shown, Sire; in calling together representatives of the people. We all believe in this path, but we are well aware that not every representative body can serve the noble aims which You place before it. It should, after all, serve the institution of internal peace, [serve] creation, not destruction; unification, not partition; and finally it should serve the "reorganization of the State," as You Yourself have said. We do not consider ourselves authorized to speak here of the final forms which the national representation [*narodnoe predstavitel'stvo*] should take, nor the means of its election. If You shall permit, Sire, we can only say that which unites all of us, which unites the majority of the Russian people who sincerely wish to follow the path pointed out by You.

It is essential that all Your subjects, equally and with no distinctions, consider themselves Russian citizens, that parts of the population and [various] civic groups not be excluded from the national representation and thus become enemies of the renewed system; it is essential that there be none outside the law and no unfortunates. We would want all Your subjects, although foreign to us by faith and blood, to see in Russia their motherland and in You its Sovereign; to feel themselves the sons of Russia and to love Russia just as we love her. The national representation should serve the task of unification and of internal peace. It is impossible, therefore, to hope that the representative assembly be a class one. As the Russian Tsar is not the Tsar of the nobility, not the Tsar of the peasants or of the merchants, not the Tsar of classes, but the Tsar of all Rus', so also the elected people [*vybornie liudi*] from the whole population, called to work with You at the affairs of State [*delo gosudarevo*], should serve general and not class interests. Class representation will inevitably give rise to class strife even where none now exists.

To continue: the national representation should serve the task of "state re-organization." Bureaucracy exists everyplace, in all countries, and condemning it we did not criticize individuals but the *prikaz* system. In the reformed structure the bureaucracy should take the place which behooves it. It should not usurp Your State rights, it should become responsible.

The calling together of a representative body should aid in the realization of such a task. The representative body cannot be a token payment to the old system of bureaucratic organization. It should be independent lest between it and You a new form of bureaucratic wall arise. You Yourself will become convinced of this point of view once you gather those elected by the people and once You see them face to face, as You see us now.

Finally, the reforms charted by You touch the Russian nation and society so intimately that it, being called upon to take part in State work, not only cannot, but should not, remain indifferent to [these proposals].

Therefore, it is essential to vouchsafe the widest possibility for the re-organization of the State not only at the first session of the elected representatives, but today, in print and in civic meetings. It would be destructive to invite civic forces to State activity and, at the same time, not to permit free discussion. It would undermine the trust for the materialization of reforms, it would stand in the way of their active implementation.

[Only the *zemstvo* civic forces of the land can build the new Russia.] Sire! The renewal of Russia should be based on trust.

After Trubetskoi, M. M. Fedorov, the Chairman of the St. Petersburg City Duma, in a very brief comment, urged the Tsar, for purposes of the economic progress and the well-being of Russia, to turn to the people to find out the true needs of the country.[67]

The whole audience was an emotionally charged experience. The deputies did not know how the Tsar would receive them. It was, after all, their own Tsar, the Russian Tsar, speaking directly and without a bureaucratic barrier to the closest surrogate Russia had at that time to a national representation. Not only did the Tsar listen carefully to them, his conduct and his words during the audience seemed to show that he agreed with the essential demands, or rather suggestions, of the delegation.

In his answer the Tsar expressed the desire to call an assembly and his hope that the *zemtsy* would co-operate with him in governing Russia on the basis of indigenous Russian principles.

I was happy to hear you. I have no doubts that you, gentlemen, were motivated by the feeling of ardent

love to the motherland when you turned directly to
me. Together with you and with my whole nation, I
have suffered and continue to suffer with my whole
soul at the realization of the hardships which the
war has brought upon Russia and which will yet continue, and about all our internal disorders.[68]

Throw away your doubts. My will — the Tsar's will —
to call together national representatives [*narodnye
predstaviteli*] is unchanging. Attracting them to the
work of the State will be done in an orderly fashion.
I look after this matter daily.

You can say so to those close to you, in the land and
in the cities. I firmly believe that Russia will come out
of her trial renewed. Let the old unity between the
Tsar and all Rus' be re-established; the communion
between me and the *zemstvo* people, which shall form
the basis for the order compatible with original principles.

From this day on, I see in you my helpers.[69]

The deputies found this last sentence particularly significant.

  After the official address the Tsar exchanged some
words with members of the delegation. Trubetskoi used
the opportunity to inform the Tsar of the situation in
Russian universities. The Tsar was interested enough to ask
for a more detailed report. Nicholas II was at a loss on how
to speak to Petrunkevich; Trubetskoi later said that the
imperial expression was that of a small boy meeting a
rather strict and unpleasant uncle. Petrunkevich insisted
that the Tsar hesitated briefly before shaking his hand.[70]

  The court took their cue from the Tsar, and after

the audience, as the deputies were relaxing in their shirt-sleeves and exchanging their impressions "of the historical moment" at a meal served to them in Peterhof, even Prince Putiatin, a courtier, embraced Petrunkevich and kissed Rodichev. Praises were heaped upon the speech by Trubetskoi.[71]

The following day, when Trubetskoi brought his text of the speech to Baron Fredericks, he found Kovalevskii in a heated argument with Fredericks. The Tsar had asked that the term "national representatives," which he had used, be replaced by "elected people," since the former contradicted the usage in the Rescript. Trubetskoi did not consider the issue substantive; he had used both terms in his speech. But Kovalevskii accused Trubetskoi of retreating from positions won in battle. The Tsar, naturally, was informed of Kovalevskii's "scandalous behavior," and, suspicious as he was, thought that the *zemtsy* were trying to catch him off guard.[72]

The Tsar had second thoughts on the whole audience. The two most striking phrases of his speech were deleted from the official transcript, a special circular was issued commanding that only a full version of the Tsar's speech as appearing in *Pravitel'stvenni vestnik* be published, and the press was urged to refrain from comments on the whole affair.[73] Two weeks later, receiving a gentry deputation, the Tsar spoke on the advantages of a class system of representation.[74]

For Trubetskoi, the audience with the Tsar was particularly important. He realized that the preservation of Russia depended on the co-operation of the Tsar with society, and that he had been, for whatever reasons, the representative of society fortunate enough to speak to the Tsar. Although he thought that the way he spoke was more forceful than the written reconstruction of his speech, he wanted to follow up his speech with a note to the Tsar to make certain that the Tsar saw in the *zemtsy* his loyal, patriotic supporters.

> Sire! Do not misconstrue our turning to You. Believe us, only love for our country and the realization of our debt to You brought us here. We are not as bold as to consider ourselves representatives of the country, we are only her sons and feel what all Russian people feel today — the desire to weld ourselves together so that by our combined efforts and joint reason [we] might save Russia. We speak with You as with a Russian Tsar; in Your throne we see a sign of our unity; of our past and future glory.

> Sovereign! Heavy are our defeats, but at the present moment the internal danger is greater than the external foe and it is that danger which paralyzes the nation's powers.

> All the dark hate which settled from age-long injustices . . .75

Trubetskoi never finished the note, probably because he realized the futility of pinning his hopes on a Tsar whose agents could not decide whether Trubetskoi was a monarchist or an anarchist.76

The leftist press attacked the *zemtsy* for turning to the Tsar 77 while the rightists presented Trubetskoi as a traitor to him.78 Among the *zemtsy* themselves there was some criticism if not of the delegation, then of the choice of Trubetskoi as the spokesman and of the speech itself.79 But on the whole the *zemtsy* supported the delegation and used Trubetskoi's speech as the basis of their own petitions to the Tsar. The voices of criticism were few, the temper of society was still liberal, and

Trubetskoi's fame was made overnight.[80] The speech
to the Tsar was the culmination of Trubetskoi's life, the
high point of his career. It marked the apogee of his
popularity.

Trubetskoi had spoken for moderate, often in-
articulate Russia. He came to personify the dream of a
peaceful reform of the whole country. This was the
reason for his popularity, the reason for the widespread
echoes of his speech. He had expressed the political hopes
of the moderates in temperate language. The Tsar had
listened to him. Many Russians, therefore, particularly
those in the provinces, viewed Trubetskoi as the intermediary between the Tsar and the people. The city of
Trubchevsk, for instance, requested and received a photo-
graph of Trubetskoi. Pavel Dolgorukov, the more moderate
of the twins, used the speech as a basis for talks with the
.peasants. A letter to the editor of *Proletarii*, published
on September 20, 1905, described how the *zemstvos*
duplicated Trubetskoi's speech in the form of leaflets.[81]
Struve considered the delegation of the *zemtsy* an event
of supreme importance with potential revolutionary consequences that justified overlooking the few "unpleasantly
off-key notes" in the speech of Trubetskoi. But while
Trubetskoi spoke as if the audience with the Tsar would
initiate an era of co-operation between the Tsar and
society, for Struve it was an "overture to the conflict
which will inevitably take place."[82]

Trubetskoi himself was not convinced that the
Tsar was willing to co-operate with society. He was trying
to impress upon the Tsar the desirability of such co-
operation. His use of the word *kramola* [sedition], un-
fortunate in the eyes of his liberal connections, was quite
natural for him. He had criticized the revolutionary movement in Russia by that term previously, and he was willing
to do so in public. He hoped, even if he found it increas-

ingly difficult to believe in, for the possibility of co-operation between the Tsar and the moderates. For a brief moment his hopes, as the hopes of the members of the delegation, might have soared, but he would not succumb to "any illusions."

> I have not had any illusions, either after or before "the significant meeting," nor have I entertained any direct hopes. I have fulfilled my natural duty. . . . At the time, before and after, I had believed and still believe that justice is on our side and that there is no other way out of the situation than to turn to "the *zemstvo* civic forces," which alone can be constructive now. . . . At the time I spoke I was able to awaken in my interlocutor a *fleeting* impression of this. I think it was fleeting; in any case, temporary. What will you do against abulia, especially with the mass of impressions of a completely different nature? But at the moment, on the very day, the impression was distinctly strong and noticeable. Instead of the prepared answers we were told: "from this day on you shall be my helpers," and then, "national representation shall form the basis of the union of the Tsar with the people . . ." Anyway, both expressions were crossed out the next day. . . . Here is the essence of the anecdote.[83]

It was not only the bureaucracy which separated the Tsar from the people — it was the Tsar's unwillingness or inability to understand. In the realization of this lies the cause of Trubetskoi's increasing depression.

Trubetskoi nevertheless defended his speech at a congress of the *zemtsy* which was held in Moscow from July 6 to 8 despite the attempts of Trepov to prevent the meeting. Disregarding the warnings of the police, more

than two hundred persons, of the 285 invited, came to
the congress, which was held at the residence of Petr
Dolgorukov as a private gathering.[84] Trubetskoi was co-
opted to the organizational bureau because he had been
a member of the *zemstvo* delegation to the Tsar.[85]

The anti-governmental mood of the congress was
heightened at the very first session by the arrival, as
usual, of Police-officer Noskov, who found, in the words
of his report, "in the residence of Prince Dolgorukov a
green table, behind which sat a few persons of the organizational bureau, and facing the table, on chairs, sat
persons of various ages, obviously representatives of the
zemstvos and of the cities."[86] Petr Dolgorukov met the
demand of the police for the dispersal of the gathering
with a thundering remark that he could invite whom he
pleased to his home.

Deliberations of the congress began as soon as
the police, having written their report, left. The *zemtsy*
applauded Golovin's not giving in to the demands of the
government to furnish reports on the preparations of the
congress and on the actual program of the congress.
Geiden was elected chairman. The participants greeted
with laughter rumors that the government feared that
the *zemtsy* would proclaim themselves a constituent
assembly. Yet they decided, should the police ask them
to disband again, to yield only to force.[87]

Under such circumstances, Trubetskoi's report on
the *zemstvo* delegation, coming as it did right after Noskov's departure, was as much a defense as it was a report.
Stressing that the delegation represented a *zemstvo* coalition congress, Trubetskoi argued that it could not
overstep the mandate of that congress. The coalition
congress delegates had decided to base the address to
the Tsar on the necessity of universal, all-class elections,
on the need to grant Russia basic freedoms and on the

demand to have the projected state duma above the bureaucracy. It was in these terms that Trubetskoi addressed the Tsar, and the Tsar "listened very favorably to . . . the speech."[88]

Trubetskoi reported on the answer of the Tsar and on the deletions in the printed text of that answer. His final argument was brief.

> It seems to me, that as a delegation of the coalition congress, we could not say much more, and the wide-scale favorable response which we received and continue to receive, shows, I think, that the delegation of June 6 expressed the feelings and views which united the whole Russian society.[89]

He could not pass up the opportunity to show the dramatic contrast between the Tsar and the bureaucracy. Trubetskoi, like many moderates, had to keep on proving to himself the perfidy of the government. Perhaps he felt guilty at opposing it, but he had no choice.

The congress, with one negative vote, agreed to express its thanks to the delegation, supporting its statements as being valid at the time they were made.[90] The views of the congress on Trubetskoi could well be expressed by the comment of Miliukov, who was present at it as the guest of Dolgorukov:

> One must admit that Sergei Nikolaevich fully vindicated his selection. If it were at all feasible and necessary to turn at the moment to the Tsar on behalf of the congress, then only in the tone chosen by this orator-patriot, a tone imbued with real suffering for the motherland . . . The immediate aim . . . could be considered to have been reached. For the first time the Tsar was really touched by a voice of the other

world; for the first time we heard from his mouth
words resembling a sincere promise of reforms and
almost a realization of their inevitability.[91]

The *zemstvo* congress felt that the Tsar had been
given a chance. Miliukov, who would later defend Trubetskoi in his memoirs, said at the congress that it would be
hypocritical of it to condemn acts of violence which the
congress welcomed as a prelude to the revolution. In May,
the *zemstvo* congress turned to the Tsar. Now, in July,
at the initiative of Petrunkevich and Rodichev, it turned
to the people.[92]

Although other subjects were discussed,[93] the bulk
of the debates dealt with the projected Bulygin Duma.
The congress had acquired an advance copy of the project,
which was formally published on July 26,[94] and discussed
it before it became law.

The project was criticized as inadequate but it was
decided that, should it be put in operation, the *zemtsy*
should participate in the legislative body in large numbers
to try to push through their own program. Meanwhile,
all present were to write their views to the bureau, which
would then develop a separate *zemstvo* project.[95] The
congress decided to publish all pertinent material on its
meeting.

Except for his report, Trubetskoi did not take
an active part in the proceedings of the congress. He
told his sister that he was bored by the constant demagogic
repetitions of the trite phrases on the tyranny of the
bureaucracy. Informally, Trubetskoi tried to prevent
the passage of the call to the people, which he considered
a dangerous incendiary measure. He spent a whole night
trying in vain to convince Petrunkevich of the danger.[96]
Trubetskoi also did not participate in the meeting of the
constitutionalists at Novosiltsev's which was held after

the *zemstvo* congress.[97]

Yet as much as he deplored the radicalization of even the *zemtsy* he understood it. He had also resorted to public opinion for the vindication of his views in May (although he did not publish his statement), and the course of events since May did little to alter his views. He predicted further radicalization.

> I will not wager that finally the very *zemstvo*, the very civic "builders" will not become revolutionaries, for we are but a few degrees removed from the boiling point and all recent congresses and meetings show very dangerous signals.[98]

In an article written after the July *zemstvo* congress, he warned that Russia was living "a year each month," and that the issue at stake was not only the establishment of a constitutional regime in Russia, but the preservation of order.[99]

Again he urged the Tsar to call upon the *zemtsy* for an open deliberation of the Bulygin Project and for the inclusion of the *zemtsy* in governmental commissions. Otherwise, continued Trubetskoi, the situation, which the government itself created by calling on the people to participate in civic activity while at the same time keeping them away from the most important legislative work, would become worse.

> The terrible dilemma facing Russia, facing all Russians, except those who still can believe in police dictatorship after von Plehve and in "traditional-class" partitions in the midst of general collapse, is whether [the reform will come about] *through* the State Duma or *despite it. Caveant consules!*[100]

The Tsar, however, could not make up his mind.

The audience of June 6 was followed by a delegation of the marshals of the nobility which not only urged immediate reform but also told the Tsar that "you receive us graciously today, and tomorrow you will agree with the exact opposite."[101] But when the Tsar met with high court dignitaries in July, Kliuchevsky, who was the only outsider present, had to remind him of the promises he had made to Trubetskoi and the June delegation.[102]

After the July congress, the Tsar asked Senator K. Z. Postovskii to investigate the members of the June delegation. The Tsar felt that what the delegates said on June 6 clashed with their actions on July 7. The investigation was conducted very politely in an informal manner. The *zemtsy* and the other members of the delegation answered the Senator in lengthy memoranda.[103]

Trubetskoi stressed that the matter under investigation was one of personal honor and that, had the congress exhibited any treasonable overtones, none of the members of the delegation would have participated in it. On the contrary, continued Trubetskoi, what was contradictory was the conduct of the government. There was a definite contradiction between the trust in society which the Tsar had expressed in June, and the failure to authorize the *zemstvo* congress, not to mention the activity of the police. "That," wrote Trubetskoi to Postovskii, "was an open challenge to society, to the *zemstvo* and to the cities." Although Trubetskoi had not been prepared to report to the July congress, particularly at such an inopportune moment, he continued in his defense;

I had the specific permission of the Tsar, who told the deputies of the May congress to spread the joyous news of his words to those living in the country and in the cities; moreover . . . I felt a direct responsibility to do so. I continue to receive many notes in which I am asked to say what the words of the Tsar were, since official reports are customarily not believed.

The contradiction between June 6 and

what happened here on July 6 is so blatant that the revolutionaries would be most happy with it. . . . The difference between the bureaucracy and the throne was drawn up very clearly.

He almost accused the government itself of treachery and lack of patriotism:

The government which will oppose the natural, normal and the basically patriotic movement of society will harm itself and will, above all, endanger the throne and the country.[104]

Yet even in this fateful year Trubetskoi was not totally immersed in political issues; he was greatly concerned about the conditions within the universities. The fall semester of 1904 had been a period of renewed disturbances. The students no longer limited their demands to university autonomy and repeal of the Statute of 1884, but demanded political rights. The government continued its policy of repression and did not initiate any significant reform.[105]

By December most of the institutions of higher learning were on strike as a protest against police brutality, and after January 9, 1905, all of them were on strike. The universities were supported by quite a few secondary and in some cases even by elementary schools. The government closed most of the schools and placed all educational institutions under the control of governors-general who were empowered to use any security measure they considered

appropriate.106 Some of the faculty supported the students. The so-called Statement of 342, initiated by sixteen
members of the Academy of Sciences and eventually
supported by over 1200 noted scholars, was an implicit
endorsement of the position of the students.107

Trubetskoi considered the politicized university
a tragic development. In February, he drafted a plea to
the students to remain calm, but the draft was not accepted by the faculty committee.108 The Moscow University Council found it necessary to permit student
meetings to learn the views of the students on the issue
of re-opening the university. The militant outlook of the
majority of students offered no hope for the renewal
of academic activities. Students could not be calmed
until the university itself received some semblance of
power, but the government showed little inclination of
doing that. Trubetskoi made repeated trips to the capital
to intervene before whomever he could on behalf of the
university. Through his relative, A. D. Obolenskii, he
met A. S. Ermolov, the Minister of Agriculture, who had
urged the Tsar to initiate overall reform. Ermolov presented the student problem at the meeting of the Council
of Ministers; his views on the university question were
similar to those of Trubetskoi.109

Trubetskoi spoke out against the police regime
in the universities because he felt it encouraged a virtual
dictatorship of the radical students. He argued that the
interests of the state, as well as of enlightenment, were
threatened. He urged immediate reform. If the commissions studying educational problems needed more
time to work out detailed legislation, then temporary
rules, which would abrogate the Statute of 1884 and grant
power to the university councils, should be passed immediately. What the university needed most, he concluded,
was "trust without which there will be no universities

in general."110

But his arguments did not, as yet, carry much weight in the government. Instead, in view of the radicalization of the students,111 the government decided to continue its policy of repression. There were rumors that the government was planning to re-open the universities under the old system and if the disturbances would continue, to expel not only the students, but also the faculty. Trubetskoi, in an article in *Russkia vedomosti* on March 20, argued the danger of such a measure. He hoped that the rumor was false.112 He was mistaken.

On April 16, the Tsar agreed to a proposal of the Council of Ministers and of the State Soviet to keep the universities, the student dormitories, and student cafeterias closed for the rest of the academic year. Universities were to be re-opened only in the fall, new students would be accepted, and the students would not be penalized for the time lost due to the university boycott. Government-appointed officials were to be placed in charge of keeping order, accepting new students, and deciding which students could graduate. Should any disturbances occur within the re-opened universities, then the students and the faculty were to be dismissed and the universities were to be closed.113

Trubetskoi was shocked. He had argued that the students should be made to realize the gravity of the student strike by being made to repeat the last academic year. That the faculty, which was powerless in the first place, be penalized for student disturbances, seemed disastrous. And the closing of the dormitories, cafeterias and the self-help organizations of the students, continued Trubetskoi, would contribute to the unrest by cutting off the students' means of subsistence.

Although the circular was not implemented, student disturbances and the radicalization of the students continued.[114] Trubetskoi spent the summer commuting between Menshovo, Moscow, and St. Petersburg, taking part in many of the popular meetings and prodding the government to reform. He discussed the university with Trepov who tried to convince Trubetskoi of the necessity of his taking a ministerial post to push through the reform. Trubetskoi, however, made reform the prerequisite for his active co-operation in the government.[115] One result of his prodding was official permission for a congress of educators in the middle of August, 1905. The congress would have been held anyway, but its legalization gave hopes for further reform. So did Trepov's telegram to Trubetskoi on the eve of the congress: "Please be patient a few [more] days. I hope you will be satisfied with what was done."[116]

At the beginning of June, Trubetskoi, at the audience with the Tsar, told him that it was not simply "a handful of radicals" who caused all the disturbances. The Tsar asked Trubetskoi to draft a note elucidating the problems of higher education and to send it directly to him, via the court, by-passing the ministry. It was under the impact of this memorandum that the government began to consider the possibility of university autonomy.[117] The arguments Trubetskoi mustered impressed the Tsar, or those capable of impressing him.

Acting quickly, the Tsar by an *Ukaz* to the Senate of August 27, 1905, granted autonomy to the universities. Autonomy came unexpectedly and was regarded as a personal concession to Trubetskoi.[118]

The *Ukaz* introduced a few short temporary rules "changing and complementing . . . the existing statutes of Russian universities," which were to be implemented prior to the opening of the academic year in September.[119] These temporary rules abrogated the Statute of 1884. They stipulated the election by the faculty of both the rector and the deans[120] and placed under their control the whole inspectorate.[121] The faculty council, working through the faculty courts which were to have been established as far back as August 27, 1902, was given full disciplinary powers in the university.[122] The functions of the trustee, although not specifically mentioned in the new legislation, were considerably reduced because of the increased competence of the faculty in administrative matters. The unpopular inspectorate, although not formally abolished until September, 1906, virtually disintegrated by the fall of 1905. In October, 1905, concessions to some of the minorities were made.[123]

Autonomy of the university was greeted by all progressives.[124] It was victory for Trubetskoi, and there was no doubt that he would be elected rector of Moscow University. He came to Moscow from Menshovo on September 1, directly to the house of N. V. Davidov, where some of his colleagues, among them Vernadskii, Novgorodtsev, Manuilov, B. K. Mlodozeevskii, M. K. Spizharnii, and others had gathered. Trubetskoi was late, and when he did come, those present, without prior agreement, greeted him with a standing ovation. The following day, by a vote of 56 to 20, he was elected rector of Moscow University.[125]

In his acceptance speech, Trubetskoi stressed the honor and the duties of the rector. He asked for help, particularly of the twenty professors who did not vote for him. Later, in the published note of thanks to the Moscow Duma, Trubetskoi stressed "the close relationship of the university with the whole of Russian society," and asked for co-operation.[126]

As rector, however, Trubetskoi tried to preserve the university from direct political involvement. He wanted to prove that the academic community, particularly the students, were mature enough to be left in peace.

He feared that the continuation of student disturbances which might lead to the closing of the university would be disastrous not only for the cause of learning but also "for the liberation movement."[127]

The liberal professors, although they trusted Trubetskoi in his administration of the university, did not trust the government and formed a commission to draft a final university statute. The conservative faculty, on the other hand, refused to accept the need of both general reform and of university autonomy.[128]

Students on the whole accepted the temporary rules, but any normal activity in the university was out of the question. Universities offered oases of free speech and were used as such.[129] Revolutionary parties argued openly for the use of the university as a vanguard of the political struggle, while the moderates in *Osvobozhdenie* modified their earlier position and defended autonomy in the same terms as Trubetskoi.[130] But it was too late. The university was one of the centers of revolutionary activity and "questions of academic nature did not interest students at all . . . The students reflected the outlook of the masses."[131] The faculty in turn were influenced by the radicalism of the students.

Moscow students, once autonomy had been granted, decided to begin studies without giving up their meetings. Trubetskoi, fearful that the students might be drawn away from the university, tried to get St. Petersburg to legalize political discussions in general. This was not necessary, for the students themselves held political meetings at which non-students constituted the majority of the participants. One such meeting began in the morning of September 19 and lasted the whole day. Toward noon, this particular meeting was addressed by A. A. Manuilov, the assistant rector, who spoke on the sanctity of the university. Some students applauded the speech, some booed, but the meeting continued.132

To prevent disturbances, Trubetskoi legalized student meetings provided that the time and place of the meeting did not conflict with classes and was cleared with the rector or his office, and that only students were present at the meetings.133

These conditions were not met. On September 21 about three thousand people flooded the Moscow University's law auditorium, and the city administration threatened to intervene to prevent possible violence.134 Trubetskoi and the faculty council decided to close the university to prevent its overcrowding by outsiders.

The following afternoon Trubetskoi and Manuilov, the assistant rector, addressed about 800 students and explained to them the reasons for the closing of the university. Not only was there no riot, neither Trubetskoi nor Manuilov were booed. Trubetskoi urged the students not to turn the university into a public square and warned them of the existence of a party which encouraged systematic violations of the decisions of the faculty council in the hope that it would lead to the closing of the university. He expressed the wish that the students would realize the importance of the university and help preserve the shrines of higher learning.135

But Trubetskoi also said that his political views were well-known, that as a member of the party to which he had the honor of belonging, he had defended free speech before the throne itself and would continue to defend it.136 His own language, sprouting such terms as "struggle" and "liberation," became similar to the terminology used by the political intelligentsia. Trubetskoi did not ask the students to postpone their involvement in politics, but only to conduct the struggle for basic freedoms outside the university.

He himself took the struggle to St. Petersburg. The

Moscow University Council had empowered Trubetskoi
with a resolution calling upon the government to grant
freedom of assembly, the right of free speech, and the
guarantees of individual liberty as the only means of
preserving the university. Armed with that resolution,
Trubetskoi went to St. Petersburg on the night of September 28, despite a bad cold and heart palpitations.[137]

As soon as he got to St. Petersburg, Trubetskoi
spoke for over an hour with minister of education General
Glazov on the need of freedom of assembly as the only
measure which could save the university.[138] Later, Trubetskoi told G. A. Falkenbork that resolute measures to
stop meetings in the universities were demanded of him.
"I will take them when the society will get freedom of
assembly."[139] He apparently repeated the plea for freedom of assembly at an afternoon meeting of the ministry
on the projected statute, to which he had been invited by
Glazov. At about seven in the evening, while handing
Glazov some of the numerous student petitions he carried
around with him, Trubetskoi fainted. This proved to be
his mortal illness.[140]

There is no doubt that Trubetskoi's declining health
was due to the emotional strain caused by heightened
political activity. For someone as inexperienced in politics
as Trubetskoi, political activity in the period of revolutionary turmoil was a particularly traumatic experience.
He tried to seek peace of mind in a broader view of things:

> We live in such a bustle, in such a stamping mill where
> events change kaleidoscopically, that to understand
> them, to write them down, to reproduce them, to
> judge them from a point of view of the coming gener-
> ations is extremely difficult. *Sub specie aeternitatis* —
> it is a kaleidoscope; nothing particularly interesting,
> not more than each day, each congress, each meeting

gives . . . We are still playing the prelude and the
curtain is not up yet. It is funny to watch some ama-
teurs putting on make-up . . . at an amateur pro-
duction.[141]

But the possibility of an impending revolution,
which could not be precluded in view of the half-measures
of the government, depressed Trubetskoi.[142] His political
hopes had been frustrated and university autonomy had
come too late to calm even the university.

Trubetskoi realized the weakness of moderate
Russia earlier than some of his colleagues. He almost fore-
saw the tyrannical elements of Russian radicalism and he
therefore feared it as much as the violence of the lower
classes. But he saw the weakness of the Tsar and the
intransigence of his advisers first hand. He reacted to it
at times with a force worthy of a good radical.

By the end of his life he understood the reasons for
the radicalization of society. He did everything in his
power to enlighten the Tsar on the true interests of Russia.
The only step which Trubetskoi had not yet tried was to
penetrate into the government to work for reform from
the inside. That apparently had been the course urged
upon him by Trepov.

At the age of forty-three Trubetskoi was aware of
the crisis in his life. His sense of duty and the ideal of
service had forced him into political activity where those
close to him were too leftist for his tastes. The Tsar, by
his weakness and choice of advisers, frustrated Trubetskoi's plans for reform emanating from the throne. The
university took up most of his time, but there were intimations by some of his relatives that the university
rectorship would be a stepping-stone to greater things.

The possibility of Trubetskoi taking on a ministerial
post was contemplated in St. Petersburg, and A. A. Lo-

pukhin informed Trubetskoi of it. But Trubetskoi could no longer in good conscience give the government the benefit of the doubt.[143]

Trubetskoi realized that he had the support of neither the government nor of the society. He had never been a *zemets* and by the time he acted as the *zemstvo* spokesman, the *zemtsy* were irrevocably split. Trubetskoi was often considered a suitable candidate for the post of president of the projected Duma. There his oratory and conciliatory skill, as well as his enlightened patriotic views, would have served him in good stead. But there was no Duma.

By September, 1905, after his election as the first freely chosen rector of Russia's oldest university, Trubetskoi was ill, tired, nervous, exasperated, and frustrated. He could not co-operate with the government when the government refused to institute reform, and any other course, he sensed, would lead to revolution. Although rational as always, even under the stress of university disturbances, he became more emotional in private. He was persecuted by a sense of doom hanging over Russia, the Yellow Peril made more acute by Russia's failure to reform.

He had one particularly graphic nightmare. While he waited at a station for a train he saw, in terror, his friends rushing to what had been the platform but what was actually a ravine. He could not stop them in their flight to destruction.[144] He did not live long enough to interpret that nightmare.

CHAPTER 7

DEATH AND AFTERMATH

Trubetskoi suffered his fatal stroke at a meeting in the Ministry of Education in St. Petersburg on September 29, 1905, while submitting to General Glazov petitions from Polish students.[1] Because he died in St. Petersburg, Trubetskoi had the equivalent of two funerals. His body was laid out in state in the capital and later transported in a magnificent procession to the railroad station. The funeral took place in Moscow. In both cities, the memorial services culminated in spontaneous demonstrations which led to armed clashes with the police. Thus, the man who tried to maintain peace at all costs was carried to his grave amid violence and bloodshed.

The circumstances of Trubetskoi's death, coupled with his popularity among students, fired public imagination. Crowds poured in to see his body as soon as it was laid out. The coffin had to remain open because of the persistent rumors that Trubetskoi had been killed by agents of the government.[2] The fear of a rightist counter-demonstration was strong enough to prevent two of his sisters from following the coffin on foot, as was the custom.[3]

For the first time since the death of the writer Turgenev in 1883, wreaths were permitted to be carried by hand in the procession. The government had forbidden that practice earlier fearing firearms concealed in the

175

flowers. The coffin was surrounded by people carrying wreaths of flowers. The Tsar sent a wreath of white orchids and laurel. There were wreaths from the universities, *zemstvos*, workers, all major civic societies, from various student groups, and from individuals. A typical wreath from the peasants was adorned by a red streamer with the inscription: "Poor chap, you waited for freedom in vain." Almost all of the inscriptions proclaimed Trubetskoi to be Russia's "freedom fighter," and outside the churches singing of the requiem was interlaced with the singing of the revolutionary hymn, "You have fallen victim in the momentous struggle." Trubetskoi's widow had to ask repeatedly that religious rather than secular dirges be sung.[4]

In thanking the students in St. Petersburg for their participation in the religious ceremonies, Trubetskaia, the widow, mentioned that her husband had wanted students to keep order at his funeral. They did so admirably as long as there was no police. The appearance of a police detachment immediately led to violence.

Trubetskoi's body was taken on October 2 by train to Moscow and the procession was accompanied by throngs of people. There was the inevitable melee, and after the train departed, the inevitable clash with the police.[5] In Moscow, on a clear October 3, a crowd of twenty thousand met the funeral cortege; it more than doubled during the day. The funeral procession was spontaneous and varied, composed of privileged and educated classes, of students, workers, and some revolutionary leaders. Services were held at the Moscow University chapel and later at Trubetskoi's apartment. The cortege then slowly wound its way to the Don Monastery, where Trubetskoi was to be interred. The burial took place by torchlight, which heightened its emotional impact. Since the walled-in cemetery was small, the crowds that could not get in clashed with the police.[6] Harcave dated the upswing of revolutionary events in Moscow to Trubetskoi's funeral, "where revolutionary students harangued the crowds outside the monastery."[7]

But even within the monastery walls the outside world could not be kept back. Manuilov and Lopatin, eulogizing at the graveside, spoke of all facets of Trubetskoi's life including his political activities. But other speakers dwelt almost exclusively on Trubetskoi's political significance. The student Zak, representing students from Moscow University, was most outspoken.

> The death of Trubetskoi proves again that in Russia great, free men can only die. . . . There is only one guilty party in this death, and that is the present [political] structure which does not permit the existence of free learning.[8]

Golovin, representing the *zemstvo*, recalled Trubetskoi's activity there in the last two years; and Professor Chubynskii of Kharkov University compared the death of Trubetskoi to that of Mikhailovskii.[9] The student Lutskii concluded the eulogies with a poem he had already recited in St. Petersburg, in which he told how Trubetskoi

> Inflamed us by the mighty word
> And blessed us for the fight to death,
> Awakening in us the faith
> In better life and order new.[10]

The poem ended with the word "freedom," which was echoed in unison by those present.

The motley crowd which participated at Trubetskoi's burial offered proof of a united opposition to autocracy. Even a Menshevik, who attended Trubetskoi's funeral by chance, could write:

> The people thronged after Trubetskoi's coffin because
> he was the first "beloved man," an elected rector, a
> dazzling representative of the liberal opposition.[11]

In death, as on the occasion of his appearance
before the Tsar, Trubetskoi became a symbol of progressive Russia. After his death many considered him more
progressive than he really was, a martyr for freedom who,
in the words of a popular poem, "had fallen at his glorious
post of duty, with the standard in his hands." Miliukov
characterized Trubetskoi as a "fighter . . . who will go
down in history as one of the most important figures of
the transitional moment," and Petrunkevich had him
suffer his fatal attack during an altercation with representatives of the St. Petersburg bureaucracy.[12] *Birzheviia
vedomosti*, a staid newspaper, echoed the words of the
student Zak: "Russian genius always crowns those who
do not live long."[13] Another newspaper, *Nasha zhizn'*,
reflecting the popular mood, bemoaned the tragic death,
among uncomprehending bureaucrats, of the perfect
candidate for the president of the Duma.[14] A. Stolypin
in *Novoe vremia* mused that the tragedy of Russia lay
in the circumstance that its great minds were invariably
placed in frail bodies.[15] Even *Voprosy Filosofii i Psikhologii* stressed Trubetskoi's achievements in trying to save
the Russian schools from the quagmire into which the
bureaucracy had pushed them.[16]
      The tone of most articles was one of faith in the
cause for which Trubetskoi had died.[17] The liberals, in
the last issue of *Osvobozhdenie*, tried to assess his political
role realistically:

> Russian society suffered a major, and in some respects,

irreplaceable, loss in the person of Prince Trubetskoi. A man of great erudition and stable civic convictions, Trubetskoi, insofar as his background, education, psychological make-up, etc., permitted, was called to serve as the intermediary between society and the government. Society rightly trusted his sincerity, the government was impressed by his views and had to take cognizance of them. For our tastes, he was at times not consistent enough in his views, but these cases are redeemed a hundred-fold by all his glorious, selfless, and dedicated service to the task of freedom. Yes, selfless, for when Prince Trubetskoi accepted the difficult duties of rector of Moscow University his physical heart had already been irretrievably damaged. And in the fateful moment it refused to serve his other heart, the heart which beat for freedom and learning. The fragile vessel broke, and the mighty spirit has left us.

Glory to him, fallen at the glorious post![18]

Obituary writers vied with each other in characterizing the greatness of Trubetskoi and the nobility of his soul. Poems were written in his honor. One of them, an answer to the poem of the St. Petersburg student, stressed that

Blood will not spatter
The banner fallen from your hands,
Courageously, wisely, and carefully
We'll carry it, Friend.

Along the bloodless path
Keeping your glorious will.[19]

Virtually all obituary writers agreed that the issue was simple. In the words of Bulgakov, used before and after him, "the heart could not stand it."[20] Trubetskoi "concentrated in himself the movements of all Russia;"[21] he was the first to speak up for academic freedom, he defended freedom in Russia, he was an outspoken foe of the *zemskii sobor*, he was a modern Granovskii.[22] He was a fighter for freedom,[23] "the fighter for the liberation movement" who died for his noble ideals.[24] His greatness transcended political divisions.[25]

An immediate result of Trubetskoi's death could be discerned in the field of education. Since Trubetskoi had suggested the establishment of private universities, a house and some money were donated for the "S. N. Trubetskoi National University." This money, it is believed, was turned over to the "Shaniavskii National University," which was founded in Moscow in 1905/1906.[26]

The student society which Trubetskoi founded was renewed after 1905, but quickly lapsed into inactivity. A new society, named in honor of Trubetskoi himself, was founded in 1908. It inherited the library and the traditions of the former organization. When the Minister of Education Kasso forbade all student meetings and dismissed some close advisers of the Trubetskoi Society, the group liquidated itself and gave its library to the Shaniavskii University.[27]

As could be expected, the political tribulations of Russia continued to be mirrored in the educational policies of the government and in the unrest in the universities. Trubetskoi's colleagues, particularly his brother Evgenii, who transferred to Moscow University, tried to defend university autonomy from the attacks of both the Left and the Right. Evgenii used both Trubetskoi's arguments and his authority.

The group which felt the loss of Sergei Trubetskoi

most keenly were the Russian philosophers. A week after Trubetskoi's death, at a closed session of the Moscow Psychological Society, its members and Trubetskoi's family listened to eulogies delivered by Lopatin, S. A. Kotliarevskii and the students B. A. Fokht and M. P. Polivanov. Later, they discussed ways to honor Trubetskoi. It was suggested to dedicate an issue of *Voprosy Filosofii i Psikhologii* to him, to have his portrait painted and hung in the editorial offices of *Voprosy Filosofii i Psikhologii*, to publish all of his articles, to establish a prize in his name, and to get the city to name in his memory one of the streets near Moscow University. The members decided to publish an album of photographs of Trubetskoi to serve as an anthropological and psychological study.[28] A doctor present at Trubetskoi's death had previously suggested the preservation of Trubetskoi's brain "as it is done in similar cases in Western Europe."[29]

Soon afterwards a group of followers of Trubetskoi edited a slim volume describing his funeral and quoting some of the obituaries.[30] By 1907, Lopatin began editing Trubetskoi's works.

Behind all these efforts lay the realization that Trubetskoi had contributed greatly to the general popularization of philosophical interests, of the historical approach to the study of philosophy, and in particular of idealistic philosophy. His own work, as well as his labors for the universities and within the Moscow Psychological Society, formed an important chapter in Russian intellectual development.

But the importance of Trubetskoi and of his special colleagues soon began to diminish even within their own lifetimes. This decline was due, paradoxically, to the success of their work. By the turn of the century, philosophical, metaphysical and religious problems began to interest certain members of the politicized Russian intelligentsia, as well as some of the prominent literary figures. These men, possessing more facile pens, greater literary talents, more flair for simplification, were accustomed to drawing political and sociological implications of their philosophy. It was this group of men which showed the fruits of the labors of the Moscow group of professional philosophers. Struve, Merezhkovskii, Berdiaev, Bulgakov, Belyi, Frank and others made the Russian intelligentsia aware of the issues of religion, morality, and idealistic philosophy. It led to political moderation, but by a process reverse to that followed by the Moscow philosophers.

The question posed by Radlov — to what degree Soloviev was the father of *Vekhi*[31] — can also be directed toward Trubetskoi. Trubetskoi differed from the contributors to *Vekhi* in that he was more intellectually tolerant and had a greater breadth of philosophical interests. The *Vekhi* contributors were all former members of the radical intelligentsia who at the time of the publication of *Vekhi* had not outgrown the manner of thinking of that group. Trubetskoi was too stable emotionally to have been able to feel at home with his younger colleagues. The sense of guilt of the intelligentsia, which became so prominent in *Vekhi*, was foreign to him.

Evgenii Trubetskoi welcomed *Vekhi* when it appeared in 1909 although he abhorred "certain infelicitous phrases" in it and disagreed with some of its authors.[32] According to Evgenii, most of the defects of *Vekhi* stemmed from the fact that the collection really attacked only the radical intelligentsia and not, as it made out, the whole intelligentsia. He felt that the major achievement of the collection was the stress it placed upon morality and absolute principles, which alone could justify the self-sacrifice necessary for the success of the political ideal. Since "revolutionary populism," which according to

Evgenii, had been the dominant creed of the radical intelligentsia, lacked this justification, the Revolution of 1905 had been doomed to failure. With the reform of the outlook of the intelligentsia, exemplified by *Vekhi*, there was also hope for success in political reform.

The *Vekhi* discussion, as the polemics stirred up by *Problemy idealizma*, illustrated the differences between the earlier professional philosophers of the Moscow group and the later converts to idealism. The professional philosophers, among them the Trubetskois, realized the importance of a juridical definition of freedom and the danger of identifying anything short of general principles with specific guidelines of morality.[33] Keeping in mind the blind alleys into which Soloviev's attempt to establish a perfect society had led him, Evgenii Trubetskoi steered the neophytes away from philosophical excesses. He tried to inject his brother's moderation, perspective, and rationality into the *Vekhi* debate.

To a degree, *Vekhi* — which reflected a transitional stage in the development of most of its authors — had the same faults as the intelligentsia it attacked. Among these were an excess of zeal, the compulsion to convert the whole educated class to a single point of view, emotionalism vented in tones of fanaticism, lack of objectivity, and a frantic approach to the issue of the intelligentsia. But it was precisely because of its shortcomings that *Vekhi* dramatized the crisis within the intelligentsia, a crisis which could be perceived as far back as the end of the nineteenth century. *Vekhi* should be considered not only as a call to the political intelligentsia to change, but as a sign that it was already changing.

The confusion in the definition of the intelligentsia which contributed to the obfuscation of the issues raised by *Vekhi* was widespread in Russia at the turn of the century. The failure to define the term intelligentsia —

which at times referred to the entire politically aware
segment of Russian society, and at other times only to
those who were actually involved in the opposition movement — contributed to the time gap between the moderation of the intelligentsia and their realization of being
moderates.

Sergei Trubetskoi did not identify himself with the
Russian political intelligentsia, which he considered
shallow. Moreover, he lacked the requisite characteristics
of the political intelligentsia: he was not alienated, he did
not experience a need to expiate his privileged status, he
did not diagnose all of Russia's ills as the result of political
repression. Nor did he consider the revolutionary parties
to be suitable allies for the moderates in their attempts to
reform the autocracy. Trubetskoi also lacked the firm
conviction in the felicitous outcome of Russia's political
struggle which was a source of strength for the intelligentsia.[34] Neither Trubetskoi nor his colleagues were
convinced of the inevitability of a constitutional regime
in Russia, much as they desired it. The realization of
the tenuous nature of Russian liberalism prevented these
men from voicing unbounded optimism and made them
prone to expressions of self-abnegation.[35]

In Sergei Trubetskoi the pessimism was overshadowed by the exhilaration of the revolutionary years, by the
hopes and by the need for action it generated. Fortunately
the high point of his career coincided with the most
widespread belief in his own ideal, that the Tsar intended
to accept reform. Trubetskoi's followers had to work
under different conditions. Some commentators saw in
the death of Trubetskoi the death of moderation in
Russia.[36] The fact that in emigration former critics of
Trubetskoi came around to his views on the danger of a
revolutionary upheaval in Russia strengthened that conviction.

But this interpretation was by no means correct. Trubetskoi's own career provided an example of alienation of the privileged from the government.[37] He illustrated the problems which the educated in Russia faced, but he did not solve them.

Sergei Trubetskoi had insisted upon legality and upon the co-operation of all moderates with the government. He always stressed the need for enlightenment to nurture the growth of the cultural forces and to secure the effectiveness of political reform. He contributed toward the process of the popularization of constitutional ideas in Russia and toward the creation of a climate of opinion conducive to the growth of constitutional institutions. His patriotism, social background, and philosophical views helped reconcile constitutionalism, an import from the West, with the Russian heritage, while his own Westernism made certain elements in the Russian tradition more acceptable to the political intelligentsia.[38] Trubetskoi's philosophical theories could, if popularly interpreted, solve the problem of the alienation of the individual, particularly the intellectual, from society. His approach, scholarly yet urgent, foreshadowed the efforts of such popular Russian thinkers as Berdiaev. Trubetskoi's colleague, L. M. Lopatin, who was not politically active, in a speech delivered on the occasion of the tenth anniversary of Trubetskoi's death, drew patriotic lessons from Trubetskoi's theories and from his life. This approach illustrated Lopatin's own politicization.[39]

Trubetskoi's life, views and career illustrated the dynamic interaction between intellectual interests and the pressures of the environment. The complexity of the views and attitudes within the educated and politically aware segment of Russian community are reflected in his life and work.

The difficulties of the intellectuals in Russia are further illustrated in the political career of Evgenii Trubetskoi. The reaction against the indecisive policies of the government was strong enough for Evgenii (and Shipov and Stakhovich) to decline an offer from Witte to enter the government.[40] It also enabled his joining the Constitutional Democratic Party. But Evgenii was revolted at what he considered the unwise, ineffective and unjustified intransigence of the liberal party.[41] Along with the dissidents from both the Kadets and the Octobrists, of whom Geiden, Stakhovich, Efremov, N. N. L'vov and Rumiantsev were the most prominent, Evgenii helped found the Party of Peaceful Regeneration [*Partiia Mirnogo Obnovleniia*]. The aim of the party was the reconciliation of all moderates and the fostering of their concerted action for a peaceful development of Russia.[42] The party was never numerous nor extremely popular, but it served the important function of crystallizing the self-consciousness of the moderates. Despite its brief existence, it was instrumental in the formation of the Progressivist faction in the Third and Fourth Dumas.

In an attempt to realize Sergei's dream to found a newspaper as a rallying point of the moderates, Evgenii, with his younger brother Grigorii, founded the *Moskovskii ezhenedel'nik* in 1906. Although he denied it, the journal was a mouthpiece of the Party of Peaceful Regeneration. Its aim, following the policy charted by Sergei Trubetskoi, was not so much to make the Russian intelligentsia moderate, as to make it realize its own moderation. Using not only his brother's reasoning and style, but often referring directly to his articles and borrowing his phrasing, Evgenii Trubetskoi argued with the Kadets and with the Octobrists, exhorting members of both parties to establish a strong bloc of moderates to offset the dangerous radicalization of Russian public opinion.[43] He placed all of his hopes upon such a bloc, which he, echoing Sergei, called "the government party."[44] He did not spare the society, which he, like his brother, held partly responsible for the type of government in Russia.

The characteristics of Evgenii Trubetskoi's approach, of the journal and of the party, were intellectualism and gradualism. The intransigence of the regime contributed toward turning these characteristics into weaknesses. In 1909, *Slovo*, the official organ of the Party of Peaceful Regeneration, on whose editorial board Evgenii served, was forced to close down for lack of subscribers. It later resumed publication as a more outspoken organ of the progressive faction under the title *Utro Rossii*. The following year, *Moskovskii ezhenedel'nik* ceased publication and members of its editorial board joined Struve's more radical *Russkaia mysl'*.

But even this radicalization within the moderates was a reaction to the unwillingness of the government to pursue real reform. Russia had aware, moderate, articulate and politically responsible citizens who were capable of working toward the implementation of reforms which would result in a viable constitutional regime. For that, however, the country also needed peace and a government at least slightly willing "to acculturize itself to constitutional institutions, for the constitutional institutions to adapt themselves to Russia."[45] This precisely had been the aim of Sergei Trubetskoi. The charge voiced by some members of the intelligentsia that its unwillingness to co-operate with the government was the major reason for the failure of reform is unwarranted.[46] The moderates, exemplified by Sergei Trubetskoi, desperately tried to warn the Russian government of the dangers facing it. They met with little understanding.

The fate of the three brothers of Sergei Trubetskoi further illustrates the tragedy of the failure. Evgenii, patriot that he was, rejoined the Kadets, who came to represent Russia; he died in the Caucasus, politically active to the last in the struggle against Bolshevism. Grigorii in emigration turned from foreign affairs to those of Russian Orthodoxy, seeing in the Church a mainstay of Russia. Petr, the prominent and rich oldest half-brother was killed in October, 1911, by his own nephew, the son of Senator Kristi. The motive was partly political; the liberal newspaper, *Rech*, deplored the act.[47]

NOTE ON TRANSLITERATION AND DATES

All Russian terms and names are transliterated according to the simplified Library of Congress system, except names with which the American reader is familar in a different transliteration (such as Kliuchevsky) or which the individuals themselves used (such as Vinogradoff or Guerrier).

All dates are given according to the Old Style Calendar.

LIST OF ABBREVIATIONS

PSZ   *Polnoe Sobranie Zakonov Rossiiskoi
                          Imperii* (3rd series) [St. Petersburg,
                          1881-1916]

SURP   *Sobranie uzakonenii i rasporiazhenii
                          pravitel'stva, izdavaemoe pri pra-
                          vitel'stvuiushchem senate* [St. Peters-
                          burg, 1809-1917]

Zhurnal MNP   *Zhurnal Ministerstva   Narodnogo
                          Prosveshcheniia*   [St. Petersburg,
                          1834-1917]

VFP   *Voprosy Filosofii i Psikhologii* [Mos-
                          cow, 1889-1922]

SPV   *Sanktpeterburgskiia   Vedomosti*
                          [1728-1914]

Unless otherwise indicated, references in the notes to *Sobranie* and Trubetskaia refer to Sergei N. Trubetskoi, *Sobranie Sochinenii kn. Sergeia Nikolaevicha Trubetskogo*, ed. L. M. Lopatin (Moscow, 1907-1912) and Olga N. Trubetskaia, *Kn. S. N. Trubetskoi: Vospominaniia sestry* (New York: 1953), respectively. References to Maklakov refer to *Vlast' i obshchestvennost'* (Paris, c. 1930).

NOTES TO CHAPTER 1

THE YOUTH

1. On the history of the family see V. K. Trutovskii, *Skazanie o rode Trubetskikh* (Moscow: 1891).

2. Evgenii N. Trubetskoi, *Iz proshlago* (Vienna: n. d.), p. 80.

3. Nikolai's first wife, who probably died in 1860, was Countess Liubov Orlov-Denisova. With her, Nikolai had three children: Petr (1857-1911), the marshal of nobility of Moscow, married to A. V. Obolenskaia, a sister of Sergei's wife; Sophia (1854-1901), married to V. P. Glebov; and Maria (1859-1926), married to G. I. Kristi, a highly-placed bureaucrat. These three children lived with an uncle. The children from the second marriage, in addition to Sergei, were Evgenii (1863-1920), a professor at Moscow University, married to V. A. Shcherbatova; Antonina (1864-1901), married to F. D. Samarin, a relative of Iurii; Elizaveta (1865-1935), married to M. M. Osorgin; Olga (1867-1947), suffered from infantile paralysis and dedicated all her life to collecting notes on her family; Varvara (1879-1932), married to G. G. Lermontov; Aleksandra (1872-1935); Grigorii (1873-1930), for a time Russia's envoy to Serbia; and Marina (1877-1924).

4. He lived from 1798 to 1871, and had been a military governor of Smolensk and Orlov, a Senator, a general in the cavalry and a Cavalier of the Order of St. Aleksandr Nevskii; see *Skazanie*, p. 299. Evgenii gives a graphic description of the private life of his grandfather in *Iz proshlago*, particularly pp. 10-17.

5. Evgenii wrote his memoirs, both *Vospominaniia* (Sofia, 1921) and *Iz proshlago*, in 1917, consciously retreating into his childhood, trying to find in it comfort for the difficult times of the war and the Revolution of 1917.* The closeness of both brothers and the similarity of their development justifies our analyzing Sergei's development on the basis of Evgenii's reminiscences. The quotation is taken from *Iz proshlago*, p. 7.

6. *Iz proshlago*, pp. 11-12.

7. She strengthened her influence by sharing the grown-up interests of her children. When the boys were studying Latin, she learned the language herself to be able to help them. N. V. Davydov, "Iz proshlago: Kn. S. N. Trubetskoi," *Golos minuvshago*; No. 1 (January, 1917), 5-6. At one point, Sergei complained to the editor of *Voprosy Filosofii i Psikhologii* that if his mother had done the proofreading for his article there would have been no mistakes. Letter of Trubetskoi to Grot from February of 1891, in *Nikolai Iakovlevich Grot:v ocherkakh, vospominaniiakh i pis'makh tovarishchei i uchenikov, druzei i pochitatelei* (St. Petersburg, 1910), p. 300. Henceforth, this source is referred to as *Grot*.

8. Evgenii's *Iz proshlago*, pp. 21-24. See also V. A. Obolenskii, *Ocherki minuvshago* (Belgrade, 1931); N. N. L'vov, "Bylye gody," *Russkaia mysl'*, (1923), Vols. I-II, 96-116; VI-VIII, 111-128; IX-XII, 5-26; and T. J. Polner, *Zhiznennyi put' Kniazia Georgia Evgenievicha L'vova. Lichnost'. Vzgliady. Usloviia deiatel'nosti* (Paris, 1932) for descriptions of family life of this type of gentry.

9. E. N. Trubetskoi, *Iz proshlago*, p. 41.

10. The word Evgenii used was *ukhod*. A character-istic of this *ukhod* was extreme absent-mindedness in everything but the object of interest. Nikolai Petrovich confused wife and manager in letters; his son, Sergei Nikolaevich, engrossed in conversation, often forgot he had come to eat.

11. N. G. Rubinshtein, the brother of Antonii, was a close friend of the Trubetskois; *Iz proshlago*, pp. 54-60. For the importance of music in the development of the brothers, particularly in the 1880's, see Evgenii's *Vospominaniia*, pp. 92-112. The impossibility of free ex-pression in any other sphere but the musical must be kept in mind. Sergei wrote two musical reviews, both on Scri-abin. One was in the form of a letter to *Kurier* in 1902, the other apparently as a note. Both published in Sergei N. Trubetskoi, *Sobranie*, I, 383-388.

12. *Iz proshlago*, p. 43; L. M. Lopatin, "Intro-duction" to Trubetskoi's *Sobranie*, I, iii.

13. Some of the tutors were bad choices, and none of them established lasting friendships with the brothers. See *Iz proshlago*, p. 69.

14. *Iz proshlago*, pp. 34-35. The children also made fun of their ancestors. Evgenii is at his best when he describes these scenes of early rebellion — from the grum-bling about the etiquette surrounding the grandfather to the burning of the nose on the portrait of a sour female ancestor (*Ibid.*, p. 11).

15. *Ibid.*, pp. 61-62. The tombstone of the woman bore the inscription she wanted — "The nanny of the Trubetskois."

16. *Ibid.*, p. 77. See also N. N. L'vov, "Bylye gody," *Russkaia mysl'*, I-II, 97-98.

17. Sergei and Evgenii, despite the one year's difference in age, always attended the same class.

18. One exception was a Latin teacher who gave Sergei bad grades in the hopes of getting extra paid lessons. The father refused to hire the teacher for private lessons and Sergei had to repeat the fourth term. Evgenii had been ill that year, and the maneuver enabled the two brothers to remain together in the same grade.

19. Sergei's "Pamiati V. P. Preobrazhenskogo," originally in *Voprosy Filosofii i Psikhologii* in 1900, also in *Sobranie*, I, 329.

20. Evgenii Trubetskoi, *Vospominaniia*, p. 29.

21. *Ibid.*, pp. 30-31.

22. *Ibid.*, p. 36.

23. In Lopatin's introduction to Trubetskoi's *Sobranie*, I, iv. The negative attitude toward the gymnasia is supported by Obolenskii, pp. 65-80; P. N. Miliukov, *Vospominaniia* (New York, 1955), I, 48-54; V. A. Maklakov, *Iz vospominanii* (New York, 1955), pp. 37-43; and others. I have been unable to identify Kokurin more closely.

24. Evgenii dated the development of his national consciousness from this time. *Vospominaniia*, pp. 14-21.

25. Evgenii's *Vospominaniia*, p. 54.

26. Lopatin in Trubetskoi's *Sobranie*, p. vi. On the conservatives of Kaluga see Obolenskii, p. 57.

27. Lopatin, *supra*, p. v. The phrase "accursed problems of life" was a favorite one of educated, moderate Russians. See for instance N. V. Davydov, *Iz proshlago* (Moscow, 1913), p. 250.

28. Evgenii's *Iz proshlago*, p. 81.

29. Evgenii's *Vospominaniia*, p. 56.

30. Quoted in A. F. Koni, *Ocherki i vospominaniia* (St. Petersburg, 1906), p. 202. For an "obligatory program of the self-education of the progressive intellectual" see Obolenskii, *op. cit.*, p. 124.

31. Evgenii's *Vospominaniia*, p. 56.

32. *Ibid.*, pp. 57-58.

33. *Ibid.*, p. 72.

34. The attachment of the Trubetskois and others to Dostoevsky enabled N. L. Losskii in *Dostoevskii i ego khristiianskoe miroponimanie* (New York, 1953), p. 346, to argue that Dostoevsky's religion was a happy one.

35. Soloviev had lost his faith at the age of thirteen, and, as the Trubetskois, had gone through all the classics of modern positivism, firmly believing in everything he read. He characterized his own development as a change from one faith to that of another, "going from Orthodoxy to Büchner," S. M. Lukiianov, *O Vl. S. Solovieve v ego molodye gody:Materiialy k biografii* (Petrograd, 1916), I,

117. Evgenii Trubetskoi was the first to point out the influence of Schelling upon Soloviev. See E. N. Trubetskoi, *Mirosozertsanie Vl. S. Solovieva* (Moscow, 1913), I, 51-56.

36. Georgii Florovskii, *Puti russkago bogosloviia* (Paris, 1937), p. 310; also V. Zenkovskij, *Aus der Geschichte des Aesthetischen Ideen in Russland im 19 und 20 Jahrhundert* (Hague, 1958), p. 49.

37. Evgenii's *Vospominaniia*, p. 115.

38. *Ibid.* We shall discuss Sergei's views on Sophia in a later chapter. Most of the manuscript has been lost but parts of it were published by Olga Trubetskaia as "*O sviatoi Sofii, Russkoi Tserkve i vere Pravoslavnoi*," in the Parisian journal *Put'*, No. 47, April-June, 1935. Almost the whole article was later incorporated into her book.

39. Evgenii Trubetskoi, *Mirosozertsanie Vl. S. Solovieva*, I, v. Even in the 1880's they both disagreed with Soloviev on certain problems.

40. Gershenzon published Chaadaev's "Philosophical Letters" in *VFP* in March/April, 1906, after Trubetskoi had died. In the only specific reference to Chaadaev, Trubetskoi, in an article on Leontiev published in *Vestnik Evropy* in 1893, mentioned that Chaadaev recognized in "Byzantinism" the reason for Russia's backwardness. See Trubetskoi, *Sobranie*, I, 178.

41. Evgenii's *Vospominaniia*, p. 67.

42. *Ibid.*

43. *Ibid.*

44. This trend was always much more pronounced in Evgenii than in Sergei, although by the time Evgenii wrote his memoirs he realized its limitations.

45. Evgenii's *Vospominaniia*, p. 71.

46. *Ibid.*, p. 82.

47. *Ibid.*, p. 74.

48. The same observation was made by Soloviev. See a letter of 1899 to S. N. Syromiatnikov in E. L. Radlov, ed., *Pis'ma V. S. Solovieva* (St. Petersburg, 1908), I, 220.

49. Evgenii's *Vospominaniia*, p. 82. Soloviev called the university "an absolute vacuum." See K. V. Mochul'skii, *Vladimir Soloviev: Zhizn' i uchenie* (Paris, 1936), p. 23. The significant exception was Kliuchevsky, whose lectures, although carefully rehearsed and repeated year after year, were popular among students.

50. His sister wrote in *Vospominaniia sestry*, p. 19: "Until 1891-92, Prince Sergei Nikolaevich was interested exclusively in philosophical, scientific and family matters and the sphere of politics was completely foreign to him." For V. A. Maklakov, see his *Vlast' i obshchestvennost'* (Paris, c. 1930) as well as his *Iz vospominanii.*

51. We shall discuss the content of Trubetskoi's satiric works when we discuss his political views. For a description of charades and home operas based on them, see Evgenii's *Vospominaniia*, pp. 131-132.

52. Evgenii's *Vospominaniia*, pp. 116-117.

53. Radlov, ed., *Pis'ma Solovieva*, I, 260; N. V. Davydov, "Iz proshlago" in *Golos Minuvshago*, No. 12, December, 1916, p. 197. Trubetskoi's oratory soothed even hostile crowds; see V. N. Khvostov, "S. N. Trubetskoi" in *VFP*, January/February, 1906, pp. 9-15 and A. A. Manuilov, "Iz vospominanii o Kn. S. N. Trubetskim" in *ibid.*, pp. 1-3.

54. Evgenii's *Vospominaniia*, pp. 181-183. On characterization of Lopatin see A. I. Ognev, *Lev Mikhailovich Lopatin* (Petrograd, 1922), particularly pp. 14-64, and S. I. Ognev, *Zasluzhennyi professor V. V. Ognev (1855-1928)* (Moscow, 1948), pp. 82-85. On Lopatin's philosophical views see a convenient summary in V. V. Zenkovskii, *Istoriia Russkoi Filosofii* (Paris, 1950), II, 187-199. Lopatin was born in 1855 and died in 1920. [Zenkovskii's book is available in English].

55. Her older sister was married to Sergei's half-brother. A former student of Sergei Trubetskoi, M. P. Polivanov, in a series of interviews held in New York in 1963 and 1964, was extremely helpful in many respects, particularly in describing and characterizing Sergei's wife, who is rarely mentioned by other writers.

56. The eldest son, Nikolai (1890-1938), was a noted philologist and a leading exponent of "Eurasianism." On the latter aspect see N. V. Riasonovsky, "Prince N. S. Trubetskoy's 'Europe and Mankind'," *Jahrbücher für Geschichte Osteuropas*, 1964, vol. 12, pp. 207-220. The younger son was named Vladimir, the daughter Maria.

57. Letters to Grot from Berlin, particularly one

from 1891 in which Trubetskoi mentions that he is not interested in local "luminaries," Grɔt, p. 297.

NOTES TO CHAPTER 2

THE SEARCH FOR UNITY

1. B. V. Iakovenko, *Ocherki russkoi filosofii* (Berlin, 1922), p. 73. See bibliography for a detailed listing of Trubetskoi's works.

2. Evgenii Trubetskoi, *Iz proshlago*, p. 74.

3. V. Zenkovskii, *Istoriia Russkoi Filosofii*, II, 343.

4. As shall be seen, Trubetskoi felt he was expounding a cosmic process, rather than only developing a philosophical theory. Among later Russian philosophers who grappled with issues in a manner similar to that of Trubetskoi were Berdiaev and Losskii.

5. From an early manuscript on Sophia, Wisdom of God, part of which has been preserved and published by Olga Trubetskaia in *Put'*, No. 47, April/June, 1935, pp. 3-13 and later incorporated into her *Vospominaniia sestry*. Phrase quoted taken from latter book, p. 200.

6. Trubetskoi, *Sobranie*, III, 400.

7. *Ibid.*, V, 205. Also see *ibid.*, III, 401-458.

8. *Ibid.*, VI, 5. Italics throughout the book follow the original.

9. *Ibid.*, III, 401. Fermentation — *brozhenie* — was

the term used in Russia to illustrate the state of intellectual and moral strivings of the Russian intelligentsia at
the turn of the century.

10. *Ibid.*, V, 9.

11. *Ibid.*, III, 43-44; see also V, 17.

12. *Ibid.*, IV, 7; also II, 205.

13. Most outspoken attack on the unconscious
metaphysics of empiricism, "the modern scholasticism,"
in *Sobranie*, III, 26-29; also II, 215.

14. *Sobranie*, V, 6; see also III, 3-31 and 336-342.
Trubetskoi based his reasoning largely on the arguments
of Soloviev and Lopatin on this issue.

15. *Sobranie*, III, 3.

16. *Ibid.*, 2-8; also IV, 4; clearest brief statement in
Vol. V, pp. 12-14. Trubetskoi was careful, however, to
disassociate himself from Hegelianism.

17. *Ibid.*, V, 1; see also III, 31 and IV, 4.

18. *Sobranie*, V, 12.

19. *Ibid.*, pp. 1-10.

20. *Sobranie*, III, 2.

21. *Sobranie*, II, 2.

22. *Ibid.*, p. 203.

23. *Sobranie*, III, 373.

24. *Sobranie*, II, 10.

25. Particularly in *ibid.*, p. 259; and vol. III, pp. 23 and 97.

26. *Sobranie*, II, 397.

27. *Ibid.*, p. 4.

28. *Ibid.*, p. 67; on p. 22 Trubetskoi acknowledged his debt to Spencer.

29. *Ibid.*, p. 13. Zenkovskii, *Istoriia*, II, 335, calls the phrase "celebrated formula."

30. *Sobranie*, II, 64.

31. *Ibid.*, p. 10.

32. *Ibid.*, p. 259.

33. *Ibid.*, pp. 162-163; most concise statement in polemics with Chicherin, in *ibid.*, p. 289.

34. *Ibid.*, pp. 170-181.

35. *Ibid.*, p. 184 and following; also see his introduction to the Russian translation of Caird's *Hegel* in *ibid.*, pp. 330-346.

36. *Ibid.*, p. 191. As proof, Trubetskoi discussed the post-Hegelian split and the philosophy of the unconscious.

37. *Ibid.*, p. 195.

38. *Ibid.*, p. 196.

39. *Ibid.*, p. 231, Trubetskoi's rather unclear argument on the soul is based on an article by Lopatin, "Poniatie o dushe po dannym vnutrenniago opyta," *VFP*, April, 1896.

40. *Sobranie*, II, p. 234.

41. Even Lopatin, a close friend of Trubetskoi and the author of one of the most thorough analyses of Trubetskoi's philosophy, in *Filosofskiia kharakteristiki i rechi* (Moscow, 1911), p. 234, considered Trubetskoi a mystic, although he rehabilitated such mystics who "live as they believe."

42. Trubetskoi, *Sobranie*, II, 252.

43. *Ibid.*, pp. 258-259.

44. *Ibid.*, pp. 270, 272. See also a repetition of the argument for the benefit of Chicherin on pp. 289-290.

45. *Ibid.*, p. 274.

46. *Ibid.*, p. 275.

47. In polemics with Chicherin in *ibid.*, p. 299.

48. As noted earlier, it has been published by Trubetskaia in *Put'* in 1935 and later incorporated into her *Vospominaniia*.

49. *Sobranie*, IV, 3.

50. He especially wanted to prove the authenticity of the Gospel of St. John and the fact that it was contemporaneous with the other gospels. (*Ibid.*, p. 390).

51. *Ibid.*, pp. 261 and 372-373.

52. *Ibid.*, pp. 453-454.

53. *Ibid.*, pp. 274-301.

54. *Ibid.*, p. 140.

55. Trubetskoi, *Sobranie*, II, 148.

56. *Ibid.*, p. 141.

57. Particularly forceful in *Sobranie*, IV, 417-420.

58. The argument was made in the Sophia manuscript but not elaborated later in view of the obvious drawbacks of the Russian church.

59. Trubetskoi argued forcefully with Renan and Harnack. He did not go into the various splits within the Christian faith, but spoke only of Christianity or Nicene Christianity. Trubetskoi's views on Renan were elaborated in a public lecture, "Renan i ego filosofiia," which was published in *Russkaia mysl'* in 1898, reprinted in *Sobranie*, I, 287-328.

60. *Sobranie*, II, 61.

61. *Ibid.*, p. 146.

62. *Sobranie*, IV, 4.

63. *Sobranie*, II, 107.

64. See particularly *ibid.*, pp. 142-149 and vol. IV, p. 380.

65. *Sobranie*, II, 74, and IV, 5.

66. *Sobranie*, II, 66.

67. *Sobranie*, IV, 5.

68. *Sobranie*, II, 79. See also the Sophia manuscript.

69. *Sobranie*, II, 79; also IV, 377 where the active role of the individual is stressed more than in earlier works.

70. *Sobranie*, II, 81.

71. *Ibid.*, p. 131; see also pp. 112-116.

72. *Ibid.*, p. 119.

73. *Ibid.*, pp. 118-124.

74. *Ibid.*, p. 107.

75. *Ibid.*, pp. 77-78.

76. *Ibid.*, p. 387; see also p. 374.

77. *Ibid.*, pp. 399 and 401-402.

78. *Ibid.*, pp. 407-417.

79. *Ibid.*, p. 349.

80. He considered philosophy and religion to be related in their aim — the attempt to know the truth. As a youth he had argued that the duty of every Christian was to philosophize, i.e., to search for wisdom and truth; see the Sophia manuscript in *Put'*, p. 6.

81. The relationship of Trubetskoi to Soloviev, as well as to other philosophers, can be best illustrated by a brief glance at the work of Evgenii Trubetskoi, the author of the most complete presentation of Soloviev's views. For a long time Evgenii could not expound either his own philosophy or that of Soloviev, for he could not tell them apart. After the death of Sergei, Evgenii's problems were compounded since now he could not distinguish his views not only from those of Soloviev but also from those of Sergei. He finally decided to stop worrying about what aspect of which theory belonged to whom and to set down his own views in their totality, along with the development of Soloviev's philosophy.

NOTES TO CHAPTER 3

"PHILOSOPHICAL PROSELYTIZATION"

1. Phrase used by A. A. Vvedenskii in an obituary article on N. Ia. Grot in *Moskovskiia vedomosti*, No. 141, 1899.

2. E. L. Radlov, *Vladimir Soloviev: Zhizn' i uchenie* (St. Petersburg, 1913), p. 170; N. Ia. Grot, "K voprosu ob istynnykh zadachakh filosofii," *Russkaia mysl'*, No. 11,

1886, pp. 21-42, and his "O zadachakh zhurnala," *VFP*, No. 1, 1889.

3. Grot, *K voprosu o reforme logiki. Opyt novoi teorii umstvennykh protsessov* (Leipzig, 1882), vii-viii; see also P. P. Sokolov, "Filosofskie vzgliady i nauchnaia deiatel'nost N. Ia. Grota," in *Grot*, p. 132. Preobrazhenskii was a self-effacing trained philosopher who did not choose to pursue a university career, see Trubetskoi, "Pamiati Vasiliia Petrovicha Preobrazhenskogo," *VFP*, October, 1900, pp. 481-500.

4. Trubetskoi, writing to Grot from Finland on August 26, 1895, in *Grot*, pp. 306-308.

5. *Ibid.*, p. 48.

6. Best source on Grot's life is *Grot*; his mother's memoirs, Natalia Grot, *Vospominaniia dlia detei i vnukov*, stop short of the birth of the children. A contemporary Soviet analysis of Grot's philosophy, in its progressive phase, in D. Kh. Ostrianyn, *Rozvytok materialistychnoii filosofii na Ukraiini* (Kiev, 1971).

7. There had been attempts to organize a Philosophical Society in St. Petersburg in February, 1880. Soloviev, because at that time he worked in the Ministry of Education, drafted the by-laws, but apparently doubted the success of the venture from the very beginning. K. Bestiuzhev-Riumin, F. G. Terner and Nikolai Strakhov were among the would-be founders. The Minister of Education, Delianov, blocked the formation of the Society because he feared it would become a forum for political discussion for the intelligentsia; see Soloviev's letter to Kireev in E. L. Radlov, *Pis'ma V. S. Solovieva* (St. Peters-

burg, 1908-1923), vol. II, 112; see also Radlov, "Golosa iz
nevidimykh stran," in *Dela i dni*, I, 1920, especially page
120. A brief history of the first twenty-five years of the
Moscow Society in N. D. Vinogradov, "Kratkii istoricheskii ocherk deiatel'nosti Moskovskago psikhologicheskogo obshchestva za 25 let," *VFP*, May 1910, 249-
262. Otherwise, information on the Society is scattered;
minutes of some of the meetings were published in *VFP*.
On the first decade of its existence, see *VFP*, March
1895, 252-258. Among the founders of the Society were
N. V. Bugaev, the mathematician, father of the poet
Andrei Bely; N. A. Zverev; M. M. Kovalevskii, the liberal
specializing in institutional history; S. A. Muromtsev,
later president of the Duma; A. I. Chuprov; full list in
VFP, March, 1893, pp. 124-125. On the early growth
of the Society, see Grot's report of 1890 in *VFP*, July,
1891, pp. 144-148.

8. Trubetskoi suggested honorary membership
for Kuno Fischer, and, on the occasion of Grot's tenth
term as chairman, also election of Grot to honorary
membership, *VFP*, May 1897, p. 368; *Grot*, pp. 345-346.

9. Letter of Grot to father, December 14, 1890; in
Grot, 333-334. The Society found it difficult to get
Russian intellectuals interested even in the serious study
of Comte. In 1891 Chicherin won half the prize; the other
half remained open until after 1905. The prize was funded
by A. A. Stolypin, a relative of the Prime Minister.

10. Trubetskoi was elected assistant treasurer in
1897; (*VFP*, May 1897, 368); he became deputy-chairman
in 1899, (*ibid.*, March, 1901, 169); he had been alternate
deputy-chairman in 1892-1893 (*ibid.*, January, 1893,
112). He served on the scholarship commission and tried,

with Grot and Lopatin, to organize a student group
(*VFP*, March 1896, 175). He was even more active in
the publishing ventures of the Society, working in 1895
in its editorial committee (*ibid.*, January 1896, 68),
working on various translations and helping with the
editorial work before he took over the editing of the
VFP.

11. Full report of the published works in the editorial statement in the November, 1895 issue of *VFP*. A
significant publication was L. M. Lopatin's *The Moral
Teaching of Schopenhauer*, which first appeared as volume
I of *Trudy* of the Psychological Society; reprinted in
Lopatin's *Filosofskie kharakteristiki i rechi* (Moscow,
1911), 70-86.

12. Letter of April 7, 1889, in *Grot*, 332, and
VFP, book I, 1889, x, respectively.

13. By O. Gerasimov, "Étude on the internal psychological life of Lermontov."

14. The preface to Bulgakov's "O zakonomernosti
sotsiialnykh iavlenii," in *VFP*, November, 1896 read "We
publish this article in line with our policy of permitting
freedom of expression for all philosophical views, although
we do not consider the essay all-encompassing or con-
vincing, and in general we do not share the author's
sociological views."

15. A good account of Grot as editor in the memoirs
of the secretary of *VFP*, Ia. K. Kolubovskii, "Iz litera-
turnikh vospominanii," *Istoricheskii vestnik*, April, 1914,
pp. 134-149.

16. See *VFP*, May 1897, p. 362 and January, 1900, p. 58.

17. Grot once removed an article by Kolubovskii on Lavrov after it was already set in type. In an interview of Grot and some of the members of the projected editorial board with Pobedonostsev, the Ober-procurator of the Synod objected only to Soloviev's participation in the journal; see Kolubovskii, p. 138. Although Robert Byrnes in his biography of Pobedonstsev, discounts the powerful influence of the man, he looms large in the thinking of the philosophers as one of the most influential members of the government.

18. See Kolubovskii, 146-147, for Grot's attempts to use even John of Kronstadt, the popular priest, to get the articles published. The articles on Nietzsche, prefaced by a careful warning, were written by Preobrazhenskii, Grot, Lopatin and Astafiev.

19. *VFP*, January, 1898, 78, minutes of the meeting of November 15, 1897.

20. Merezhkovskii spoke on December 8, 1901 on "Russian Culture and Religion", Trubetskoi took part in the discussion, *VFP*, January 1902, 633. Although they were the same age, Merezhkovskii considered himself a representative of the younger generation and did not expect to be understood by the "professors." An ironic eye-witness account of the evening in Boris Bugaev [Andrei Bely] *Nachalo veka* (Moscow, 1933), 172-181.

21. S. Bulgakov, "Kn. S. N. Trubetskoi kak religioznyi myslitel'," *Moskovskii ezhenedel'nik*, 1 April, 1908, 11-22 and "Kn. S. N. Trubetskoi," *Voprosy zhyzni*,

October/November, 1905, 280-289. See also S. Soloviev, "Smert' S. N. Trubetskogo," *Vesy*, September/October, 1905, 76-78.

22. Because of overall political reaction and lack of religious interests, continued infractions on the powers of the Church passed without public interest. In 1885 only Soloviev protested the abdication of the rights of the Church to examine aspirants to the bar in canon law. See *Osvobozhdenie*, 1902, No. 4, p. 59. Soloviev constantly pleaded for religious toleration, see for instance a letter he sent to Pobedonostsev in 1892, in *K. P. Pobedonostsev i ego korrespondenty. Pis'ma i zapiski* (Moscow, 1923), vol. 1^2, pp. 969-970. An interesting illustration of Soloviev's relations with the Church is in G. Florovskii's "Chteniia po filosofii religii magistra filosofii V. S. Solovieva," in *Orbis Scriptus Dmitrij Tschizewskij zum 70. Geburtstag* (Munich, 1966), pp. 221-236. On the Church in Russia during this period see Igor Smolitsch, *Geschichte der russischen Kirche, 1700-1917* (Leiden, 1964) and J. S. Curtiss, *Church and State in Russia: The Last Years of the Empire, 1900-1917* (New York, 1940), as well as Nicholas Zernov, *The Russian Religious Renaissance of the Twentieth Century* (New York, 1963).

23. From a review of a Russian translation of A. Menzies *History of Religion*, published in St. Petersburg in 1897. Trubetskoi's review was originally published in *VFP*; reprinted in *Sobranie*, II, 526-527. Trubetskoi's views on the relationship of religious and political matters were often similar to those expounded in *Osvobozhdenie*; see particularly 1902, No. 5, pp. 72-73 and No. 6, pp. 86-87.

24. From "Nauchnaia deiatel'nost A. M. Ivantsova-

Platonova," first published in *VFP* in 1895, in Trubet-skoi *Sobranie*, I, 230. Soloviev had studied under Ivantsov-Platonov, see K. V. Mochulskii, *Vladimir Soloviev:zhizn' i uchenie* (Paris, 1936), 44-45.

25. The work had merited extremely favorable reviews by Soloviev in *Russkoe obozrenie*, 1890, No. 10, pp. 931-945; reprinted in Soloviev's *Sochineniia*, 2nd ed. (St. Petersburg, 1888), VI, 267; another favorable review by Grot in *VFP*, 1890, book 2, pp. 105-106; V. Rozhkov in an article on Russian philosophical thought in *VFP*, 1890, book 3, p. 6, called Trubetskoi's *Metafizika* "a capital work."

26. Trubetskoi did not know where to publish a rebuttal to the "popovskaia drian' " directed against him. See *Grot*, pp. 297 and 301 for pertinent letter by Trubet-skoi to Grot. *Pravoslavnoe obozrenie* was a mouthpiece of the reformers in the Church. Trubetskoi's answer to Butkevich is reprinted in *Sobranie*, I, 149-171.

27. Count Pavel Kapnist, the trustee of Moscow University and a relative of Trubetskoi, was on the side of the Society. Grot tried to intervene through him and through his father to get to K. P. Pobedonostsev, the powerful procurator of the Synod. See Grot's letter to his father, October 26, 1891, in *Grot*, pp. 334-335. Grot's letter and note to Pobedonostsev in *Pobedonostsev i ego korrespondenty*, vol. 1^2, pp. 956-957. Text of Soloviev's lecture in *VFP*, January, 1892.

28. Discussion of these meetings in Jutta Scherrer, *Die Petersburger Religiös-Philosophischen Vereinigungen* (Forschungen zur osteuropäischen Geschichte, Berlin, 1973) and Peter Scheibert, "Die Petersburger religiös-

philosophischen Zusammenkünfte von 1902 und 1903,"
Jahrbücher für Geschichte Osteuropas, Band 2, February,
1965, pp. 513-560; some stenographic minutes in *Novyi
Put'*, 1904.

29. The fragment published in *Sobranie*, I, 446-
451, under the title "Proektirovannoe chtenie na 'bogoslovskikh besedakh'."

30. "O sovremennom polozhenii russkoi tserkvi,"
first published in *Moskovskii ezhenedel'nik* in 1906. In
Sobranie, I, 438-446. The text ends in mid-sentence;
there are no notes or an outline.

31. A short presentation of Trubetskoi's views on
religion in his article on that subject in Brockhaus-Efron,
reprinted in *Sobranie*, I, 504-509.

32. *Sobranie*, I, 440.

33. *Ibid.*, 438.

34. Boris Melioranskii, "Teoreticheskaia filosofiia S.
N. Trubetskogo," *VFP*, March, 1906, p. 220. Some clerics,
as P. Pospelov, the tutor of Trubetskoi's children, stressed
the deep religiosity of Trubetskoi's life and defended him
from the charges that he was an atheist. A group of clergy
placed a wreath on Trubetskoi's coffin in St. Petersburg to
attest to his being a practicing member of the Church.
See ENPE, ed., *Kniaz' Sergei Nikolaevich Trubetskoi:
Pervyi borets za pravdu i svobodu russkago naroda* (St.
Petersburg, 1905), particularly pp. 111-115. I have not
been able to decipher who was the editor of the work, to
which we shall subsequently refer as ENPE. It might
stand for Evgenii and Petr, a brother and half-brother

of Trubetskoi.

35. For example, the populist-terrorist Lev Tikhomirov wrote "Why I stopped being a revolutionary" not
because he broke with revolutionary ideology and tactics,
but because "the forty-year old man had a moral obligation to share his views, just as the twenty year old
youth did," Tikhomirov, *Pochemu ia perestal byt' revoliutsionerom* (Moscow, 1895; originally published in
French in 1888), p. 23. Tikhomirov accepted the notion
of the separation of Church and State, but he also argued
that within the Church, the individual should subordinate
himself completely to it. Soloviev took him to task for
that view, see December, 1892 issue of *Vestnik Evropy*.
A favorable account of Tikhomirov in V. A. Maevskii,
Revoliutsioner-monarkhist:Pamiati L'va Tikhomirova (Novyi Sad, 1934).

36. Sergei Makovskii, *Na parnase serebriannogo
veka* (Munich, 1962), p. 32.

37. At a closed meeting of the Society on May
11, 1902, Novgorodtsev spoke on behalf of the interested
authors, among them both Trubetskois, Bulgakov, P. B.
Struve (whose article appeared under the pseudonym P.
G.), Berdiaev, S. L. Frank, S. A. Askoldov, B. A. Kistia-
kovskii, A. S. Lappo-Danilevskii, S. F. Oldenburg and
D. E. Zhukovskii.

38. *VFP*, Jan., 1903, book 1 (66), pp. 156-157. The
members of the Society insisted on the disclaimer because
they did not want the Society to be identified with any
one particular philosophical or political school of thought.

39. P. I. Novgorodtsev, ed., *Problemy idealizma*

(Moscow, 1903), introduction.

40. *Problemy idealizma* generated a heated discussion, although by no means as extended as the one caused by *Vekhi*. One result was the publication of S. Dorovatovskii and A. Charushnikov, eds., *Ocherki realisticheskogo mirovozreniia* (St. Petersburg, 1904) which tried to exploit philosophical interest for the study of Marxism. Among the contributors were Lunacharskii, Bogdanov, and Maslov.

41. Iu. Aikhenval'd's review of *Problemy idealizma* in *VFP*, March/April, 1903, quotations from pp. 356 and 333.

CHAPTER 4

THE STRUGGLE FOR THE UNIVERSITY

1. Among the introductory works on Russia's educational development see S. V. Rozhdestvenskii, *Ocherki po istorii sistem narodnogo prosveshchenia v Rossii v XIX v.* (St. Petersburg, 1912), vol. I; Nicholas Hans, *History of Russian Educational Policy, 1701-1917* (London, 1931 and New York, 1964) and his *Russian Tradition in Education* (London, 1963); W. H. E. Johnson, *Russia's Educational Heritage. Teacher Education in the Russian Empire, 1600-1917* (Pittsburgh, 1950) and P. L. Alston, *Education and the State in Tsarist Russia* (Stanford, California, 1969). An extremely logical and coherent presentation of the argument for greater control of the universities was given in A. I. Georgievskii, *Kratkii istoricheskii ocherk pravitel'stvennikh mer i prednachertanii protiv studencheskikh bezporiadkov* (St. Petersburg, 1890). It was published in a limited edition and later

virtually destroyed by the government. The book was considered damning enough for Struve to publish an abstract of the work as the first volume of his *Materialy po universitetskomu voprosu* in Stuttgart, in 1902. Georgievskii's abstract shall be referred to as Georgievskii, *Materialy* . . . . On the student movement in Moscow University see P. S. Tkachenko, *Moskovskoe studenchestvo v obshchestvennopoliticheskoi zhizni Rossii vtoroi poloviny XIX veka* (Moscow, 1958) and V. I. Orlov, *Studencheskoe dvizhenie v moskovskom universitete* (Moscow, 1954) and V. I. Orlov, *Studencheskoe dvizhenie v moskovskom universitete* (Moscow, 1934), as well as the various articles and sources listed in the bibliography. The earlier Orlov edition is cited here.

2. The term trustee is a rather weak translation of the Russian *popechitel'* which connotes a more active function than the English equivalent. Text of the Statute of 1884 in *Svod Zakonov Rossiiskoi Imperii*, vol. XV, Part I, *Svod ustavov uchenykh zavedenii vedomstva ministerstva narodnogo prosveshcheniia* (St. Petersburg, 1893). A conveniently brief summary of the university statutes can be found in V. V. Glinskii, "Universitetskie ustavy (1755-1884)" *Istoricheskii Vestnik*, LXXIX (Jan./ Feb., 1900), pp. 324-351 and 718-742. Conditions of the students are described in countless memoirs; a convenient presentation of student life, particularly of the social conditions of the students in Moscow, can be found in P. Ivanov, *Studenty v Moskve:Byt. Nravy. Tipy* (Moscow, 1903).

3. Most forceful in a censored article entitled "Na rubezhe," written in 1904 but published only in 1906, *Sobranie*, I, 484.

4. ENPE, p. 6. The first private university in Russia was founded only after the Revolution of 1905.

5. Letter to Chicherin, fall, 1899, in Trubetskaia, pp. 196-197.

6. Writes Trubetskaia, pp. 81-82 of 1904/1905, which gives some indication of family connections earlier: "Our family . . . was in an extremely favorable position to get information on current social and political problems. Brother Peter Nikolaevich [a half brother] was the marshal of the nobility of the Moscow province; Grigorii Ivanovich Kristi, married to my sister [Maria] was [for a time] the Governor of Moscow; . . . [Fedor Dimitrievich] Trepov (Moscow chief of police, later Governor-General of St. Petersburg) had just become related to our family, having married his daughter to a relative of mine, P. V. Glebov. My cousin, A. A. Lopukhin, was director of the police department, and finally Prince Aleksei Dmitrievich Obolenskii (later ober-procurator of the Synod), the cousin of my mother, was particularly close to Sergei." Another uncle, S. A. Lopukhin, was the prosecutor in Kiev. Family connections helped Trubetskoi in his interventions and academic ventures; see his letters to Evgenii of April, 1899 and January, 1903, in Trubetskaia, pp. 190 and 217.

7. "Po povodu pravitel'stvennogo soobshcheniia o studencheskikh bezporiadkakh"; published originally 24 Dec., 1896 as the lead article of *Sanktpeterburgskiia vedomosti*, reprinted in *Sobranie*, I, 1-13. Trubetskaia incorrectly dated the article as appearing in 1899.

8. *Sobranie*, I, 7; from an article of 1896. Also letter to Evgenii of May, 1899, in Trubetskaia, p. 194;

similar view in "Universitet i studenchestvo," originally in *Russkaia mysl'*, 1897. See *Sobranie*, I, 265.

9. *Sobranie*, I, 6, the article of 1896.

10. *Ibid.*, p. 73.

11. From an article of 1896 in *SPV*; in *Sobranie*, I, 11.

12. March, 1902, in Trubetskaia, p. 212.

13. Trubetskoi, "Sumlevaius' shtop," 27 April, 1901, in *SPV*; in *Sobranie*, I, 52; see also "Urok klassitsizma," 27 July, 1901 in *SPV*; in *Sobranie*, I, 65-69.

14. The term was taken over from German. For Trubetskoi's criticism see his "Ochen' somnevauis," 26 May, 1901, in *SPV*, in *Sobranie*, I, 53-57 and "V vysshei stepeni somnevauis'," 19 July, 1905, in *SPV*, in *Sobranie*, I, 57-65. Trubetskoi made fun of the failure of Russian students to learn the correct orthography.

15. Among the critics of the system, chosen at random from among the political moderates, are F. E. Sollogub in N. V. Davydov, *Iz proshlago*, pp. 197-199; M. M. Novikov, *Ot Moskvy do Niu Iorka:moia zhizn' v nauke i politike* (New York, 1952), p. 27; V. N. Speranskii in *Pravo*, No. 42, in ENPE, p. 19. Novikov was the last freely elected rector of Moscow University.

16. "Universitet i studenchestvo," 1897 in *Russkaia mysl'*, in *Sobranie*, I, 261; also see *Osvobozhdenie* (1903), 20/21, 347.

17. Vinogradoff shared Trubetskoi's views: see his "Uchebnoe delo v nashykh universitetakh," *Vestnik evropy*, October, 1901, No. 10, 537-573. Vinogradoff predicted the worst for Russian universities and emigrated in December of 1901, accepting a post at Oxford, England.

18. A. I. Anisimov, "Kniaz' S. N. Trubetskoi i moskovskoe studenchestvo," *VFP*, book 1 (81), 1906, pp. 148-149.

19. Letter from 1895, in Trubetskaia, pp. 183-184.

20. *Grot*, p. 311.

21. On the St. Petersburg disturbances see P. S. Vannovskii, *Doklad po povodu studencheskikh bezporiadkov 1899-1900*, published by Tipografiia Rabochego Znameni in 1900. Also useful is a collection of allegedly first hand accounts by the students themselves edited by V. Chertkov, *Studencheskoe dvizhenie* (Purleigh, England, 1900), pp. 1-62.

22. Tkachenko, pp. 239-240; Orlov, p. 348.

23. Orlov, p. 344.

24. A new Ispolkom was formed in Moscow University in March, 1900, which called for a continued boycott; Chertkov, p. 39. The members of this committee and their alternates were arrested before any activity could bear results. A new flurry of unrest developed when the students staged demonstrations in April to commemorate German Liven, a student who had burned himself in Butyrka prison, where he was being kept in connection with the distribution of a booklet by Kautsky; Tkachenko,

pp. 245-250; see also Trubetskaia, pp. 190-191 and *Osvobozhdenie*, No. 10, 2/15 November, 1903, p. 179. The situation was so bad that Professor Sokolovskii of the Katkov Lycee wanted his charges to stop sitting in on university lectures because contact with the university students made the Lycee pupils restless; *Osvobozhdenie*, No. 10, 2/15 February, 1903, p. 285.

25. Vannovskii presented his report on May 25, 1899.

26. *PSZ*, Svod II, vol. 19^1, article 17333.

27. The problem of student service in the army as punishment for disturbances was discussed ever since Pobedonostsev suggested the measure in the 1870's. But the army did not want any revolutionary students who might cause trouble in its ranks. The measure was used only two years later in Kiev, and the drafting of students caused serious student unrest. The decree of July 29, 1899, in *PSZ*, Svod III, vol. 19^1, pp. 395-396.

28. The government was able to get advance information on a plan to reactivate the *zemliachestva* and arrest the students involved; Orlov, pp. 362-371.

29. Text of the resolution in R. C. Vydryn, *Osnovnye momenty studencheskogo dvizheniia v Rossii* (Moscow, 1908), p. 51.

30. Trubetskaia, pp. 41-42. Before deciding to go to St. Petersburg in person, Trubetskoi jotted down his views in a note to Vannovskii, which is reprinted in *ibid.*, pp. 204-207. Allegedly Vannovskii had not been informed of the arrests. He learned of them only from Trubetskoi.

Trubetskaia, p. 42.

31. See *Rech i otchet*, 1901, p. 62; Evgenii Trubetskoi, *Vospominaniia*, pp. 84-85; and N. V. Davydov, "Iz
proshlago:Kn. S. N. Trubetskoi," *Golos minuvshago*, No.
1, January, 1917, p. 17. Also interview with Polivanov,
January 17, 1964.

32. In "Universitet i studenchestvo," published in
Russkaia mysl' in 1897, Trubetskoi criticized the students
as he tried to prod the government into legalizing student
organizations. The article reprinted in *Sobranie*, I, 261-
286; see particularly p. 285.

33. Letter to Evgenii in Trubetskaia, p. 190.

34. *Ibid.*, p. 210. The letter was written probably
in 1901.

35. In Trubetskaia, p. 205.

36. Guerrier was not only a pioneer in female
education in Russia; in 1882 he had been excluded from
government-sponsored discussions on universities since
he was considered to be too liberal, P. A. Zaionchkovskii,
Krizis samoderzhaviia na rubezhe 1870-1880 gg. (Moscow,
1964), p. 448.

37. Trubetskaia, pp. 207-208 and p. 42.

38. *Ibid.*, p. 209, from a letter to Evgenii; see also
A. I. Anisimov, "Kniaz' S. N. Trubetskoi i moskovskoe
studenchestvo," in *VFP*, Book 1 (81), 1906, pp. 146-196.

39. Trubetskaia, p. 44.

40. From a speech to the students of Moscow University, 1903, in *Sobranie*, I, 73.

41. An article originally published in 1897; in *ibid*., p. 20.

42. "Zapiska ordinarnogo professora kn. S. N. Trubetskogo o nastoiashchem polozhenii vysshikh uchebnykh zavedenii i o merakh k vozstanovleniiu akademicheskogo poriadka," 21 June, 1905; in *Sobranie*, I, 401-412. Similar views earlier.

43. Article from 1897 in *ibid*., p. 265.

44. "[The faculty], because of the shortage of educated personnel, would probably remain the same even if the professors were elected." *Ibid*.; see also pp. 5, 273-274 and 281.

45. According to the provisions of the Statute of 1884 the student could choose his courses, but these provisions were soon so modified that a rigid program made it virtually impossible to take electives; eventually students were forbidden to take courses outside their faculties. The ministry of education had to approve all courses.

46. These views were similar to those expressed by Kavelin in the 1860's and to those of the German professors whose opinion was solicited at the same time, as well as to those of Pirogov; see William L. Mathes, *The Struggle for University Autonomy in the Russian Empire during the First Decade of the Reign of Alexander II (1855-1865)* (unpublished Ph.D. dissertation, Columbia University, 1966).

47. *Sobranie*, I, 267-271 and 4-8, articles from 1897 and 1896; also letter to Evgenii from May, 1899, in Trubetskaia, p. 193. The *zemliachestva* were associations of students who came from the same home area and who banded together in Moscow for purposes of financial aid, social contact, and academic interests. They levied an income tax on their members and received some funds from the home town which were distributed among the needy members. Sometimes, the *zemliachestva* set up housekeeping apartments and libraries. On the whole, the *zemliachestva*, until the 1890's tried to avoid politics and student disturbances. The *zemliachestva* at times managed to establish a central union to co-ordinate policy and a network or courts which originally judged students but which eventually began trying the faculty *in absentia*. These organizations were considered illegal and were constantly hounded by the police. The result was the radicalization of the membership. For a fuller discussion, see the works by Tkachenko and Orlov cited earlier, as well as V. A. Obolenskii, *Ocherki minuvshago*, especially p. 100.

48. *Sobranie*, I, 283-284, article from 1897; ground was broken for a new dormitory in Moscow on November 2, 1901, see Moscow University, *Rech i otchet*, 1902. This publication was the annual progress report of Moscow University and usually included the lecture delivered on the celebration of the patron saint of the university, the Russian version of Founder's Day.

49. *Sobranie*, I, 277, article from 1897.

50. Factual account in *Vestnik evropy*, No. 3 and No. 4, March-April, 1901. Bogolepov did not die until March 2. Toward the end of the year serious disturbances

broke out in Kiev which resulted in almost 200 students being drafted into the army, a measure which in turn led to greater student disturbances.

51. The commission worked until May 16. It was headed by D. N. Zernov and composed of V. I. Guerrier, V. O. Kliuchevsky, P. G. Vinogradoff, N. A. Umov, K. A. Andreev, V. K. Tserakii, Count L. A. Komarovsky, I. T. Tarasov, M. B. Dukhovskii, A. B. Fokht, and A. A. Bobrov. The findings of the commission are summarized in Orlov, pp. 107-112. They were published by *Osvobozhdenie* as *Materialy po universitetskomu voprosu* (Stuttgart, 1904), vol. II. The conclusions of the commission were based on discussions of the professors as well as on the talks of the faculty with the students. The faculty urged a speedy legalization of student organizations, the ameli-oration of student economic needs, the limitation of the powers of the inspectorate and a concurrent strengthening of the competence of the faculty, as well as the freeing of arrested students. Orlov, p. 344, complained that such suggestions made the students susceptible to "the liberal point of view."

52. The answer of Moscow University professors to Vannovskii's questions in Moscow University, . . . *O peresmotre ustava i shtatov Imperatorskikh rossiiskikh universitetov:Suzhdenie Soveta Imperatorskogo Moskov-skogo Universiteta po voprosam kasaiushchimsia ustroistva universitetov, s zakliucheniem Rektora Universiteta i otzyvom Popechitelia Moskovskogo Uchebnogo Okruga* (na pravakh rukopysu) (Moscow, 1901); henceforth cited as Moscow University, . . . *O peresmotre*. As part of his policy of reconciliation, Vannovskii sent Sviatopolk-Mirskii to negotiate with the students exiled to Siberia to get them to promise good conduct if permitted to

return. For a description of the episode, see *Osvobozh-denie*, No. 9, 19 Oct./ 1 Nov., 1902, and No. 10, 2 Nov., 1902, pp. 142-143.

53. Moscow University, . . . *O peresmotre*, p. 52. Other universities, for instance Kharkov, were more vehement in their denunciation of the diarchy in university rule. See Kharkov University, *Doklad kommissii po peresmotre ustava i shtatov Imperatorskikh Rossiiskikh universitetov* (Kharkov, 1901), introduction.

54. Some faculty argued that student disturbances had always been political, others, that vacations served as incubation periods for revolutionary ideas, while the father of the poet Andrei Bely, Professor Nikolai Bugaev, complained that the primary task of the university, the preparation of civil servants, had been lost from sight.

55. The student movement seemed all the more serious to the government in view of the renewed wave of terrorism, noted by Cherevanin in L. Martov, P. Maslov, A. Potresov, *Obshchestvennoe dvizhenie v Rossii v nachale XX veka* (St. Petersburg, 1909-1910), I, 283. For examples of legislation against the students see the laws of June 25, 1899, in *PSZ*, Svod III, vol. 19^1, article 17333; June 29, 1899, in *ibid.*, article 17484 (this article provided for the drafting of students who were expelled from the university). Mass arrests of the students continued.

56. This legislation was known as Vannovskii Rules; text in *Zhurnal MNP*, vol. CCCXXXIX (February, 1902), pp. 171-181; see also letter of Sergei Trubetskoi to Evgenii from January, 1903, in Trubetskaia, p. 217.

57. There had been earlier attempts to organize

student societies whose purpose would be extra-curricular study. An important one was the Student Scientific-Literary Society founded in St. Petersburg University in 1882 and dissolved in 1887 because some of its members had participated in the assassination attempt on the Tsar. Prof. Orest F. Miller served as the adviser to this society. For an account of the Society, see A. K. Borozdin, "Studencheskoe nauchno-literaturnoe obshchestvo pri St. Peterburgskim universitete," *Istoricheskii vestnik*, vol. 74 (January/February/March, 1900), pp. 302-312 and S. G. Svatikov, "Opal'naia professura 80-tykh gg.," *Golos minuvshago*, No. 2, 5-78. Alexander Ulianov, Lenin's older brother, served for a time as the secretary of the Society; for his views see B. D. Wolfe, *The Three Who Made a Revolution* (Boston, 1959), pp. 60-65. Ulianov participated in the assassination plot. The majority of the students had wanted the Society to be apolitical, and A. F. Geiden, whose idea it was to organize a group which would combat radical propaganda, resigned in protest. Orlov, pp. 189-190, accused the Society of being run by the reactionary *Sviashchennaia Druzhina* and of lacking both science and literature; Georgievskii, *Materialy* . . . , p. 39, also referred to the Society as a quasi-literary one. The dissolution of the Society led to the establishment of a spate of circles of self-education which trained students in revolutionary ideology and conspiratorial tactics; Obolenskii, pp. 87-88.

58. Orlov, 84, 249; Tkachenko, 232, N. N. Tikhomirov, ed. *Istoriia Moskovskago universiteta*, vol. I (Moscow, 1955), 374; Georgievskii, *Materialy* . . . , p. 20.

59. See Trubetskaia, p. 48, and I. Kheraskov in V. B. Yel'iashevich, A. A. Kizevetter and M. M. Novikov, eds., *Moskovskii universitet* (Paris, 1930), p. 445.

60. A. I. Anisimov, "Kn. S. N. Trubetskoi i moskov-skoe studenchestvo," *VFP*, book 1 (81), January, 1906, p. 159. I. Kheraskov in V. B. Yel'iashevich, *et al.*, eds., *Moskovskii universitet*, p. 442, wrote of a split within the academics. The right faction was composed of such moderates as A. I. Anisimov, M. A. Geineke, and B. N. Fokht, while the left faction called itself democratic and included among its leaders Kheraskov, V. S. Protopopov, V. V. Sher, and D. P. Konchalovskii. In an earlier generation, Maklakov and Miliukov had shared the "academic" view. See Maklakov, *Vlast'*, pp. 96-104 and 124-126, and Miliukov, pp. 96-97.

61. According to Anisimov, p. 166; also N. Knorring, "Iz zhizni moskovskogo studenchestva v nachale XX veka (Pamiati professora Kn. S. N. Trubetskogo)," in Yel'iashevich *et al.*, *op. cit.*, p. 452.

62. Letter to Evgenii, March, 1902, in Trubetskaia, p. 213.

63. Trubetskoi's letter to Chicherin, spring, 1903, in Trubetskaia, p. 214; Kheraskov in Yel'iashevich *et al.*, p. 446.

64 Anisimov, p. 165; Trubetskaia, pp. 48 and 218; letter of Sergei to Evgenii, March, 1902, in *ibid.*, p. 213; but Polivanov in an interview of January 3, 1964, mentioned that the Society was "a *kollektiv* of students," with apparently student officers. Polivanov seems to be mistaken in this respect. Trubetskoi was considered chairman of the Society, not its adviser. But Polivanov leaves no doubts as to Trubetskoi's key role in the Society, regardless of his official position.

65. Trubetskaia, p. 49; Kheraskov in Yel'iashevich *et al.*, p. 446.

66. Anisimov kept stenographic notes of Trubetskoi's speech; text in Anisimov, pp. 168-169; also see Kheraskov in Yel'iashevich *et al.*

67. Trubetskoi to Evgenii, March, 1902, in Trubetskaia, p. 213.

68. *Ibid.*; also letter to Chicherin in *ibid.*, p. 214. See also Kheraskov and Knorring in Yel'iashevich *et al.*, pp. 446 and 452; and Polivanov interview, January 3, 1964.

69. Trubetskaia, p. 53. Knorring, p. 453.

70. Anisimov, p. 173; Trubetskaia, p. 53; and Trubetskoi to Chicherin in Trubetskaia, pp. 213-214.

71. Trubetskaia, pp. 66 and 217; letter of Trubetskoi to Evgenii, July, 1902, in *ibid.*, p. 216. Again, it was not an original idea. In answering the Vannovskii questions, the Moscow University professors specifically mentioned scientific excursions as being a desirable means of contact between the students and the professors. They did not, however, envisage as spectacular a journey as this one. The specific idea was wholly Trubetskoi's. See Anisimov, p. 177. A very favorable secondhand account is given by the son of one of Trubetskoi's colleagues, S.I. Ognev, *I. V. Ognev*; the Greek excursion is described on pp. 97-101. This account is often based on N. V. Davydov, "Iz proshlago," in *Golos minuvshago*, January, 1917, pp. 5-34.

72. Trubetskaia, pp. 67-68. Trubetskoi's health was undermined by an inflammation of the liver and gall bladder trouble in the summer of 1901. In the spring of 1903 he caught pneumonia from his wife, who, according to Olga, got it when her carriage overturned and she fell into a puddle.

73. Trubetskoi managed to import duty-free some tropical suits for the members of the excursion. The suits shrank during the first rainfall. The opponents of the whole excursion considered the suits to be uniforms provided by the government; Knorring, p. 455.

74. Ognev, *Ognev*, p. 99.

75. Trubetskoi's letter to his wife in Trubetskaia, p. 220, Knorring, p. 456.

76. Trubetskoi to his wife in Trubetskaia, p. 220.

77. *Ibid.*, p. 223; other letters from the excursion on pp. 219-235; see also p. 70.

78. Knorring, pp. 454-460; also Ognev, *op. cit.*

79. Trubetskaia, pp. 246-249; also *Osvobozhdenie*, No. 10 (34), 2/15 November, 1903, pp. 180-181; text of leaflet is also there. Trubetskoi's speech is also in *Sobranie*, I, 72-76.

80. Trubetskoi was hurt by the deaths of those close to him: Grot died in 1899; Trubetskoi's father, Soloviev and Preobrazhenskii in 1900; and his sister Antonina and his mother died in March, 1901.

81. Kheraskov, p. 448; also N. S. Arsenev, interview on December 13, 1963.

82. Letter in Trubetskaia, pp. 253-254.

83. In Trubetskaia, p. 72; see also *Osvobozhdenie*, No. 10, 2/12 November, 1903, pp. 180-181.

84. The Moscow University Soviet supported the government in what it called "its policy of implementation of moral ideals," text of the council resolution in *Listok Osvobozhdeniia*, No. 6, 15 (28), April, 1904. See also E. Maevskii in Martov, *et al.*, eds., *Obshchestvennoe dvizhenie*, II, 36. S. I. Ognev, *Ognev*, pp. 101-102, cites cases of women students wanting to go to the front.

85. See Evgenii Trubetskoi, "Die Universitätsfrage," in J. Melnik, ed. *Russen über Russland* (Frankfurt am/ Main, 1906), p. 40; on the Kazan' Square demonstration of March 4, 1901 at which Struve and Tugan-Baranovskii were arrested see L. Martov *et al.*, eds., *Obshchestvennoe dvizhenie*, I, 385, and Ariadna Tyrkova-Williams, *Na putiakh k svobode* (New York, 1952).

86. Trubetskaia, pp. 254-255; also *Listok Osvobozhdeniia*, 10 (23), April, 1904.

CHAPTER 5

THE ENLIGHTENMENT OF TSAR AND SOCIETY

1. Evgenii Trubetskoi, *Vospominaniia*, pp. 130-134.

2. For a ful list of Trubetskoi's satires, see the bibliography. Soloviev made fun of Trubetskoi's satiric

attempts; see his letters to Grot in *Grot*, pp. 283, 285 and 288, but one of Trubetskoi's poems has been incorrectly attributed to Soloviev. The poem, "The Prayer of Butonov," is from "Pravdivaia istoriia 'Zdravago Slova'," written in 1895, and published in *Sobranie*, I, 413-430; the poem on pp. 427-428.

3. The differences between Moscow and St. Petersburg and the political effect both have had on various Russians have been discussed by many authors. Miliukov, *Vospominaniia*, p. 270, had this to say on the subject: "In Petersburg political programs are worked out, in Moscow scientifically and systematically legislative projects . . . which Moscow firmly believed would materialize some day." Law in Moscow was quite different from a statute. See also F. A. Stepun, *Byvshee i nesbyvsheesia* (New York, 1956), vol. I, as well as almost all memoirs about Moscow. S. I. Ognev, *Zasluzhennyi prof. I. V. Ognev*, p. 74, stressed the extremely active social life of the Moscow professors, which naturally contributed to an informal approach to political problems. On the other hand, because of an essentially different conception of politics, V. I. Gurko, *Features and Figures of the Past* (Stanford, Calif., 1939), pp. 16-17, accused Moscow of lack of political interest in general.

4. D. N. Shipov, *Vospominaniia i dumy o perezhitom* (Moscow, 1918), p. 27, considered the socioethical tasks of the *zemstvo* to be of prime importance. In an obituary on V. S. Soloviev, published in *Vestnik evropy*, 31 July, 1900, reprinted in *Sobranie*, I, 344-352, Trubetskoi noted with full agreement that "[Soloviev] compared his publicistic activity to the 'obedience' manifested by the monk who cleans out the garbage and dirt from the premises of the monastery." *Ibid.*, p. 350.

Also in an article on Soloviev in *VFP* in 1901; in *Sobranie*, I, 367.

5. The famine was so intense because the reserves of the peasants had been eaten up by governmental taxes. See Theodore H. von Laue, *Sergei Witte and the Industrialization of Russia* (New York, 1963), p. 30. At first the government tried to keep the famine a secret, but the *zemstvo*, its connection with the peasants, the magnitude of the disaster and the existence of an alert public opinion brought the famine out into the open. News of the plight of the villages travelled quickly. Public opinion was incensed. Even *VFP* had articles on the relationship of ethics to the famine by Soloviev and Lev Tolstoi. These articles, however, were censored and removed from the galleys; *Grot*, p. 359. Soloviev, with whom Trubetskoi was very close, prodded the government to reform in a series of articles in *Vestnik evropy, Russkaia mysl'* and *Severnyi vestnik*. Both he and Trubetskoi thought that the government's inability to handle the crisis caused by the famine "freed the opposition from the hypnosis of its weakness," and encouraged the activity of the non-opposition intelligentsia. See A. Potresov in L. Martov, *et. al.*, *Obshchestvennoe dvizhenie*, I, 539. See also Maklakov, p. 127 and Trubetskaia, *Vospominaniia sestry*, p. 20.

6. Letter to Evgenii, April, 1892, in Trubetskaia, p. 178.

7. He acknowledged the influence Soloviev exercised upon him within this context. See Trubetskoi's obituary on Soloviev, originally published in *Vestnik evropy*, 1900, in *Sobranie*, I, 344-352, and his "Osnovnoe nachalo ucheniia V. Solovieva," originally a speech de-

livered before the Moscow Psychological Society• on February 2, 1901, published that year in *VFP*; in *Sobranie*, I, 352-367.

8. Trubetskoi expounded his views in an article on Leontiev, "the disillusioned Slavophile," who was so different from the Slavophiles, and in resulting polemics with a minor epigone of the Slavophiles, General Alexander Kireev. Both articles were originally published in 1893 in *Vestnik evropy*, both reprinted in *Sobranie*, I, the article on Leontiev, "Razocharovannyi slavianofil," on pp. 173-211; the other article, "Protivorechiia nashei kul'tury," on pp. 212-229. The phrase quoted is on p. 176.

9. Soloviev argued that *narodnost'*, transformed into nationalism, contradicted Christianity and led to the dissolution of Slavophilism. His views were most fully developed in "Natsional'nyi vopros," which is volume V of the second edition of his *Sochineniia*. Despite all his criticism of the Slavophiles, Soloviev also kept certain elements of Slavophile ideology. Trubetskoi on Soloviev's criticism of the Slavophiles in *Sobranie*, I, 183.

10. Trubetskoi nevertheless felt that the religion of the early Slavophiles was best portrayed by Soloviev; see *ibid.*, pp. 178-183 and 205-208. Trubetskoi wrote the article in Norway and did not have the works of Khomiakov at hand. He was afraid that he had been imprecise in his formulation of the religious views of the Slavophiles; see letter to Grot in *Grot*, pp. 304-305.

11. Trubetskoi, *Sobranie*, I, 222, from "Protivorechiia nashei kul'tury," originally published in 1893 in *Vestnik evropy*.

12. Letter to Grot, 13 August, 1894, in *Grot*, p. 303; Trubetskaia, p. 106.

13. D. N. Shipov, *Vospominaniia i dumy*, p. 154; Trubetskaia, pp. 35-36.

14. Trubetskoi met Chicherin often, was familiar with all of his works and valued them highly; Trubetskaia, *passim*, as well as Evgenii's memoirs. Trubetskoi, in "Sushchestvuet li obshchestvo," originally in *SPV*, 9 August 1900; in *Sobranie*, I, 37, directed his conservative opponent to Chicherin's works for an analysis of basic concepts in politics and sociology.

15. The article, "Chuvstvitel'nyi i khladnokrovnyi," was originally published in *Russkaia mysl'* in 1896; in *Sobranie*, I, 251-261. The passage quoted is from pp. 260-261.

16. "Vera v bezsmertie," first published in *VFP*, 1901; in *Sobranie*, II, 348-349. *VFP* were subject to censorship, as were books published by the Psychological Society. See letter of Trubetskoi to Grot, July, 1894, in *Grot*, pp. 302-303.

17. "Delo Dreifusa i frantsuzkie generaly," published under a pseudonym in *SPV* in June, 1899; reprinted in *Sobranie*, I, 33-36.

18. Trubetskoi used this characterization of the Russian intelligentsia in the Sophia manuscript; in Trubetskaia, p. 200. At times he accused the whole Russian society of shallowness. For instance, in an article on Scriabin in the *Kurier* in 1902 he even criticized the musical tastes of the Russian public as being formed by

"ready made criticism and cliches," in *Sobranie*, I, 385.

19. Miliukov, *Vospominaniia*, p. 152; see also the
letter of Soloviev to Grot, in *Grot*, p. 270. Miliukov's
"Razlozhenie slavianofil'stva," first in *VFP*, May, 1893;
reprinted with very slight stylistic changes in his *Iz istorii
russkoi intelligentsii:sbornik statei i etiudov* (St. Petersburg, 1903), pp. 266-306; Miliukov's answer to Soloviev
in *ibid.*, pp. 307-308. Specific references to latter source.

20. Soloviev, "Zamechaniia na lektsiiu P. N. Miliu-
kova," in *VFP*, 1893, book 18; also in his *Sochineniia*, 2nd
ed., VI, 424-446.

21. "Po povodu zamechanii V. S. Solovieva," in
Miliukov, *Iz istorii*, pp. 307-308.

22. The sectarianism of the intelligentsia was also
proverbial, but the similarity of its views to some of the
moderates, even within the bureaucracy, is rarely noted.
A dramatic example of this similarity was offered by
Gurko, *Features and Figures of the Past*, p. 348, note.
He described his chance collaboration with a member
of the Socialist Revolutionary Party in 1917: "most
surprising of all, [I] found that I had much in common
with him." Gurko was a highly placed bureaucrat in the
Tsarist government.

23. In a letter to Evgenii, April, 1899, in Trubetskaia, p. 198, Trubetskoi considered one of the leading
liberals, Pavel Miliukov, almost a rabble rouser.

24. "Lishnie liudi i geroii nashego vremeni," published posthumously in *Sobranie*, I, 368-382, apparently
written after 1901.

25. Trubetskoi's "Sumlevaius' shtop," in *SPV*, April 27, 1901; also in *Sobranie*, I, 51. See also his "Tatianin den'," in *SPV*, January, 1904; in *Sobranie*, I, 78, and his analysis of Soloviev's "Tri razgovora" and the negative Russian public opinion of the work in *Sobranie*, II, 581-586, originally published in May, 1900, in *VFP*, book 53 (III), as well as his article on Chekhov and Gorki mentioned earlier, in *Sobranie*, I, particularly p. 380.

26. Quoted by Polivanov, interview of January 3, 1964.

27. "Delo Mortara," published originally in *SPV*, 7 November, 1897; in *Sobranie*, I, 20-22.

28. From "Na rubezhe," an article written in the winter of 1904 but first published only in Evgenii Trubetskoi's *Moskovskii ezhenedel'nik* (1906); see *Sobranie*, I, 458-492. Quotations are from pp. 479 and 478. This article is a convenient presentation of Trubetskoi's political credo. The views expressed in it are the result of long time deliberation, and had been expounded in private by Trubetskoi prior to the time of writing the article. This article is dedicated to Chicherin ard harks back to Chicherin's anonymously published *Rossiia nakanune dvadtsatago stoletiia* (Berlin, 1900).

29. "Vtoroi otvet kniaziu Tsertelevu," originally in *SPV*, 10 June, 1899; in *Sobranie*, I, 32.

30. From "Na rubezhe," in *Sobranie*, I, 487. Included in the article is a long and emotional call to the Tsar to act immediately. The anti-bureaucratic note characterized much of Russian conservative thought. General Fadeev, for instance, felt that bureaucrats pre-

vented the full use of educated talent in Russia; Edward C. Thaden, *Conservative Nationalism in Nineteenth-Century Russia* (Seattle, 1964), p. 155.

31. Letter to Evgenii in Trubetskaia, pp. 184-185. Symptomatic of the manner in which educated Russians viewed their bureaucracy is the fact that Shipov in 1896 declined a rather high bureaucratic post because bureaucratic work repelled him; Shipov, p. 60.

32. Trubetskoi, "Na rubezhe," in *Sobranie*, I, 468.

33. *Ibid*. Underlined in the original.

34. Obolenskii owed his influence on the Tsar to his brother, who was close to the Tsar. Obolenskii himself was an admirer of V. S. Soloviev, was slightly pro-*zemstvo*, and was given to the formulation of broad theories. He supported Witte, knew provincial Russia, and served in various capacities in St. Petersburg at the beginning of the present century. After 1917 he apparently defended the Bolsheviks; see Gurko, pp. 207-210, for and unfavorable account; see *ibid*., pp. 641-642, for a list of positions held by Obolenskii.

35. In contrast to Obolenskii, Lopukhin was an intimate of Plehve; Gurko, p. 212. He accepted the post of the Director of the Police because he was under the impression that Plehve would institute a series of reforms within the police structure. Lopukhin himself was a moderate liberal. In January, 1905, he argued the ineffectiveness of the Temporary Rules of 1881; see *Dokladnaia zapiska direktora departamenta politsii Lopukhina, razsmotrennaia v Komitete Ministrov . . . Ian. 1905*. In 1907 he again urged the reform of the police, after he

resigned from service. Two years later he was implicated in the Azef case, tried by the Senate, and despite his attestations of innocence, was found guilty of abetting revolutionary activity by informing some revolutionaries of Azef's connection with the police. See *Delo A. A. Lopukhina v osobom prisutsvii Pravitel'stvuiushchogo Senata*. Stenograficheskii Otchet (St. Petersburg, 1910). This source and Lopukhin's *Otryvki iz Vospominanii (po povodu Vospominanii gr. S. Iu. Witte)* (Moscow, 1923) are useful for Lopukhin's political views. Because of his position, Lopukhin was of interest to the revolutionaries. The *précis* of his *Dokladnaia zapiska* was published in Geneva by *Vpered* in 1905, with an introduction by Lenin.

36. See particularly "I ty tozhe, Brut," written in August, 1904, published in *Sobranie*, I, 494. This article was banned by censorship, but Trubetskoi incorporated its ideas into another article, "Dva puti," which was published in *Pravo*, No. 44, October 31, 1904, pp. 3006-3009, as the lead article. "Dva puti" was not republished in *Sobranie*.

37. From "Na rubezhe," in *Sobranie*, I, 486. See also "Skazka o Senie i Vasie," a satire written in May, 1905, on how censorship aided the popularity of forbidden books; published posthumously in *ibid.*, pp. 125-128.

38. From "Na rubezhe," in *ibid.*, p. 472.

39. *Ibid.*, p. 487.

40. From "Na rubezhe," in *ibid.*, p. 461; see also his articles of May, 1905, in his censored newspaper, also

in *ibid.*, pp. 120 and 101, as well as "Pered resheniem," originally published in *Russkie vedomosti*, 12 July, 1905; in *Sobranie*, I, 138.

41. Letter to Chicherin in Trubetskaia, p. 196; satire "Ferkel' " written in 1895, published posthumously in 1906 in *Moskovskii ezhenedel'nik*, reprinted in *Sobranie*, I, 430-435; see also *Moskovskaia nedelia*, in *ibid.*, p. 102.

42. Most forceful in "Na rubezhe," *ibid.*, p. 467.

43. Best stated in Chicherin's *O narodnom pred-stavitel'stve* (Moscow, 1866), p. 144.

44. From articles in Trubetskoi's banned newspaper, *Moskovskaia nedelia*, in 1905, in *Sobranie*, I, 103-104.

45. See *Moskovskaia nedelia*, May, 1905, which was censored, published in *Sobranie*, I, 103.

46. See especially Trubetskoi's "Pered resheniem," originally in *Russkiia vedomosti*, 12 July, 1905, in *Sobranie*, I, 135; his articles in *Moskovskaia nedelia*, in *Sobranie*, particularly p. 112, as well as his "K sovremmennomu politicheskomu polozheniiu," in *SPV* in March, 1900, in *Sobranie*, I, 42. Soloviev's views on this issue in *Sochineniia*, 2nd ed., V, 4-8.

47. Letter to wife from Greece in Trubetskaia, pp. 242-243. Trubetskoi's brother Evgenii later argued for the annexation of the Straits; Grigorii, the older brother, with whom Trubetskoi stayed during part of his Greek excursion, was connected with the Russian foreign service

in the Balkans. On Grigorii's views, see his *Krasnaia Rossiia i sviataia Rus'* (Paris, 1931) and *Russland als Großmacht* (Stuttgart, 1913). A brief statement of Evgenii's views on the issue, in very emotional terms, in a speech he delivered in Moscow in 1915, published as a separate pamphlet under the title *Natsional'nyi vopros, Konstantinopol' i Sviataia Sofia*.

48. From Trubetskoi's letter to the editor of *SPV*, 31 August, 1900, in *Sobranie*, I, 46-50; the quotation is from p. 49. Trubetskoi shared his fear of the "Yellow Peril" with Soloviev. For an example of Soloviev's views on this issue, see his "Kitai i Evropa," written in 1890, in *Sochineniia*, 2nd ed., VI, 93-150.

49. Letter to Chicherin, in Trubetskaia, pp. 218-219, and Trubetskoi's letter to the editor, *SPV*, August, 1900, in *Sobranie*, I, 50. Trubetskaia, p. 67.

50. "Rossiia na rubezhe," in *Sobranie*, I, 78-80; not to be confused with "Na rubezhe," which was published only posthumously.

51. *Ibid.*, pp. 491-492, from "Na rubezhe."

52. Letter to Evgenii from 1892, in Trubetskaia, pp. 178 and 181.

53. *Sobranie*, I, 122-124, from *Moskovskaia nedelia*, 1905.

54. *Sobranie*, I, 136, from "Pered resheniem," 12 July, 1905, in *Russkiia vedomosti*.

55. *Sobranie*, I, pp. 116-117, from *Moskovskaia*

nedelia, June, 1905.

56. *Ibid.*, pp. 108-109.

57. From "Otkrytoe pis'mo kn. E. E. Ukhtomskomu," April 13, 1899, in *SPV*; in *Sobranie*, I, 22-25;
quotation is from p. 24.

58. See "Vtoroi otvet kn. Tsertelevu," 10 June,
1899, in *SPV*; in *Sobranie*, I, 29-32; and "Otvet kn. D. N.
Tsertelevu," in *SPV*, May 3, 1899; in *Sobranie*, I, 25-28.

59. From "Vtoroi otvet Tsertelevu," in *Sobranie*,
I, 30. Katkov had been what was considered a conservative
Russian journalist; see Marc Raeff, "Reactionary Liberal,
M. N. Katkov," *Russian Review*, XI (July, 1952), 157-
167.

60. From "Otkrytoe pis'mo kn. E. E. Ukhtomskomu," in *SPV*, 1899; *Sobranie*, I, 24.

61. From "Otvet kn. D. N. Tsertellevu," in *SPV*,
May 3, 1899; *Sobranie*, I, 28.

62. In Trubetskaia, p. 83.

63. The two satires are "Freilein," which was published by Struve and "Skazka o Senie i Vasie," which was
published in *Russkiia vedomosti*, May 25, 1906. Both in
Sobranie, I, 70-72 and 125-128, respectively.

64. The statement of resignation was not published
for the same reason; *Sobranie*, I, 93-95.

65. "Medlit' nel'zia," 9 April, 1905, in *Russkiia*

vedomosti; in *Sobranie*, I, 98.

66. From "Na rubezhe," the censored article written in 1904, in *Sobranie*, I, 488.

67. *Sobranie*, I, 459; from "Na rubezhe."

68. "Liberation" is used in quotation marks by Trubetskoi; *ibid.*, p. 488; also from "Na rubezhe."

69. From a philosophical article, "O prirode chelovecheskogo soznaniia," published in *VFP*, in 1889; in *Sobranie*, II, 9. See also Trubetskoi's "Vorwort zu den *Drei Gesprächen* von Solowiof," written in 1903 but not published for a lack of an interested publisher. Published in *Sobranie*, II, 611-619.

70. "Kanun novago goda, 31 Dek. 1901," due to the opposition of the censor published only posthumously in *Moskovskii ezhenedel'nik* in 1906; in *Sobranie*, I, 452.

71. "Sushchestvuet li obshchestvo," originally in *SPV*, 9 Aug., 1899; in *Sobranie*, I, 40.

72. He was beside himself when the illegal organ of the liberals, *Osvobozhdenie*, published one of his satires which dealt with censorship, "Freilein," *Osvobozhdenie*, No. 31, 1903, p. 116; reprinted in *Sobranie*, I, 70-72. Trubetskoi had originally wanted to publish it in *SPV* and when censorship made that impossible, as a note in *VFP*, but *Osvobozhdenie* got it first. The article was signed "Strubin"; Trubetskoi's reaction as a note of the editor of *Sobranie*, I, 70.

73. In Trubetskoi's *Sobranie*, I, 144, as well as

Trubetskaia, *Vospominaniia sestry*, p. 118.

74. From the article, "Dva puti," in *Pravo*, No. 44, Oct. 31, 1904, p. 3006.

75. An article written by Trubetskoi in May, 1905, for his newspaper, which was banned by the government; in *Sobranie*, I, 113.

76. In *Moskovskaia nedelia*, Trubetskoi's ill-fated newspaper of May, 1905; in *Sobranie*, I, 109.

77. *Ibid.*, p. 112.

CHAPTER 6

TSAR AND SOCIETY:1905

1. See part of a letter of Trubetskoi's wife to his sister, in Trubetskaia, p. 255; also a letter of Sergei to Evgenii, in *ibid.*, pp. 256-257.

2. Polivanov, interview of January 16, 1964. Gurko, p. 321, writing about December, 1904, computed that by that time "a case of urgent necessity," requiring the use of a special statute on censorship, occurred once every thirteen days. Sidney Harcave, *First Blood:The Russian Revolution of 1905* (New York, 1964), p. 15, wrote: "By the beginning of 1904 more than half of Russia, including most of her major cities, were under some form of extraordinary bureaucratic protection."

3. *Sobranie*, I, 100; from Trubetskoi's projected but censored newspaper, *Moskovskaia nedelia* of May, 1905.

4. From "Na rubezhe," pp. 462 and 480.

5. Letter to Evgenii, in Trubetskaia, p. 258. But even Trubetskoi's closest friends did not realize how prominent his political role would be. See P. I. Novgorodtsev, "Pamiati kn. S. N. Trubetskogo v ego otnoshenii k universitetskoi nauke," in *Moskovskii ezhenedel'nik*, 1 April, 1908, No. 14, 23-26; and S. A. Kotliarevskii, "Pamiati Kn. S. N. Trubetskogo," in *ibid*., pp. 29-30.

6. See Trubetskoi's letter to Evgenii, December, 1904, in Olga Trubetskaia, "Iz perezhitogo," *Sovremennyia zapiski* (Paris) 1937, No. 64, 291.

7. See especially his letter to P. G. Vinogradoff in Trubetskaia, p. 128.

8. Written after Tsushima, on May 23, 1905, for Trubetskoi's censored newspaper; published in *Sobranie*, I, 112-113. In the previous year Trubetskoi had defended Kuropatkin in *SPV* and his role in the leadership of the army; in *ibid*., pp. 81-82. According to Olga, only the defeat at Tsushima seemed to elicit any sorrow from Russian society, Trubetskaia, pp. 130-131. She now lived in the same house as her brother and kept a diary, parts of which she often quotes in her book.

9. B. B. Veselovskii, *Istoriia zemstva za sorok let* (St. Petersburg, 1909), III, 555; I. P. Belokonskii, *Zemstvo i konstitutsiia* (Moscow, 1910), p. 105; Melnik, ed. *Russen über Russland*, p. 161; Terence Emmons, "The Beseda Circle, 1899-1905," *Slavic Review*, September, 1973, pp. 461-490.

10. For a full discussion see Richard Pipes, *Struve:*

Liberal on the Left (Cambridge, 1971), first volume of a projected two-volume study of the man central to *Osvobozhdenie*. *Osvobozhdenie* used the group to influence the moderate *zemtsy*, George Fischer, *Russian Liberalism* (Cambridge, 1958), p. 145, calls it a "front organization." See also Shmuel Galai, *The Liberation Movement in Russia, 1900-1905* (Cambridge, England, 1973). In February, 1904, a congress of *zemstvo*-constitutionalists opposed official cooperation of *zemstvo* and *Osvobozhdenie*; I. P. Belonkonskii, *Zemstvo i konstitutsiia*, p. 129. Gatherings at private homes for political lectures became fashionable at the time, Miliukov, *Vospominaniia*, p. 276.

11. Trubetskoi's support of the war was echoed by many *zemtsy*; see Veselovskii, *Istoriia zemstva*, III, 590-592, Egorov in Martov *et al.*, *Obshchestvennoe dvizhenie*, I, 393; also Maklakov, p. 179.

12. Shipov, pp. 233-237; Veselovskii, Belokonskii, Fischer, *passim*.

13. Shipov, it will be recalled, wanted a consultative assembly, was against a popularly drafted constitution, and did not share the democratic views of the majority of the *zemtsy*.

14. Plehve's assassination was met with general feelings of relief. Even former supporters of Plehve, Prince Meshcherskii, for example, now criticized him. Trubetskoi directed his banned "I ty tozhe, Brut," against Meshcherskii. Although this article was published only posthumously in *Sobranie*, I, 492-495, the bulk of its arguments was incorporated by Trubetskoi into another article, "Dva puti," published in *Pravo*, a journal of the

liberals, on October 31, 1904, as the lead article. (*Pravo*, No. 44, 3006-3009). Maklakov, in *Vlast'* . . . pp. 317-320, describing the general joy which greeted Plehve's death, recalled that Evgenii Trubetskoi almost crossed himself in relief upon hearing the news. On Prince Mirskii, see Belokonskii, "K istorii zemskogo dvizheniia v Rossii," *Istoricheskii sbornik*, 1907, No. 1, 26; Gurko, pp. 294-297; and V. N. Kokovtsev, *Iz moego proshlago. Vospominaniia. 1903-1919* (n.p., 1933), vol. I.

15. The program served as the basis for the eleven thesis resolutions adopted by the congress.

16. According to Gurko, p. 307, many civil servants took part in the congress, and the congress was generally considered legal. The very careful *Novoe vremia* even published its resolutions. The congress met in St. Petersburg rather than in Moscow, the site of all subsequent *zemstvo* meetings, because Mirskii had insisted it be held in the capital. Shipov recalled that telegrams addressed simply to St. Petersburg, the *Zemstvo* congress, were delivered promptly, one of them, from political exiles in Archangelsk, by a clerk of the Ministry of Interior; Shipov, p. 259.

17. Maklakov was rather derisive about the aspirations of the *zemtsy*; see his *Vlast'*, p. 268. In addition to Fischer, p. 181, M. P. Polivanov, *Zemstvo*, an unpublished manuscript, p. 280; Veselovskii in Martov *et al.*, I, 312; Belokonskii, *Zemstvo i konstitutsia*, p. 52; and D. I. Shakhovskoi, "Politicheskie techeniia v russkom zemstve," in B. B. Veselovskii and Z. H. Frenkel, *Iubileinyi zemskii sbornik, 1864-1914* (St. Petersburg, 1914), p. 466, as well as Gurko, pp. 305-306, and Shipov, *passim*.

18. Text of the theses in Shipov, pp. 261-265; full discussion in Fischer, pp. 181-188, from which the translated passage is taken. For a different analysis see Victor Leontovitch, *Geschichte des Liberalismus in Russland* (Frankfurt am Main, 1957), who for the most part agreed with Maklakov's analysis. The Shipov faction is often regarded as Slavophile, but Shipov himself did not consider the characterization apt; Shipov, p. 270. Contemporary commentators, as Golubew in Melnik, ed., *Russen über Russland*, p. 174, did not shy from using the term party to characterize the factions. Outspoken liberals, such as Miliukov, chided the *zemtsy* for not using the word constitution; see Miliukov, *Vospominaniia*, p. 246.

19. According to Shipov, Mirskii could not see the difference between the position of the majority and that of the minority.

20. See particularly Shipov, p. 283; Veselovskii, III, 624. The journal *Rus'* was forbidden to publish a facsimile of the signatures of the *zemtsy* lest it, in the words of the censor, "excite public opinion"; V. Botsianovskii and E. Gollerbakh, *Russkaia satira pervoi revoliutsii 1905-1906* (Leningrad, 1925), p. 12.

21. Trubetskaia, p. 89. His contacts with both Obolenskii and Lopukhin were also instrumental now, as well as the circumstance that the daughter of F. D. Trepov, the Moscow chief of police who became the Governor-General of St. Petersburg and the Assistant Minister of Interior, had married a relative of the Trubetskois; see Trubetskaia, p. 82.

22. Shipov, pp. 278-280; Trubetskaia, p. 89; the phrase quoted is Miliukov's, Miliukov, p. 289. The mem-

bers were Shipov, M. V. Chelnokov, Prince Petr D. Dolgorukov, F. A. Golovin, V. E. Iakushkin, N. N. Khelev, F. F. Kokoshkin, Prince G. E. L'vov, N. N. L'vov, I. I. Petrunkevich, R. A. Pisarev, N. F. Rikhter and Prince D. E. Shakhovskoi.

23. Petrunkevich, p. 382, was also favorably impressed by Trubetskoi, whom he first met at the home of V. I. Vernadskii, the scientist.

24. Shipov, p. 281; Trubetskaia, p. 90, and letter to Evgenii in *ibid.*, p. 257. The only difference in the text given by Shipov and the one in Trubetskoi, *Sobranie*, I, is that Shipov uses once *tiazhkiia* and Trubetskoi, *tiazhiolyia*.

25. "Zapiski" to Mirskii; in *Sobranie*, I, 389-397.

26. *Ibid.*, p. 392. Italics are Trubetskoi's.

27. Gurko, pp. 302-303 and 316; Shipov, pp. 285-288; Kokovtsev, p. 48.

28. Kliuchevsky's phrase, in Trubetskoi's letter to Evgenii, Dec. 15, 1904; in Trubetskaia, *Sovremennyia zapiski*, No. 64, 295. See also Gurko, pp. 302-303. Bekbulatovich, a Tatar prince, helped Ivan the Terrible in the establishment of autocratic rule. Ivan pretended to withdraw from power and vested sovereignty in Bekbulatovich. Muscovites pleaded with the Tsar to return, which he did, on his own terms.

29. In Trubetskaia, p. 260, from a letter to Evgenii.

30. *Ibid.*, p. 101.

31. Text of the minority petition in *Sobranie*, I, 397-399; quotation is from p. 398. On the meeting of the nobility see Veselovskii, III, 611-612; Trubetskaia, pp. 107-108. Petr Trubetskoi sided with Sergei and it was thanks to him that an open discussion of the address took place. Petr explained his reasons for permitting the discussion in a note to Mirskii; in Trubetskaia, pp. 99-100 and 108. In general, Petr Trubetskoi was closer to Shipov than to Sergei. He accompanied Shipov in October, 1905, to discuss the possibility of forming a cabinet with Witte; Shipov, p. 334. See also Maklakov, *Iz vospominanii* (New York, 1954), pp. 313-319.

32. The Manifesto and the *Ukaz* caught even the ministers, who were aware only of the preparation of the Rescript, by surprise. Kristi, who tried to placate Olga Trubetskaia by promising her a pleasant surprise from St. Petersburg, was himself surprised by the documents. The same was the case with Lopukhin. See Trubetskaia, pp. 113-114. On the actual discussions in St. Petersburg and on the reaction of the ministers, see Gurko, pp. 367-370 and S. Iu. Witte, *The Memoirs of Count Witte*, translated and edited by Abraham Yarmolinsky (Garden City, N.Y., 1921), pp. 227-228. The Manifesto was a reproof for the assassination of Grand Duke Sergei and an exhortation to all Russians to stand firm in the support of autocracy. The *Ukaz* to the Senate bade the Council of Ministers, presided over by the Tsar, "to examine and consider the ideas and suggestions presented to Us by private persons and institutions concerning improvements in the state organization and the betterment of the people's existence", Gurko, p. 369. Shipov was particularly hurt by the *Ukaz*, for the *zemtsy* had been denied the right of petition which now seemed to be granted as a result of the revolutionary disturbances

which the *zemstvo* had avoided. A secret circular, which became known only in April, accompanied the *Ukaz*. The circular warned that the *Ukaz* should not be interpreted in terms of a greater freedom of the *zemstvo*; Belokonskii, *Zemstvo*, p. 155.

33. In Trubetskaia, pp. 110-111. The discussions preceding the Rescript in Ministerstvo Vnutrennikh Del, *Soobrazheniia . . . 18 Fevralia 1905 goda* (n.p., n.d.). It was Ermolov, the Minister of Agriculture, who intiated the discussion and pressed for reform; Gurko, p. 370.

34. Trubetskaia, pp. 118-119.

35. Shipov, pp. 295-297.

36. Trubetskaia reported the rumors prevalent in her sphere: A. A. Lopukhin had uncovered many bombs and a merchant-sponsored defense organization, while Petrunkevich was planning to get together six hundred *zemtsy* in order to proclaim a constituent assembly; Trubetskaia, pp. 110 and 112. The latter rumor apparently originated when Vodovozov, at an *ad hoc* meeting of the *literati* in St. Petersburg in January, which was electing a delegation to the government, pleaded for more regularity in the election since "we do not know the role the delegation shall play." See I. V. Gessen, *V dvukh vekakh: zhiznennyi otchet* in *Arkhiv Russkoi Revolutsii* (Berlin, 1937), XXII.

37. According to Veselovskii, III, 622, small protorightist groups were organized before May.

38. Letter to Evgenii; in Trubetskaia in *Sovremennyia zapiski*, No. 64, 287.

39. *Ibid.*, pp. 318 and 315.

40. Trubetskaia, *Vospominaniia*, p. 127. She gives Petrunkevich the wrong patronymic. V. I. Gurko in his memoirs, p. 120, expressed similar sentiment.

41. Trubetskaia, p. 127.

42. Letter to his wife, June 2, 1905; in Trubetskaia, *Vospominaniia*, p. 136.

43. Trubetskoi to P. G. Vinogradoff, in Trubetskaia, *Sovremennyia zapiski*, No. 64, 317.

44. This conference, in contrast to the previous congresses, was an elective one; Maevskii, in Martov *et al.*, eds., *Obshchestvennoe dvizhenie*, II, 58. A minority of 54 disagreed in varying degrees with the decision and suggested the use of *zemstvos* as electoral organs.

45. See Trubetskoi's contributions to the discussion; published in D. P. Dolgorukov and I. I. Petrunkevich, *Agrarnyi vopros*, 1st ed. (Moscow, 1906), and reprinted in Trubetskoi's *Sobranie*, I, 400-401. See also Trubetskaia in *Sovremennyia zapiski*, No. 64, 315-316.

46. *Sobranie*, I, 473; the article, which has been discussed in the preceding chapter, was originally published in *Moskovskii ezhenedel'nik* in 1906.

47. *Sobranie*, I, 107-109.

48. *Ibid.*, p. 112.

49. Trubetskaia, p. 132; Shipov, p. 317.

50. Trubetskaia, pp. 134-135.

51. *Ibid.*, p. 134.

52. Miliukov, *Vospominaniia*, pp. 289-291.

53. Minutes of the Congress in *Osvobozhdenie*, 1905, No. 74, 403-408. Maklakov, *Vlast'*, recalled that someone suggested that the *zemstvo* congress go *in corpore* to St. Petersburg to be shot if necessary. See also D. I. Shakhovskoi, "Soiuz Osvobozhdeniia," *Zarnitsy: Literaturno-politicheskii sbornik*, II (1909), 155-161, as well as "Iz zapisok F. A. Golovina," *Krasnyi Arkhiv*, vol. 58 (1933), 142-149, and V. D. Nabokov, "Piat' let nazad," *Russkaia mysl'*, November, 1910, 195-198.

54. Trubetskaia, pp. 132-134; Shipov, p. 320. Shipov's resignation was caused also by other disagreements. B. B. Golitsyn disagreed with the phrase "the *prikaz* system," meaning a government by personal fiat by an arbitrary appointee of the Tsar, as had existed in Russia prior to Petrine reforms. Przheval'skii did not consider the address radical enough. Consequently, neither signed it.

55. In ENPE, pp. 11-12; when *Le Matin* published the petition unsigned, Trubetskaia hurried home from France, where she had gone for a family wedding. She wanted to be close to Sergei in the historical moment; *Vospominaniia*, p. 134.

56. ENPE, p. 13.

57. *Osvobozhdenie*, 1905, No. 72, 365-367.

58. The list of the members of the delegation in the order given in *Pravitel'stvennyi vestnik*, Wed., 9 (21) June, 1905; No. 121; functions in Belokonskii, p. 169. The position of each delegate was determined by the number of votes received; *Osvobozhdenie*, 1905, No. 74, 408: P. A. Geiden, Marshal of the Nobility of Pskov, received 161 votes; Prince G. E. L'vov, Marshal of the Nobility of Tula, 141 votes; N. N. L'vov of Saratov, 113 votes; I. I. Petrunkevich of Tver, 106 votes; D. N. Shipov, 103 votes (did not accept); Prince Petr D. Dolgorukov, Marshal of the Nobility of Ruza, 92 votes; A. F. Golovin of Moscow, 91 votes; Prince Pavel D. Dolgorukov, 84 votes; N. N. Kovalevskii of Kharkov, 81 votes; N. A. Novosil'tsev, Marshal of the Nobility of Temnikov, 78 votes; F. I. Rodichev, candidate for Marshal of the Nobility of Tver, 72 votes; Prince D. I. Shakhovskoi of Iaroslavl', 68 votes; N. N. Shchepkin and N. A. Khomiakov received 64 and 62 votes respectively and were chosen as alternates. Also included in the delegation were Baron P. L. Korff, M. P. Fedorov, and A. N. Nikin, as representatives of the St. Petersburg city duma. The most significant development was the resignation of Shipov, who felt that the proposed petition was more of a demand than a petition. For this reason, and because of his other disagreements with the majority, he did not take part in further *zemstvo* work in Moscow; Shipov, pp. 319-330. Harcave, *First Blood*, p. 160, mistakenly included him in the delegation, while N. N. Kovalevskii was mistakenly not included in the list as given in Trubetskoi's *Sobranie*, I, 129. Both Petrunkevich and Rodichev offered to resign from the delegation for fear of compromising the congress, but the congress did not accept their offer.

59. Letter to his wife, June 2, 1905, in Trubetskaia, p. 135.

60. *Ibid*., p. 136.

61. *Ibid*.

62. Both men had offered to resign from the delegation, but the *zemtsy* would not hear of it. Significantly enough, Petrunkevich in his memoirs referred to the delegation as representing society rather than the *zemstvo*.

63. Petrunkevich, p. 376, and Miliukov, p. 289. There is some discrepancy in the two accounts. It is possible that Trubetskoi rehearsed twice — once before the delegation only, in Petrunkevich's room, and later in a restaurant (as mentioned by Miliukov) before a somewhat broader, but still a very limited audience. It was apparently Guchkov who managed to convince the Tsar to see the deputies; P. E. Shchegolev, ed., *Padenie tsarskogo rezhima* (Petrograd, 1917), VI, 250.

64. The account of the audience is based mainly on Trubetskaia in *Sovremennyia zapiski*, No. 65, 210-217. See also Petrunkevich, pp. 377-381. Gurko, describing the affair, pp. 376-380, said that like everyone else meeting the Tsar for the first time, the *zemstvo* delegation was charmed by him.

65. Shchegolev, *Padenie*, V, iii and 32, refers to him as "one of the pillars of the regime." Gurko, p. 267, described him as a man of limited intelligence but of unimpeachable honor and chilvalry.

66. Text in *Pravitel'stvennyi vestnik*, 8 (21) June, 1905, No. 121; in Trubetskoi's *Sōbranie*, I, 129-133; also in ENPE, pp. 6-11 and Belokonskii, pp. 169-171; parts in brackets are from Trubetskaia in *Sovremennyia za-*

piski, No. 65, 217; in her *Vospominaniia*, p. 144 and from a letter to one of the possible contributors of Trubetskoi's paper in *ibid.*, p. 263. Petrunkevich also quoted the speech in his memoirs for the edification of youth, but he used a published source.

67. Fedorov's speech in Trubetskoi's *Sobranie*, I, 133.

68. This part of the speech was from *Pravitel'-stvennyi vestnik*.

69. *Sobranie*, I, 134; and Trubetskaia, p. 145. In *Pravitel'stvennyi vestnik* the last sentence was changed to "I hope you will cooperate with me in this work."

70. Trubetskaia, p. 264; Petrunkevich, pp. 377-378.

71. Trubetskaia, p. 143. Trubetskoi was apparently subject to special ovations but was reluctant to discuss his success, Olga commented.

72. Trubetskaia, pp. 145-156, called Kovalevskii's behavior "scandalous." A. Obolenskii, speaking later with the Tsar, told him that "elected people" was a stronger term than the nebulous "national representatives." The Tsar was startled by this unexpected interpretation, as well as by Trubetskoi's youth; *ibid.*, p. 146.

73. *Osvobozhdenie*, 1905, No. 73, 369, with no comments "for fear of misconstruing the contents of the document." *Zritel'*, a satiric journal in which Iu. K. Artsybashev cooperated, published the text of Trubetskoi's speech and the Tsar's reply with no comment but with

imp figures lurking in the background; Botsianovskii and Gollerbakh, *Russkaia satira*, p. 64. Compare the Tsar's reply in versions given in *Pravitel'stvennyi vestnik* and *Osvobozhdenie*, 1905, No. 75, 427.

74. Trubetskaia in *Sovremennyia zapiski*, No. 65, 212; Harcave, *First Blood*, p. 161.

75. Trubetskaia, *Vospominaniia sestry*, p. 144.

76. In B. P. Koz'min, *S. V. Zubatov i ego korrespondenty: sredi okhrannikov, zhandarmov i provokatorov* (Moscow, 1928), p. 112.

77. Lenin's article on "Bor'ba proletariata i kholopstvo burzhuazii," in *Proletarii*, 20 June, 1905, in Akademiia Nauk SSSR, *Revoliutsionnoe dvizhenie v Rossii vesnoi i letom 1905 goda* (Moscow, 1957), I, 60-63. Various leaflets deprecating the delegation and Trubetskoi personally appeared, with RSDRP using the delegation as proof of the double-dealing of the *zemstvos*; *ibid.*, pp. 142-144; 574-576 and 57-59.

78. Letter of Trubetskoi complaining of the criticism from the rightists in ENPE, pp. 73-74.

79. In an open letter an old *zemets* complained in *Osvobozhdenie*, 1905, No. 73, 370, that old *zemtsy*, such as Rodichev and Petrunkevich were by-passed for Trubetskoi, who did not express *zemstvo* sentiments. Another article, *ibid*, No. 74, 393-394, chastised the *zemtsy* for failing to insist on a written transcript of what had been said at the time it was said and for failing to come out openly with their views. Trubetskoi was attacked for using the word *kramola* and for crediting

the Tsar with the understanding of suffering. Struve
defended Trubetskoi, No. 73, 369, note. S. S. Oldenburg, *Tsarstvovanie Imperatora Nikolaia Vtorogo* (Munich,
1949), II, 288, suggested that "old *zemets*" was Miliukov's
pseudonym.

80. Harcave, pp. 161 and 191; Maklakov, p. 380;
Belokonskii in *Istoricheskii sbornik*, p. 101; Leontovitsch,
p. 320.

81. ENPE, pp. 72-75; *Revoliutsionnoe dvizhenie*, I,
643.

82. "Nezhnaia uvertiura k groznomu konfliktu,"
signed P. S. in *Osvobozhdenie*, No. 73, 369.

83. Letter of Trubetskoi to G. B. Mgunov, a prospective contributor to his paper; in Trubetskaia, pp. 263-
264.

84. Trubetskaia, p. 151, claims that Trepov opposed
Bulygin and the Governor of Moscow A. A. Kozlov on the
issue of the congress. The latter resigned. Kozlov is to have
said, arguing for permission for the congress: "Except for
talk, there will be no scandal; they'll probably talk of the
constitution," *Revoliutsionnoe dvizhenie*, I, xvi. Full
discussion of attempts of government to forbid the congress in Belokonskii in *Istoricheskii sbornik*, where some
of the correspondence of G. I. Kristi, representing the
government, and F. A. Golovin, representing the *zemstvo*,
is published; see particularly pp. 91-93; also *Osvobozhdenie*, 1905, No. 75, 418 and 432.

85. His co-option, along with three other persons,
was approved at the first session of the congress. Minutes

of the congress in *Osvobozhdenie*, 1905, No. 76, 447.

86. *Ibid.*, No. 75, 423; Miliukov, p. 295.

87. *Osvobozhdenie*, No. 76, 448 and 452. N. N. Shchepkin of Moscow said, "Even if we destroy ourselves, we will not destroy Russia."

88. *Ibid.*, p. 448.

89. *Ibid.*, pp. 448-449.

90. The negative vote came from a new, reactionary deputy of Kursk, N. F. Kasatkin-Rostovskii, whose comments on the Jewish-inspired rebellion were met with jeers and laughter.

91. Miliukov, *Vospominaniia*, p. 289.

92. *Osvobozhdenie*, No. 78/79, 502; Maklakov, p. 384.

93. Among the topics were the relationship of the *zemstvo* to bureaucratic commissions on the study of the agrarian problem, the issues of censorship, famine, agrarian problems, equality of women, the Jewish question, and the minorities.

94. Gurko, p. 387.

95. *Osvobozhdenie*, No. 75, 424-425; No. 76, 452.

96. By the time Petrunkevich wrote his memoirs, in emigration, he agreed with Trubetskoi. (Petrunkevich, p. 384). See also Max Weber, "Russlands Übergang zum

Scheinkonstitutionalismus," *Archiv für Sozialwissenschaft und Sozialpolitik* (1906), XXIII, 355.

97. Evgenii was there and suggested, among other things, the opening of free universities in the fall if regular universities remained closed. There were more than 100 persons present, and Geiden defended Trubetskoi's speech. This meeting decided on the creation of the Kadet Party; see *Osvobozhdenie*, 1905, No. 78 and addenda of No. 75; also Belokonskii, *Zemstvo*, pp. 176-178; and Trubetskaia, p. 148. Lopukhin in a letter to Trubetskoi, *ibid.*, p. 154, said that S. S. Manukhin, the Minister of Justice, who had defended the *zemtsy*, would probably be replaced by Baron Nolde. The *zemstvo* congress had been disbanded by the police; Gurko, p. 388, and this fact contributed to the popularity of the subsequent gathering.

98. In Trubetskaia, pp. 264-265.

99. "Pered resheniem," 12 July, 1905, in *Russkiia vedomosti*, in *Sobranie*, I, 134-139; the quotation is from p. 134.

100. *Ibid.*, p. 139.

101. The petition was drafted by Iu. N. Miliutin and the delegates, V. V. Gudovich and Petr N. Trubetskoi, Sergei's half-brother, were chosen by lot. Petr allegedly made the above statement to the Tsar. The Tsar paled on hearing it, and Petr paled whenever he recalled it. Right after the audience Petr went to Karlsbad to cure his shattered nerves; Trubetskaia, p. 149; on the audience see *Osvobozhdenie*, No. 75, 431-432. At another audience, the Tsar sided with the conservatives. A. G. Shcherbatov and F. D. Samarin protested openly against the position

of Petr Trubetskoi; unpleasant polemics developed as a result. (Trubetskaia, p. 150).

102. Kliuchevsky informed Miliukov of the discussion; Miliukov, pp. 298-299.

103. *Osvobozhdenie*, No. 78-79, 501-503 and addenda, 14-16; No. 76, 460-461; Trubetskaia, pp. 148-149; Belokonskii in *Istoricheskii sbornik*, pp. 94-95; Petrunkevich, p. 389.

104. The above quotations are from Trubetskoi's answer to Postvoskii, taken from Trubetskaia, pp. 267-268.

105. Among the problems which the government did discuss were the need for a higher academic level in all educational establishments and the teacher shortage in the Empire.

106. On student disturbances, see *ibid.*, pp. 91-93 and *passim*; *Osvobozhdenie*, particularly 1904, No. 59, 159; No. 60, 183-184; No. 61, 198-199; No. 56, 97-99; No. 63 (1905), 229; and Pilenko, *Zabastovki v srednikh uchebnykh zavedeniiakh* (St. Petersburg, 1906); on governmental policies see a report on the meeting of trustees with the Minister of Education in *Zhurnal MNP*, Nov., 1904, pp. 9-15; on pertinent legislation see *PSZ*, III, 1905, article 25642, Jan. 11, p. 24.

107. Vydryn, *Osnovnye momenty studencheskogo dvizheniia*, p. 57; Harcave, *First Blood*, p. 101; and N. A. Gredeskul, "Rol' universiteta v sovremennom dvizhenii," *Pravo*, Oct. 9, 1904, No. 40, 3309-3310. Gredeskul maintained that over 1800 scholars signed.

108. Trubetskaia, pp. 112 and 115; see an unpublished open letter to D. N. Anuchin, March, 1905, in *Sobranie*, I, 96.

109. Trubetskaia, p. 116.

110. "Byt' ili ne byt' universitetu," 25 February, 1905, in *Russkiia vedomosti*, No. 54; in *Sobranie*, I, 86-88. As a result of this article Trubetskoi was attacked for downgrading university personnel and university faculty. He defended himself in the same newspaper by saying that he was against the rotten institutions, not against individuals; *Sobranie*, I, 88-89.

111. One example will suffice. On February 7, 1905, the students of St. Petersburg University were permitted to hold a meeting at which foreign correspondents could be present. The agenda of the meeting included political and academic issues. After discussing the political situation, the students decided on the need of a constituent assembly as a preliminary to any discussion of reform. Before such were called, the students felt they could not discuss any academic problems. They therefore decided to continue the student boycott; see Vydryn, *Osnovnye momenty*, p. 56.

112. *Sobranie*, I, 92-93.

113. *PSZ*, III, 1905, April 16, article 26124, pp. 256-257, also *Sobranie uzakonenii i rasporiazhenii pravitel'stva*, No. 90, 1007-1008, 719; henceforth as *SURP*.

114. An example of radical student activity: "A Union of Students of the Northern District" issued a leaflet on May 1 urging revolution "for without it even

academic freedom could not exist." In all seriousness
the students referred to the school as their prison and
forced labor camp; *Revoliutsionnoe dvizhenie*, I, 896
897. Maklakov, p. 187, relegated the academics of 1905
to the conservative faction and suggested that they were
sponsored by the "Union of the Russian People."

115. Ministerial offer mentioned in Trubetskaia,
p. 147; fuller discussion later.

116. In Trubetskaia, p. 153. In November, 1904,
Sergei was dissuading Evgenii from holding a congress
on the grounds that it would not be permitted; *ibid.*,
p. 88. Trubetskaia in *Sovremennyia zapiski*, No. 64, 232,
and Polivanov, who spent the summer close to Menshovo
and bicycled frequently to see Trubetskoi; interview
of January 17, 1964, on Trubetskoi's state of health.
On educational policies, see Hans, *Educational Policies*,
p. 196.

117. "Zapiska ordinarnogo professora S. N. Trubetskogo o nastoiashchem polozhenii vysshikh uchebnykh
zavedenii . . ." in *Sobranie*, I, 401-412; Ognev, *Ognev*,
pp. 103-104.

118. *Zhurnal MNP*, Oct., 1905, pp. 67-68; Hans,
op. cit., p. 196; Maklakov, p. 393; Miliukov, p. 305; Trubetskaia, *Vospominaniia*, p. 157.

119. Quotations are from *SURP*, 28 August, 1905,
No. 154, part I, 1418 and note, p. 2221.

120. Text of the *Ukaz*, paragraph I.

121. Paragraph 3, subsections v, g, a, b.

122. Hans, pp. 196-197. At that time the power of the inspectorate made the courts useless.

123. *SURP*, 19 Sept., 1905, No. 170, part I, 1571. Polish and Lithuanian languages were to be used in certain schools; *SURP*, 7 Oct., 1905, No. 182, part I, 1634, Law of October 1, 1905.

124. Maklakov, pp. 394-395, noted that the Right was either passive or *schadenfroh*. He personally considered the hasty law of August 27 to be dangerous, since it contradicted the formally existing law. Witte also criticized the granting of autonomy at this time as a factor contributing to the upsurge of revolutionary violence. "The university autonomy was the first breach in the Government's fortifications, through which the revolution burst forth into the open." (Witte, p. 230).

125. Ognev, *Ognev*, pp. 105-106.

126. The note to the Moscow City Duma was published in *Russkiia vedomosti*, Sept. 21, 1905, in *Sobranie*, I, 140-141. Text of the acceptance speech has been reconstructed from notes taken when it was delivered; in *ibid.*, pp. 139-140.

127. *Ibid.*, p. 141, from Trubetskoi's note to the Moscow City Duma.

128. Gredeskul in *Pravo*; *Osvobozhdenie*, 1905, No. 76, 445-447; and F. F. Zelinskii, "Universitetskii vopros v 1906 g." in *Zhurnal MNP*, August, 1906, pp. 111-113. The proposed statute of professors in *Pravo*, 1905, No. 40.

129. Harcave, p. 167, that a student congress in September, 1905, met in Vyborg and supported the Menshevik plan of returning to the universities to make use of the new immunities for political purposes. See also P. A. Garvi, *Vospominaniia sotsial-demokrata* (New York, 1946), pp. 529-532, on the importance of the students and the university autonomy to the revolutionary movement. Garvi was a prominent Menshevik who happened to be in Moscow at the time.

130. Maevskii in Martov *et. al.*, eds., *Obshchestvennoe dvizhenie*, II, 74-81; Vydryn, p. 59; *Iskra*, 1905, No. 107 as quoted in *Osvobozhdenie*, No. 78/79, 495-498; Miliukov, p. 305; and Maklakov, p. 396, as well as Garvi, p. 321.

131. Trubetskaia, p. 158; also Novikov, *Ot Moskvy*, p. 80, describing one of the popular student meetings which Trubetskoi tried to direct to purely academic problems.

132. Ognev, *Ognev*, p. 106 and Trubetskaia, p. 160. Manuilov, later a member of the Kadet party, served as the Minister of Education in the Provisional Government from March to July, 1917.

133. From Trubetskoi's speech to the students, originally in *Russkiia vedomosti*, 23 Sept., 1905; in *Sobranie*, I, 142.

134. Trubetskaia, p. 160; Ognev, *Ognev*, estimated up to 4,000 participants. Garvi, *Vospominaniia*, pp. 531-532, on the participation of the workers in the university meetings.

135. *Sobranie*, I, 142; also Trubetskaia, pp. 160-162, and Ognev, *Ognev*, pp. 106-107. Gurko, *Features and Figures of the Past*, p. 392, bitterly complained that Trubetskoi was the only one who spoke out against the use of the university by the radicals. That is not quite true. *Osvobozhdenie* at this time defended the autonomy of the university.

136. *Sobranie*, I, 144, from the speech to the students.

137. ENPE, p. 25. The press made fun of what it considered Trubetskoi's political illness, and the last note Trubetskoi wrote was a bitter reply to the insinuations that "by the way, the rector fell ill" when the student meeting was held; published only in *Sobranie*, I, 144-145; see also Trubetskaia in *Sovremennyia zapiski*, No. 65, 236.

138. Trubetskaia, *Vospominaniia sestry*, p. 166.

139. In ENPE, p. 60.

140. Trubetskoi's death initiated a series of new student disturbances which were exploited eventually by the left and the right and which led to the resignations of Trubetskoi's closest collaborators and to the closing of the universities. See Ognev, pp. 108-112; Novikov, p. 81, Maklakov, p. 185; Maevskii in Martov *et al.*, eds., II, 74; and A. Syromiatnikov, "Moskovskii universitet v oktiabrskie dni 1905 g." *Krasnii arkhiv* (1936), vol. 74, 200-204.

141. Letter to Mgunov, one of the prospective contributors to Trubetskoi's newspaper, in Trubetskaia,

pp. 263-265.

142. Shipov, p. 328, wrote that the Manifesto was proof that the Tsar wanted to preserve the old bureaucratic structure. Kliuchevsky's son asked Trubetskoi to intervene about the recently arrested Miliukov and the Kliuchevsky papers which had been impounded at Miliukov's apartment; Trubetskaia, p. 152. Weber, "Russlands Übergang zum Scheinkonstitutionalismus," p. 241, characterized all legislation after August as "a chain of disappointments."

143. Trubetskaia, p. 147, and letter of Lopukhin to Trubetskaia, 2 September, 1905, in *ibid.*, pp. 153-154.

144. Trubetskaia, p. 159.

CHAPTER 7

DEATH AND AFTERMATH

1. Trubetskaia, pp. 163-165; ENPE, pp. 25-27.

2. Olga's first reaction to the news of Trubetskoi's illness was that he had actually been arrested; Trubetskaia, p. 164. An anonymous doctor, in ENPE, pp. 30-31, made the tacit rebuke that proper medical care had been purposefully withheld from Trubetskoi.

3. Trubetskaia, p. 171.

4. Based mainly on ENPE and Trubetskaia; see also Novikov, 81.

5. Olga was almost trampled in the melee; Trubet-

skaia, 171-172.

6. ENPE quotes accounts from *Novoe vremia* and *Novosti*. Also see Trubetskaia, pp. 173-174, and B. B. Glinskii, "Kn. S. N. Trubetskoi," *Istoricheskii vestnik*, 1905, No. 102, 598-614. Novikov, *op. cit.*, p. 81, says that the crowd was relatively small, but he is contradicted by all sources, and particularly by Polivanov, interview May 14, 1964.

7. Harcave, *First Blood*, p. 179. His source seems to be P. A. Garvi, *Vospominaniia sotsial-demokrata* and the phrase Garvi quoted to conclude his description of the events, p. 538, "Osmelel narod," "the people has grown courageous" or "the people has dared." See Garvi, pp. 534-538 for a description of the funeral procession.

8. ENPE, p. 51; the speeches of Lopatin and Manuilov in *ibid.*, pp. 48-50.

9. N. N. Bazhenov also spoke at the graveside, as did the student Lopatin from St. Petersburg; *ibid.*, pp. 51-55.

10. *Ibid.*, p. 37.

11. Garvi, p. 537. For him the funeral illustrated the need of the Mensheviks to build a bridge with the semi-open opposition, since the workers seemed to support that opposition.

12. *Pravo*, No. 39, Oct. 1, 1905. Miliukov, in *Russkiia vedomosti*, No. 269; in ENPE, pp. 117-120, Petrunkevich, 381.

13. No. 9059, in ENPE, p. 76.

14. No. 293/4, in ENPE, p. 78.

15. No. 10, pp. 625-626, in ENPE, pp. 87-88.

16. V. M. Khvostov, "Pamiati dorogogo tovarishcha, kn. S. N. Trubetskogo," *VFP*, Jan./Feb., 1906, book 1 (81), pp. 9-15.

17. For instance, Vladimir Umanskii in *Russkoe slovo*, No. 261 in *ENPE*, pp. 115-117.

18. The obituary is by Struve, in *Osvobozhdenie*, No 78-79, 504.

19. Vladimir Zhukovskii in *Novoe vremia*, No. 10641, in ENPE, pp. 134-135.

20. Bulgakov in *Voprosy zhyzni*, Oct./Nov., 1905, pp. 280-289.

21. *Peterburgskaia gazeta*, No. 261, in ENPE, p. 91.

22. *Razsvet*, No. 188, and *Novosti*, No. 197, in ENPE, pp. 131-133.

23. V. N. Speranskii in *Pravo*, No. 42, in ENPE, pp. 90-91.

24. A. Bely, "Kn. S. N. Trubetskoi," *Vesy*, Sept./Oct., 1905, No. 9/10, 79-80.

25. *Russkoe slovo*, No. 261, in ENPE, p. 108.

26. ENPE, p. 6; Polivanov interview on May 14, 1964.

27. *Moskovskii ezhenedel'nik*, 1 April, 1908, No. 14, 8; N. Davidov, "Kniaz' S. N. Trubetskoi," in *ibid.*, pp. 3132, and his article in *Golos minuvshago*, 1917, pp. 18-19. *Moskovskii ezhenedel'nik* henceforth as *ME*.

28. In the posthumous fame of Trubetskoi, his philosophical contributions were often overshadowed by his political importance. See *VFP*, March/April, 1906, book 82 (II), 135-137; Lopatin's speech at Trubetskoi's grave in ENPE, pp. 49-50; E. L. Radlov, "Kniaz' S. N. Trubetskoi," *Zhurnal MNP*, Nov., 1905, pp. 44-51; Evgenii Trubetskoi, "Svoboda i bezsmerite," *VFP*, 1906, book 84 (IV), 368-370; Boris Melioranskii, "Teoreticheskaia filosofiia S. N. Trubetskogo," *VFP*, March/April, 1906, book 82 (II), 197-198; Bulgakov, in his article on Trubetskoi in *Voprosy zhyzni*, noted that he almost wanted to thank the censor for banning Trubetskoi's newspaper and thus giving him more time for philosophy. As late as 1923, Georges Florovskii in *Russkaia mysl'*, pp. 419-431, in a review of three histories of Russian philosophy written by Ershev, Shpet, and Iakovenko, complained of their failure to analyze Trubetskoi's philosophical views.

29. In ENPE, p. 31.

30. ENPE had been ready for publication in October but it was delayed by the general strike until November or even December, 1905.

31. Radlov, *Soloviev*, p. 70.

32. Evgenii's review of *Vekhi* — "*Vekhi* i ikh kritiki" — in *ME*, 13 June, 1909, No. 23, 2-18.

33. Evgenii, for example, forcefully argued against the establishment of a Christian political party, since he maintained that all parties should be guided by Christian principles and that no single party should dare act as the interpreter of Christianity, see especially *ME*, 7 July, 1907, No. 24/25, 25, as well as 10 November, 1910, No. 44, 24-28.

34. The optimism of the intelligentsia is illustrated by the words with which Pavel Miliukov concluded his *Russia and Its Crisis* (original publication in 1905 based on a series of lectures delivered in the U.S.A. in 1903 and 1904; Collier edition, 1962), p. 409. "History may have its whims, but it also has its laws; and if the law of Russian history is progress, as we have tried to demonstrate, political reform may not be avoided. To deny it is to despair of the future of Russia." Similar views held by A. Tyrkova-Williams, *Na putiakh k svobode* (New York, 1952), pp. 96-97.

35. Noted by the Tsar; see Oldenburg, I, 365; and by Witte, p. 322; also by Miliukov, in *Tri popytki* (Paris, 1921), p. 13.

36. Most graphic and recent in Leontovitsch, p. 323, but also evident in Maklakov, Oldenburg, Tyrkova-Williams, and others.

37. Discussed in a somewhat different context by Leopold Haimson, "Social Stability in Urban Russia, 1905-1917," *Slavic Review*, XXIII, No. 4 (Dec., 1964), 619-642 and XXIV, No. 1 (March, 1965), 1-22.

38. Unlike many members of the intelligentsia at the time, Trubetskoi was a patriot of the Russian state and not only a patriotic Russian. Later, the consciousness of their patriotism "de-radicalized" many members of the intelligentsia. Here again the "converts" went further than the original patriots. See, for instance, Evgenii Trubetskoi's article on "Velikaia Rossiia" in *ME*, 11 March, 1908, No. 11, 6-13. Evgenii, because of his stress on the rights of the Jews, the Poles and the Finns, was at times accused of wanting to dismember the Russian Empire.

39. The speech was printed as "Sovremennoe znachenie filosofskikh idei S. N. Trubetskogo," *VFP*, January, 1916, book 131 (I), pp. 1-39.

40. The offer was probably insincere, since Witte kept P. N. Durnovo, who was not acceptable even to the most moderate of the liberals, and relegated Prince Urusov, with whom the liberals were willing to co-operate, to second place. See Shipov, pp. 334-349; Witte, pp. 319-322, Gurko, p. 405, Miliukov, *Tri popytki*, pp. 1-25, also E. D. Chermenskii, *Burzhuaziia i tsarism v revoliutsii 1905-1907* (Moscow, 1939), p. 317; Max Weber, "Zur Lage der bürgerlichen Demokratie in Russland," *Archiv für Sozialwissenschaft und Sozialpolitik*, 1906, XXII (N.F. 4), 344; and Oldenburg, I, 360. It had been Gessen who suggested Evgenii Trubetskoi as a suitable candidate for the post of Minister of Education; Gessen, pp. 206-207.

41. Evgenii, together with M. A. Stakhovich and N. N. L'vov, tried to dissuade the deputies of the First Duma from issuing the Vyborg Manifesto; see Tyrkova-Williams, p. 329; Oldenburg, pp. 363-371, and especially Evgenii's articles criticizing the Kadet policy in *ME*,

passim, but particularly in No. 1, Jan., 1907. At one point, *ibid.*, p. 10, he predicted that the conciliatory tactics of the liberals toward the revolutionaries "will relegate us into the archives, where there will be much room for everything indecisive and incomplete." Significantly enough, Evgenii accused only some Kadets of radicalism, i.e., of overestimating the strength of the liberals in Russia; *ME*, 13 January, 1907, No. 2, p. 7. He wrote: "The fall of the center signifies a long period of troubles and internal struggle. The extremists understand that and enter this path consciously. . . . I understand them, but I must admit that I can't understand anymore many of those who share my views — men of the center," *ME*, 6 January, 1907, pp. 11-12. His main criticism of the Kadets was that they practiced self-deception by not realizing their own moderation and by continuing to use revolutionary rhetoric.

42. See especially an article by Efremov on the First Duma in *ME*, 27 January, 1907, No. 4, and an article by Evgenii in *ibid.*, for a discussion of the policies of the party. Also see Shipov, pp. 513-516.

43. Political parties were recognized by the government only in October, 1905. The Octobrists, a party to the right of the Kadets, considered the concessions granted by the government in the October Manifesto adequate. Evgenii, according to Shipov, p. 498, predicted that the Octobrist Party, which considered the Manifesto of Oct. 17 its standard, would turn into a party of "the lost charter." Evgenii argued that the Octobrists were too compromised by the cooperation with a reactionary regime to be able to provide real leadership for Russia; see particularly *ME*, 21 July, 1907 and 28 July, 1907.

44. In *ME*, 19 May, 1907, No. 19, 7. Evgenii had naturally always criticized the bureaucracy. His first really famous publicistic article had dealt with the short-comings of the bureaucracy as the reason for the defects suffered by Russia in the Russo-Japanese war. This article had been published in *Pravo*. When in January, 1907, the Kiev governor closed the local branches of the Party of Peaceful Regeneration, Evgenii considered it as further proof that the government was incapable of carrying out even rudimentary state functions; *ME*, 27 January, 1907, No. 4, 8-9.

45. This is how Evgenii Trubetskoi characterized the immediate tasks facing Russia in *ME*, 14 April, 1907, No. 15, 8.

46. There are various stages of this argument; Maklakov provides a convenient illustration of it. It was reinforced by the tendency of some Kadets to traditional radical verbiage.

47. See issues of October 5 and 6, 1911.

BIBLIOGRAPHY

I. WORKS BY S. N. TRUBETSKOI

Sobranie sochinenii kn. Sergeia Nikolaevicha Trubetskogo edited with an introduction by L. M. Lopatin. 6 vols. in 5. Moscow, 1907-1912. This collection includes almost all of Trubetskoi's published and unpublished works written since 1896.

[The following is a chronological list of his articles and works, arranged topically.]

Philosophy

Most of Trubetskoi's philosophical works appeared originally in *Voprosy Filosofii i Psikhologii (VFP)*. The numeration of the journal is not always consistent; I shall use the one appearing in the particular issue.

Metafizika v drevnei Gretsii. Published as a separate book in 1890; reprinted as vol. III of *Sobranie* in 1910.

"O prirode chelovecheskogo soznaniia," first appeared in *VFP* in the following issues: Oct., 1889, book 1, pp. 83-126; 1890, book III, pp. 159-192; 1891, book 6, pp. 132-156; March, 1891, book 7, pp. 21-56; *Sobranie*, II, 1-110.

"Psikhologicheskii determinizm i nravstvennaia svoboda," *VFP*, Nov., 1894, book 25 (5), pp. 494-521; *Sobranie*, II, 111-133.

"Etika i dogmatika," *VFP*, 1895, 29 (4), pp. 484-517;

Sobranie, II, 134-160.

"Osnovaniia idealizma," *VFP*, Jan., 1896, 1 (31), pp. 73-106; March/April, 1896, 2 (32), pp. 226-263; May/June, 1896, 3 (33), pp. 405-430; Sept./Oct., 1896, 4 (34), pp. 552-578; Nov./Dec., 1896, 5 (35), pp. 733-765, *Sobranie*, II, 161-284.

"V zashchitu idealizma," *VFP*, March/April, 1897, 2 (37), pp. 288-327, and "Neskol'ko slov v otvet B. N. Chicherinu," *VFP*, May/June, 1897, 3 (38), pp. 504-512; *Sobranie*, II, 285-329.

"Renan i ego filosofiia," a public lecture, published in 1898 in *Russkaia mysl'*; *Sobranie*, I, 287-328.

"Vera v bezsmertiie," originally a speech in the memory of Grot, *VFP*, May/June, 1902, 3 (63), pp. 1195-1220; Nov./Dec., 1903, 5 (70), pp. 497-515; Jan./Feb., 1904, 1 (71), pp. 62-83; Nov./Dec., 1904, 75 (V), pp. 539-561; *Sobranie*, II, 348-417.

Uchenie o Logose v ego istorii. The final version was published in 1900; *Sobranie*, vol. IV (1906).
[The following are the preliminary articles on the subject (not included in *Sobranie*)]

"Uchenie o Logose v drevnenei filosofii v sviazi s razvitiem idealizma," *VFP*, Jan./Feb., 1897, 1 (36), pp. 82-136.

"Filon i ego predshestvenniki," *VFP*, Nov./Dec., 1897, 5 (40), pp. 813-866, and Jan./Feb., 1898, 41 (1), pp. 138-183.

"Messianisticheskii ideal evreev v sviazi s ucheniem o Logose," *VFP*, 1898, 3 (43), pp. 463-494; continued under the title "Religioznyi ideal evreev," *VFP*, 1898, 44 (IV), pp. 659-695.

Kurs istorii drevnei filosofii; in *Sobranie*, vols. V and VI; (1912-1913). A history of ancient philosophy which Trubetskoi was preparing from his lecture notes.

"Protagor Platona v sviazi s razvitiem ego nravstvennoi mysli," *VFP*, May/June, 1901, 58 (III), pp. 207-228. An argument for the authenticity of Plato's work (not included in *Sobranie*).

"Pifagor i pifagoreitsy," *VFP*, March/April, 1905, 77 (II), pp. 303-325. A variant on the chapter on Pythagoras from *Metafizika*.

Trubetskoi also wrote the introduction to a Russian translation of Caird's *Hegel*, "Osnovnye momenty filosofii Hegelia," reprinted in *Sobranie*, II, 330-347; and an introduction to Barth's *Religions of India* (published in 1897), reprinted in *Sobranie*, II, 575-577; an article on the bibliography of the history of religions, in *VFP*, Jan./Feb., 1897, 1 (36), pp. 55-69; *Sobranie*, II, 524-538; an article in a collection in honor of F. E. Korsh, "Novaia teoriia obrazovaniia religioznykh poniatii," in *Sobranie*, II, 539-574; and an article in *Nauchnoe slovo* on "Etiudy po istorii grecheskoi religii," in *Sobranie*, II, 418-492. He prepared a bibliography on the history of religion for the Russian edition of P. Chantempie de la Saussaye, *Illustrated History of Religions* (Moscow, 1899).

Trubetskoi wrote review articles on the works of Chicherin, A. A. Vvedenskii, Hartman, Soloviev's "Tri razgovora," Chantempie de la Saussaye, Erwin Rohde, and Joseph Müller's *Dostoiewski, ein Charakterbild*. He also contributed articles on Logos, religion and eschatology to the Brockhaus-Efron encyclopaedic dictionary. All of these articles are included in *Sobranie*.

Publicism

Trubetskoi's publicistic works appeared in various journals and newspapers, but mostly in *Sanktpeterburgskie vedomosti (SPV)*.

Works of Social and Cultural Criticism

"Protivorechiia nashei kul'tury," *Vestnik Evropy*, 1893; *Sobranie*, I, 212-229.

"Razocharovannyi slavianofil," *Vestnik Evropy*, 1893; *Sobranie*, I, 173-211.

"Nauchnaiia deiatel'nost' A. M. Ivantsova-Platonova," *VFP*, March, 1895, VI book 27 (2), pp. 193-220; *Sobranie*, I, 229-251. (Originally a speech delivered March 5, 1895, at the Historical Society of Moscow University).

"Smert' V. S. Solovieva: v kachestve nekrologa," *Vestnik Evropy*, July, 1900; *Sobranie*, I, 344-352.

"Pamiati Vasiliia Petrovicha Preobrazhenskogo," *VFP*, Oct., 1900, book 54 (IV), pp. 481-500; *Sobranie*, I, 328-344.

"Lishnie liudi i geroi nashego vremeni," published only in *Sobranie*, I, 368-383.

Articles on Religious Problems [unfinished]:

"Proektirovannoe chtenie na bogoslovskikh besedakh," in *Sobranie*, I, 446-451.

"O sovremennom polozhenii russkoi tserkvi," first published in *Moskovskii ezhenedel'nik*, 1906; *Sobranie*, I, 438-446.

Works on Educational Problems.

"Universitet i studenchestvo," *Russkaia mysl'*, 1894, No. 4, 182-203; *Sobranie*, I, 261-286.

"Po povodu pravitel'stvennogo soobshcheniia o studencheskikh bezporiadkakh," *SPV*, 24 Dec., 1896; *Sobranie*, I, 1-13.

"Otvet 'professoru universiteta'," *SPV*, 3 Feb., 1897; *Sobranie*, I, 14-20.

"Sumlevaius' shtop," *SPV*, 27 April, 1901; *Sobranie*, I, 51-53.

"Ochen' somnevaius. . .," *SPV*, 26 May, 1901; *Sobranie*, I, 53-57.

"Urok klassitsizma nekotorym iz ego druzei," *SPV*, 27 July, 1901; *Sobranie*, I, 65-69.

"Tat'ianin den'," *Russkiia vedomosti*, 12 January, 1904; *Sobranie*, I, 77-79.

"Byt' ili ne byt' universitetu," *Russkiia vedomosti*, 25 Feb., 1905; *Sobranie*, I, 85-88.

─────────── (untitled note on student disturbances dated 20 March, 1905), *Russkiia vedomosti*; *Sobranie*, I, 92-93.

─────────── (a letter to the editor and a letter to Prof. D. N. Anuchin, March, 1905, on the Pedagogical Society), appeared only in *Sobranie*, I, 94-97.

"V vysshei stepeni somnevaius'," *SPV*, 19 July, 1905; *Sobranie*, I, 57-65.

Articles on Political Problems

"Chuvstvitel'nyi i khladnokrovnyi," *Russkaia mysl'*, 1896; *Sobranie*, I, 251-261.

"Delo Mortara," *SPV*, 7 November, 1897; *Sobranie*, I, 20-22.

"Otkrytoe pis'mo kn. E. E. Ukhtomskomu," *SPV*, 13 April, 1899; *Sobranie*, I, 22-25.

"Otvet kn. D. N. Tsertelevu," *SPV*, 3 May, 1899; *Sobranie*, I, 25-28.

"Vtoroi otvet kn. Tsertelevu," *SPV*, 10 June, 1899; *Sobranie*, I, 29-33.

"Delo Dreifusa i frantsuzkie generaly," *SPV*, 22 June, 1899; *Sobranie*, I, 33-36.

"Sushchestvuet li obshchestvo?" *SPV*, 9 August, 1899; *Sobranie*, I, 36-40.

"K sovremennomu politicheskomu polozheniiu," *SPV*, 9

March, 1900; *Sobranie*, I, 41-46.

_____ (a letter to the editor on China), *SPV*, 31 August, 1900; *Sobranie*, I, 46-50.

"Kanun novago goda," 31 December, 1901 (censored); published in *Sobranie*, I, 452-455.

"Rosiia—na rubezhe," *SPV*, 24 January, 1904; *Sobranie*, I, 79-81.

"Na rubezhe," written in winter, 1904, censored; published in *Moskovskii ezhenedel'nik*, 1906; *Sobranie*, I, 458-492.

"I ty tozhe, Brut," 18 August, 1904, censored; published in *Sobranie*, I, 492-495.

_____ (a letter to the editor on the command of the army), *SPV*, 19 September, 1904; *Sobranie*, I, 81-82.

_____ (a letter to the editor, defending Evgenii Trubetskoi), *Russkiia vedomosti*, 20 October, 1904; *Sobranie*, I, 83-84.

"Sovremennoe polozhenie nashei pechati," *Russkiia vedomosti*, 11 March, 1905; *Sobranie*, I, 89-92.

_____ (a letter to the editor), *Russkiia vedomosti*, 4 March, 1905; *Sobranie*, I, 88-89.

"Medlit' nel'zia," *Russkiia vedomosti*, 9 April, 1905; *Sobranie*, I, 97-99.

Moskovskaia nedelia (Trubetskoi's banned newspaper), May, 1905; *Sobranie*, I, 99-125.

"Pered resheniem," 12 July, 1905; *Sobranie*, I, 134-139.

Speeches and Notes

Speech at Student Society, 9 October, 1903; published in *Osvobozhdenie*, 1903; *Sobranie*, I, 72-76.

Note to Mirskii from the *zemtsy*, November, 1904; *Sobranie*, I, 389-397.

Note from the minority at the January, 1905, meeting of the assembly of the nobility of Moscow; *Sobranie*, I, 397-399.

Speech at a *zemstvo* congress on the agrarian problem, April, 1904, first published in P. D. Dolgorukov and I. I. Petrunkevich, eds., *Agrarnyi vopros*; *Sobranie*, I, 400-401.

Address of the *zemstvo* to the Tsar, June, 1905, and Trubetskoi's speech to the Tsar; in *Sobranie*, I, 129-134.

Note to the Tsar on educational problems, June, 1905; in *Sobranie*, I, 401-412.

Speech on the election to post of rector of Moscow University and a speech to the students; in *Sobranie*, I, 139-144.

Satiric Works

"Pravdivaia istoriia 'Zdravago Slova'," written in 1895,

published in *Sobranie*, I, 413-430.

"Ferkel!" written in 1895; published in *Moskovskii ezhenedel'nik*, 1906; *Sobranie*, I, 430-438.

"Skazka ob obshchipannoi zhar-ptitse," published in *Moskovskii ezhenedel'nik*, 1906; *Sobranie*, I, 455-458.

"Freilein," written in 1903; published in *Osvobozhdenie*, 1903, No. 31, 116; *Sobranie*, I, 70-72.

"Skazka o Senie i Vasie, ili blagonamerennost ne vsegda pomogaet," published May 25, 1905 in *Russkiia vedomosti*; in *Sobranie*, I, 125-128.

Musical Reviews

"Po povodu kontserta Skriabina," a letter to the editor, *Kur'er*, 1902; *Sobranie*, I, 385-388.

"K deviatomu simfonicheskomu sobraniiu," in *Sobranie*, I, 383-385.

Trubetskaia, Olga Nikolaevna, "Kn. Sergei N. Trubetskoi o Sv. Sofii, russkoi tserkvi i vere pravoslavnoi," *Put'*, April-June, 1935, No. 47, 3-13, contains parts of an early manuscript on Sophia which are not included in *Sobranie*.

The following articles, not included in *Sobranie*, were incorporated by Trubetskoi into his other works.

"Uchenie o Logose v drevnei filosofii v sviazi s razvitiem idealizma," *VFP*, January/February, 1897, book 1

(36), pp. 82-136.

"Filon i ego predshestvenniki," *VFP*, Nov./Dec., 1897, book 5 (40), pp. 813-866; and Jan./Feb., 1898, book 41 (1), pp. 138-183.

"Messianisticheskii ideal evreev v sviazi s ucheniem o Logose," *VFP*, May/June, 1898, book 3 (43), pp. 463-494. Continued under the title: "Religioznyi ideal evreev," *VFP*, July/August, 1898, book 44 (IV), pp. 659-695.

"Protagor Platona v sviazi s razvitiem ego nravstvennoi mysli," *VFP*, May/June, 1901, book 58 (III), pp. 207-228.

"Pifagor i pifagoreitsy," *VFP*, March/April, 1905, book 77 (II), pp. 303-325.

"Dva puti," *Pravo*, No. 44 (October 31, 1904), 3006-3009.

II. MEMOIRS AND CORRESPONDENCE

Trubetskaia, Olga Nikolaevna. *Kn. S. N. Trubetskoi: Vospominaniia sestry*. New York, 1953. (Invaluable memoirs of Trubetskoi's sister, combined with a diary she kept in 1904-1905, as well as with some of Trubetskoi's correspondence).

_____ "Iz perezhitogo," *Sovremennyia zapiski*, 1937, book 64, pp. 277-318, and book 65, pp. 206-244. (Contains parts of *Vospominaniia* with slight changes).

Trubetskoi, Evgenii Nikolaevich. *Iz proshlago*. Vienna, n.d. (Memoirs on Trubetskoi's childhood and youth by his brother).

_____ *Vospominaniia*. Sofia, 1921. (Memoirs on Trubetskoi's childhood and youth).

ENPE, ed., *Kniaz' S. N. Trubetskoi:pervyi borets za pravdu i svobodu russkago narodu. V otzyvakh russkoi sovremennoi pechati, rechakh i vospominaniiakh ego posledovatelei i pochitatelei*. St. Petersburg, 1905. (Source includes reprints of newspaper articles about Trubetskoi, speeches at his funeral and some memoirs).

Grot, Nikolai Iakovlevich. *Nikolai Iakovlevich Grot: v ocherkakh, vospominaniakh i pis'makh tovarishchei i uchenikov, druzei i pochitatelei*. St. Petersburg, 1910. (Memoirs on one of Trubetskoi's closest colleagues. Contains a selection of Trubetskoi's correspondence).

III. SHORTER MEMOIRS ON TRUBETSKOI

Anisimov, A. I., "Kniaz' S. N. Trubetskoi i moskovskoe studenchestvo," *VFP*, January, 1906, book 1 (81), pp. 146-196.

Arsenev, Nikolai, "Kniaz' S. N. Trubetskoi," *Novyi Zhurnal*, XXIX (1952), 282-302.

Belyi, Andrei [Boris Bugaev]. "Kn. S. N. Trubetskoi," *Vesy*, nos. 9/10 (Sept./Oct., 1905), 79-80.

Blonskii, P. P. "Kn. S. N. Trubetskoi i filosofiia," *Mysl' i slovo*, I (Moscow, 1917), 142-176.

Bulgakov, Sergei N. "Kn. S. N. Trubetskoi," *Voprosy zhizni*. Oct./Nov., 1905, pp. 280-289.

—————— "Kn. S. N. Trubetskoi kak religioznyi myslitel'," *Moskovskii ezhenedel'nik*, No. 14 (April 1, 1908), 11-22.

Davydov, N. V. "Kniaz' S. N. Trubetskoi," *Moskovskii ezhenedel'nik*. No. 14 (April 1, 1908), 31-35.

—————— "Iz proshlago:Kn. S. N. Trubetskoi," *Golos minuvshago*, No. 1 (January, 1917), 5-34.

Florovskii, Georges. "Kniaz' S. N. Trubetskoi," *Put'*, XXVI, 1931, 119-122.

Glinskii, V. V. "Kniaz' S. N. Trubetskoi," *Istoricheskii vestnik*, No. 102 (1905), 598-614.

Kheraskov, Ivan. "Iz istorii studencheskogo dvizheniia v moskovskom universitete (vospominaniia uchasnika 1897-1903)," in Yel'iashevich *et al.*, eds. *Moskovskii universitet*, pp. 431-449.

Khvostov, V. N. "S. N. Trubetskoi," *VFP*, January/Feb., 1906, book 1 (81), pp. 9-15.

Knorring, N. "Iz zhizni moskovskogo studenchestva v nachale XX veka (pamiati prof. kn. S. N. Trubetskogo)," in Yel'iashevich *et. al.*, eds. *Moskovskii universitet*, pp. 450-466.

Kotliarevskii, S. A. "Mirosozertsanie kn. S. N. Trubet-

skogo," *VFP*, January/February, 1916, book 131
(I), pp. 40-50.

_____ "Pamiati Kn. S. N. Trubetskogo," *Moskovskii
ezhenedel'nik*, No. 14 (April 1, 1908), 27-30.

Lapshin, I. "Sergei N. Trubetskoi," in Brockhaus-Efron,
vol. 33ᵃ (66) (1901), 919-921.

Lopatin, L. M. "Pamiati kn. S. N. Trubetskogo," *VFP*,
September/October, 1905, book IV (79), pp. i-[vi].

_____ "Kn. S. N. Trubetskoi i ego obshchee filo-
sofskoe mirosozertsanie," *VFP*, January/February,
1906, book 1 (81), pp. 28-129.

_____ "Sovremennoe znachenie filosofskikh idei
S. N. Trubetskogo," *VFP*, January/February, 1916,
book 131 (I), pp. 1-39.

Manuilov, A. A. "Iz vospominanii o kn. S. N. Trubetskim,"
VFP, January/February, 1906, book 1 (81), pp. 1-3.

_____ "Kn. S. N. Trubetskoi," *Moskovskii ezhenedel'nik*, No. 14 (April 1, 1908), 9-10.

Melioranskii, Boris. "Teoreticheskaia filosofiia S. N. Trubetskogo," *VFP*, March/April, 1906, book 82 (II),
pp. 197-222.

Novgorodtsev, P. N. "Pamiati kn. S. N. Trubetskogo,"
VFP, January/February, 1906, book 1 (81).

_____ "Kn. S. N. Trubetskoi v ego otnoshenii k
universitetskoi nauke," *Moskovskii ezhenedel'nik*,

No. 14 (April 1, 1908), 23-26.

Polivanov, M. P. Personal interviews held in New York. January-June, 1964.

Rachinskii, G. "Religiozno-filosofskiia vozreniia S. N. Trubetskogo," *VFP*, January/February, 1916, book 131 (I), pp. 51-77.

Radlov, E. L. "Kniaz' S. N. Trubetskoi," *Zhurnal Ministerstva Narodnogo Prosveshcheniia*, vol. 362 (November, 1905), 44-52.

Soloviev, Sergei. "Smert' S. N. Trubetskogo," *Vesy*, No. 9/10 (Sept./Oct., 1905), 76-78.

Speranskii, V. N. "Kniaz' Sergei Trubetskoi:k 90-letiiu dnia rozhdeniia," *Russkaia mysl'*, No. 474 (August 8, 1952), 4-5 and No. 477 (August 20, 1952), 4-5.

Trubetskoi, E. N. "Svoboda i bezsmertie (K godovshchine smerti kn. S. N. Trubetskogo)," *VFP*, September/ October, 1906, book 84 (IV), pp. 368-377.

IV. FAMILY BACKGROUND

[Trutovskii, V. K.]. *Skazanie o rode Trubetskikh*. Moscow, 1891.

Burg, B. G., Count. "Kniazia Trubetskie: Kievskaia vetv," *Novik*, No. 3 (31) (New York, 1941), 22-25.

Trubetskoi, Evgenii N. and (for some time) Grigorii N., eds., *Moskovskii ezhenedel'nik*. Moscow, 1906-1910.

Trubetskoi, E. N. *Natsional'nyi vopros, Konstantinopol' i Sviataia Sofiia.* Moscow, 1915.

—————— *Umozrenie v kraskakh:vopros o smysle zhizni v drevne-russkoi religioznoi zhivopisi.* Moscow, 1916.

Trubetskoi, Grigorii N. *Krasnaia Rossiia i Sviataia Rus'.* Paris, 1931.

—————— *Russland als Großmacht.* Translated from the Russian. Stuttgart, 1913.

Nolde, B. E. *Dalekoe i blizkoe.* Paris, 1930. (On Grigorii)

Riasanovsky, N. V. "Prince N. S. Trubetskoy's 'Europe and Mankind'," *Jahrbücher für Geschichte Osteuropas*, Band 12 (1964), 207-220. (On one of Trubetskoi's sons).

V. JOURNALS USED EXTENSIVELY

Voprosy Filosofii i Psikhologii. Published by the Moscow Psychological Society, 1889-1917.

Moscow University. *Otchet o sostoianii i deistviiakh 1-go Moskovskago gosudarstvennogo universiteta.* Title varies also as *Rech i otchet . . . .* Annual reports published at intervals from 1872-1926.

Struve, P. B., ed. *Osvobozhdenie.* Stuttgart/Paris, 1902-1905.

—————— *Listok Osvobozhdeniia.* 1904-1905.

Ministerstvo Narodnogo Prosveshcheniia. *Zhurnal Ministerstva Narodnogo Prosveshcheniia.* St. Petersburg, 1834-1917.

Trubetskoi, E. N., ed., *Moskovskii ezhenedel'nik.* Moscow, 1906-1910.

VI. PRIMARY SOURCES

Books

Akademiia Nauk SSSR. *Revoliutsionnoe dvizhenie v Rossii vesnoi i letom 1905 goda.* vols. I & II. Moscow, 1957 and 1961.

Besedy o zadachakh narodnogo prosveshcheniia. Paris, 1901-1902.

Chelpanov, G. *Mozg i dusha. Kritika materializma i ocherk sovremennykh uchenii o dushe.* 5th edition. Moscow, 1912.

Chertkov, V., ed. *Studencheskoe dvizhenie 1899 g.* . Purleigh, Maldon, Essex, England, 1900.

[Chicherin, B. N.] *Rossiia nakanune dvadtsatago stoletiia.* Berlin, 1900.

Davydov, N. V. *Iz proshlago.* Moscow, 1913.

Debogorii-Mokrievich, V. K. *Vospominaniia.* Vol. I. Paris, 1897.

Doroshenko, Dmytro. *Moii spomyny pro davne mynule (1901-1914).* Winnipeg, Canada, 1949.

Dorovatovskii, S. and Charushnikov, A. *Ocherki realisticheskogo mirovozreniia (sbornik statei po filosofii, obshchestvennoi nauke i zhizni).* St. Petersburg, 1904. 2nd edition, 1905.

Garvi, P. A. [P. A. Bronstein]. *Vospominaniia sotsialdemokrata.* New York, 1946.

Gessen, I. V. *V dvukh vekakh:zhiznennyi otchet.* Vol. XXII of *Arkhiv Russkoi Revolutsii.* Berlin, 1937.

Gershuni, G. A. *Reforma Generala Vannovskago.* London (?), 1902.

Giliarov-Platonov, N. P. *Iz perezhitogo.* 2 vols. Moscow, 1886.

Grot, N. Ia. *K voprosu o reforme logiki. Opyt novoi teorii umstvennykh protsessov.* Leipzig, 1882.

Grot, N. P. *Vospominaniia dlia detei i vnukov.* St. Petersburg, 1899.

Guerrier, V. I. *Pervaia russkaia Gosudarstvennaia duma, politicheskiia vozrenia i taktika eia chlenov.* Moscow, 1906.

Gurko, V. I. *Features and Figures of the Past:Government and Opinion in the Reign of Nicholas II.* Stanford, California, 1939.

Iushkevich, P. *Novyia veianiia.* St. Petersburg, 1911.

Ivanov, P. *Studenty v Moskve:Byt. Nravy. Tipy.* Moscow, 1903.

Ivanov, R. V. *The Memoirs of Ivanov-Razumnik*. London, 1965.

Iz istorii studencheskikh volnenii (Konovalovskii konflikt z prilozheniem dokumentov). St. Petersburg, 1906.

Kharkov University. *Doklad kommissii po peresmotre ustava i shtatov Imperatorskikh Rossiiskikh Universitetov*. Kharkov, 1901.

Kizevetter, A. A. *Na rubezhe dvukh stoletii*. Prague, 1929.

Kokovtsov, V. N., Graf. *Iz moego proshlago. Vospominaniia, 1903-1919*. vol. I. n.p., 1933.

Komitet Ministrov. *Istoricheskii obzor deiatel'nosti Komiteta Ministrov*. 5 vols. St. Petersburg, 1902. (particularly vol. 4).

——————— *Zhurnaly Komiteta Ministrov po ispolneniiu ukaza 12 dekabria, 1904*. St. Petersburg, 1905.

Koni, A. F. *Ocherki i vospominaniia*. St. Petersburg, 1906.

Korostowetz, W. K. *Neue Väter—Neue Söhne:Drei russische Generationen*. Berlin, 1926.

Kotliarevskii, S. A. *Konstitutsionnoe gosudarstvo*. St. Petersburg, 1907.

——————— *Vlast' i pravo*. Moscow, 1915.

Kovnator, R.A., ed. *Moskovskii universitet v vospominaniakh sovremennikov*. Moscow, 1956.

Koz'min, B. P., ed. *S.V. Zubatov i ego korrespondenty: sredi okhrannikov, zhandarmov i provokatorov.* Moscow, 1928.

Leary, Daniel Bell. *Education and Autocracy in Russia: from the Origins to the Bolsheviki.* Buffalo, N.Y., 1919.

Lopatin, L. M. *Filosofskiia kharakteristiki i rechi.* Moscow, 1911.

Lopukhin, A. A. *Dokladnaia zapiska direktora departamenta politsii Lopukhina, razsmotrennaia v Komitete Ministrov v Yanuare, 1905.* Geneva, 1905.

_____ *Iz itogov sluzhebnogo opyta.* Moscow, 1907.

_____ *Otryvki iz Vospominanii (po povodu Vospominanii gr. S. Y. Witte).* Moscow, 1923.

_____ *Delo A. A. Lopukhina v osobom prisutsvii Pravitel'stvuiushchago Senata.* St. Petersburg, 1910. (Stenographic record).

Maklakov, V. A. *Iz vospominanii.* New York, 1955.

_____ *Vlast' i obshchestvennost'.* Paris, 1930 (?).

Materialy po universitetskomu voprosu. Vol. I. Stuttgart, 1902. (This is an abstract of A. I. Georgievskii, *Kratkii istoricheskii ocherk pravitel'stvennikh mer i prednachertanii protiv studencheskikh bezporiadkov,* which was published by the government in St. Petersburg in 1890 and which is unavailable here).

—————— Vol. II. Stuttgart, 1904. (This is a reprint of the Zernov Commission of Moscow University in 1901 on the causes of student unrest and it incorporates the views of the professors and the students. It was originally published officially in a very limited edition with limited circulation).

Mathes, W. L. *The Struggle for University Autonomy in the Russian Empire During the First Decade of the Reign of Alexander II, (1855-1865)*. Unpublished Ph.D. dissertation, Columbia University, 1966.

Makovski, S. A. *Na Parnase serebrianogo veka*. Munich, 1962.

—————— *Portrety sovremennikov*. New York, 1955.

Melgunov, S. P. *Iz istorii studencheskikh obshchestv v russkikh universitetakh*. Moscow, 1904.

—————— *Studencheskie organizatsii 80-90 gg. v Moskovskom universitete*. Moscow, 1908.

—————— *Tserkov i gosudarstvo v Rossii (K voprosu o svobode sovesti), Sbornik statei*. Moscow, 1906.

Melnik, Josef, ed. *Russen über Rußland: Ein Sammelwerk*. Frankfurt/Main, 1906.

Miliukov, P. N. *Iz istorii russkoi intelligentsii: Sbornik statei i etiudov*. 2nd edition. St. Petersburg, 1903.

—————— *Russia and Its Crisis*. New York, 1962.

—————— *Tri popytki (K istorii russkago lzhe-kon-*

stitutsionalizma). Paris, 1921.

——————— *Vospominaniia.* New York, 1955. (vol. I).

Ministerstvo Narodnogo Prosveshcheniia. *Izvlecheniia iz vsepoddaineishego otcheta Ministra Narodnago Prosveshcheniia.* Annual reports published at intervals, 1887-1901.

——————— *Obzor deiatel'nosti vedomstva Ministerstva Narodnogo Prosveshcheniia za vremia tsarstvovaniia Imperatora Alexandra III.* St. Petersburg, 1901.

Ministerstvo Vnutrennikh Del. *Soobrazhenie Ministra Vnutrennikh Del po nekotorym voprosam, voznikaiushchim pri osushchestvlenii vysochaishikh predukazanii vosveshchennykh v reskripte 18 fevralia, 1905 goda.* n.p., n.d. (governmental publication).

Minskii, N. M. *Religiia budushchago (filosofskie razgovory).* St. Petersburg, 1905.

Moscow University. *Doklad kommissii po peresmotre ustava i shtatov Imperatorskikh Rossiiskikh Universitetov.* Moscow, 1901.

Muratov, N. A. *Privet Imperatorskomu Moskovskomu Universitetu 1755-1905:Gaudeamus igitur.* Moscow, 1905.

Novgorodtsev, P. I., ed. *Problemy idealizma.* Moscow, 1903.

Novikov, M. M. *Ot Moskvy do N'iu Iorka:moia zhizn' v*

nauke i politike. New York, 1952.

Obolenskii, V. A. *Ocherki minuvshago*. Belgrade, 1931.

Petrishchev, A. B. *Tserkov i shkola:svoboda sovesty; iz istorii russkoi shkoly*. St. Petersburg, 1906.

Petrunkevich, I. I. *Iz zapisok obshchestvennogo deiatelia, vospominaniia*. Vol. XXI of *Arkhiv Russkoi Revoliutsii*. Berlin, 1934.

Pilenko, A. A. *Zabastovki v srednikh uchebnykh zavedeniiakh*. St. Petersburg, 1906.

Pobedonostsev, K. P. *Reflections of a Russian Statesman*. trans. Robert Drozier Long. London, 1898.

——————— *K. P. Pobedonostsev i ego korrespondenty. Pis'ma i zapiski*. Vol. 1¹ and 1². Moscow, 1923.

Polner, T. I. *Zhiznennyi put' Kn. Georgiia Evgenievicha L'vova. Lichnost'. Vzgliady. Usloviia deiatel'nosti*. Paris, 1932.

Polnoe Sobranie Zakonov Rossiiskoi Imperii. Sobranie tret'e, 1881-1913. 33 vols. St. Petersburg, 1885-1916.

Pravitel'stvuiushchii Senat. *Sobranie uzakonenii i rasporiazhenii pravitel'stva, izdavaemoe pri pravitel'stvuiushchem senate*. St. Petersburg, 1809-1917.

Pravitel'stvennyi vestnik. St. Petersburg, 1905.

Radlov, E. L., ed. *Pis'ma V. S. Solovieva*. 3 vols. St.

Petersburg, 1908, 1909, 1911.

Schleuning, Johannes. *Mein Leben hat ein Ziel. Lebenserinnerungen eines Rußlanddeutschen Pfarrers.* Witten, 1964.

St. Petersburg University. *Pravila organizatsii studentov vvedenoi v Imperatorskii Sanktpeterburgskii Universitet.* St. Petersburg, 1902 (?).

Shchegolev, P. E., ed. *Padenie tsarskogo rezhima.* 7 vols. Petrograd, 1917.

Shipov, D. N. *Vospominaniia i dumy o perezhitom.* Moscow, 1918.

Soloviev, V. S. *Sochineniia.* ed. S. M. Soloviev and E. L. Radlov, 10 vols. 2nd edition. St. Petersburg, 1888.

Stepun, F. A. *Byvshee i nesbyvsheesia.* Vol. I. New York, 1956.

Svod Zakonov Rossiiskoi Imperii: Svod ustavov uchenykh uchrezhdenii i uchebnykh zavedenii vedomstva Ministerstva Narodnogo Prosveshcheniia. Vol. XI, Part I. St. Petersburg, 1893.

Tikhomirov, Lev. *Pochemu ia perestal byt' revoliutsionerom.* Moscow, 1895. (Originally published in French in Paris).

Trubetskoi, E. N. *Mirosozertsanie Vl. S. Solovieva.* Vol. I, Moscow, 1913.

Trubetskoi, Michael. *Out of Chaos: A Personal Story of*

the *Revolution in Russia*. trans. Edith Livermore. London, 1907.

Tsentrarkhiv. *Revoliutsiia 1905 goda i samoderzhavie*. Moscow, 1928.

Tyrkova-Williams, A. V. *Na putiakh k svobode*. New York, 1952.

Urusov, S. D., Prince. *Memoirs of a Russian Governor*. trans. Herman Rosenthal. London, 1908.

Vannovskii, P. S. *Doklad po povodu studencheskikh bezporiadkov, 1899/1900*. Tipografiia Rabochego Znameni, 1900.

Vekhi. Sbornik statei o russkoi intelligentsii. 3rd edition. Moscow, 1909.

Velichko, V. L. *Vladimir Soloviev: Zhizn' i tvorenia*. St. Petersburg, 1902.

Vinogradoff, P. G. *Nakanune novogo goda*. Moscow, 1902.

Vvedenskii, A. A. *Sud'by filosofii v Rossii*. Speech at the first public meeting of the St. Petersburg University Philosophical Society on January 31, 1898; printed as a separate booklet; also in the same author's *Filosofskii ocherki*. Prague, 1924.

Witte, S. Iu. *The Memoirs of Count Witte*. trans. and ed. Abraham Yarmolinsky. Garden City, N.Y., 1921.

Yel'iashevich, V. B., Kizevetter, A. A., and Novikov, M.M.,

eds. *Moskovskii universitet, 1755-1930.* Paris, 1930.

Zaitsev, B. K. *Moskva.* Munich, 1960.

Articles

Arsenev, N.S. "O moskovskikh religiozno-filosofskikh i literaturnykh kruzhkakh i sobraniiakh nachala XX veka," *Sovremennik* (Toronto), No. 6 (1962), 30-42.

_____ Interview in New York, December 13, 1963.

Aikhenval'd, Iu. Review of *Problemy idealizma, VFP,* March/April, 1903, book II (67), pp. 333-356.

El'tsova, K. "Sny nezdeshnie:k 25-letiiu konchiny V. S. Solovieva," *Sovremennyia zapiski,* book 28 (1926), 225-275.

[Golovin, F. A.]. "Iz zapisok F. A. Golovina," *Krasnyi Arkhiv,* vol. 58 (1933), 142-149.

Gredeskul, N. A. "Rol' universiteta v sovremennom dvizhenii," *Pravo,* No. 40 (Oct. 9, 1904), 3309-10.

Grot, N. Ia. "K voprosu ob istinnykh zadachakh filosofii," *Russkaia mysl',* (Moscow), November, 1886, pp. 21-42.

_____ "O zadachakh zhurnala," *VFP,* 1889, bk. 1.

_____ "Ot redaktsii," *VFP,* 1890, books 2, 3, 4.

_____ "Zhiznennyia zadachi psikhologii," *VFP*

1890, book 4.

——————— "Eshche o zadachakh zhurnala," *VFP*, 1891, book 6.

——————— Review of Sergei Trubetskoi's *Metafizika v drevnei Gretsii*, in *VFP*, 1890, bk. 2, pp. 105-108.

Kapnist, Pavel, Count. "Universitetskie voprosy," *Vestnik Evropy*, book 11 (November, 1903), 167-218.

Kaufmann, P. "Novyi universitetskii ustav," *Zhurnal MNP*, No. 7 (1909), 1-27.

Kizevetter, A. A. "Moskovskii universitet i ego traditsiia," *Russkaia mysl'* (Moscow), 1905, book 1, part 2, 1-13.

Kovalevskii, M. M. "Moskovskii universitet v kontse 70-kh i nachale 80-kh gg. proshlago veka (lichnyia vospominaniia)" *Vestnik Evropy*, book 263 (May, 1910), 178-221.

L'vov, N. N. "Bylye gody," *Russkaia mysl'*, 1923, I-II, 92-116; III-V, 79-107; VI-VIII, 111-128; IX-XII, 5-26.

Melgunov, S. P. "Moskovskii Universitet v 1894 g.," *Golos minuvshago*, No. 5 (1913), 182-218.

Miliukov, P. N. "Universitety v Rosii," *Brockhaus-Efron*, LXVIII (1902), 788-800.

Moscow University. "Iz khroniki moskovskogo universiteta:Istoriia s professorom Malovym," *Russkii arkhiv,* book 1 (1901), 316-324.

_____ "Shchutochnaia khronika moskovskogo universiteta," *Russkii arkhiv,* book 1 (1912), 125-128, 279-289.

Nabokov, V. D. "Piat' let nazad," *Russkaia mysl',* Nov. 1910, pp. 195-198.

Osorgin, Mikhael. "Deviat'sot piatyi god," *Sovremennyia zapiski,* XLIII (1930), 268-299.

Panina, S. V. "Na peterburgskoi okraine," *Novyi Zhurnal,* XLVII (1957), 162-196, and XLIX (1957), 189-203.

Plekhanov, G. V. "Chto dal'she," *Sochineniia,* XII (Moscow, 1924), 137-178.

Raskol'nikov, F. "Zabytoe pis'mo F. Dostoevskogo k moskovskim studentam," *Krasnaia nov',* book 4 (1932), 149-155.

Rodichev, Fedor. "The Liberal Movement in Russia, 1855-1917," *Slavonic and East European Review,* II, No. 4 (June, 1923), 1-13, and no. 5 (December, 1923), 249-262.

_____ "The Veteran of Russian Liberalism," *Slavonic and East European Review,* VII (1929), 316-326.

Rostovtsev, G. "Studencheskie volneniia v moskovskom universitete v 1887 g.," *Russkaia starina,* No. 1 (1906), 132-146.

Rozhkov, N. "Znachenie i sud'by noveishogo idealizma v Rossii. (Po povodu knigi *Problemy idealizma*)," *VFP*, March/April, 1903, book II (67), pp. 314-32.

Rudakov, V. E. "Studencheskie nauchnyia obshchestva," *Istoricheskii vestnik*, No. 12 (1899), 1143-1156.

Shakhovskoi, D. I., Prince. "Soiuz Osvobozhdeniia," *Zarnitsy: Literaturno-politicheskii Sbornik*, II (1909), 81-171.

Shchetinin, B. A., Prince. "Pervye shagi," *Istoricheskii vestnik*, No. 9 (1905), 501-514.

_____ "Svobododeistvuiushchie vosmidesiatniki," *Istoricheskii vestnik*, No. 9 (1905), 936-943.

Soloviev, V. S. Review of Sergei Trubetskoi's *Metafizika v drevnei Gretsii*, in *Russkoe Obozreniie*, No. 10 (1890), 931-945.

Syromiatnikov, A. "Moskovskii universitet v oktiabrskie dni 1905 g.," *Krasnyi arkhiv*, vol. 74 (1936), 195-204.

Svatikov, S. G. "Opal'naia professura 80 gg.," *Golos minuvshago*. No. 2 (February, 1917), 5-78.

Trubetskoi, E. N. "Die Universitätsfrage," in J. Melnik, ed., *Russen über Rußland*. Frankfurt/Main, 1906, pp. 16-53.

_____ "Krushenie teokratii v tvorchestve V. S. Solovieva," *Russkaia mysl'* (Moscow), book 1, part 2 (1912), 1-35.

Valentinov, N. "Vstrechi s Andreem Belym:plenenie Andreia Belogo '*Vekhami*' Gershenzona," *Novyi Zhurnal*, XIL (March, 1957), 170-188.

Vinogradoff, P. G. "Uchebnoe delo v nashikh universitetakh," *Vestnik Evropy*, No. 10 (October, 1901), 537-573.

Vinogradov, N. "Kratkii istoricheskii ocherk deiatel'nosti Moskovskogo Psikhologicheskogo Obshchestva za 25 let," *VFP*, 1910, book 103, pp. 249-262.

Zelinskii, O. F. "Universitetskii vopros v 1906 g.," *Zhurnal MNP* (August, 1906), pp. 111-159.

VII. SECONDARY SOURCES

Books

Askol'dov, S. A. *Alexei Alexandrovich Kozlov*. Moscow, 1912.

Belokonskii, I. P. *Zemstvo i konstitutsiia*. Moscow, 1910.

Botsianovskii, V. and Gollerbakh, E. *Russkaia satira pervoi revoliutsii 1905-1906 goda*. Leningrad, 1925.

Butiagin, A. S. and Saltanov, Iu. A. *Universitetskoe obrazovanie v SSSR*. Moscow, 1957.

Chermenskii, E. D. *Burzhuaziia i tsarizm v revolutsii 1905-1907*. Moscow, 1939 and 1970.

Curtiss, J. S. *Church and State in Russia: The Last Years of the Empire, 1900-1917*. New York, 1940.

Edie, James M., Scanlan, James, P., and Zeldin, Mary-Barbara, eds., with the collaboration of George L. Kline. *Russian Philosophy:Pre-revolutionary Philosophy and Theology, Philosophers in Exile, Marxists and Communists.* Vol. III. Chicago, 1965.

Ershov, M. N. *Puti razvitiia filosofii v Rossii.* Vladivostok, 1922.

Fischer, George. *Russian Liberalism.* Cambridge, Mass., 1958.

Florovskii, Georgii. *Puti russkago bogosloviia.* Paris, 1937.

Frank, S. L., ed. (posthumously ed. V. S. Frank). *Iz istorii russkoi filosofskoi mysli kontsa XIX i nachala XX veka. Antologiia.* n.p., 1965.

Geiger, T. *Aufgaben und Stellung der Intelligenz in der Gesellschaft.* Stuttgart, 1949.

Gratieux, Albert. *Unam Sanctam:Le Mouvement slavophile à la Veille de la Revolution.* Paris, 1953.

Gruzenberg, Semen. *Ocherki sovremennoi russkoi filosofii. Opyt kharakteristiki sovremennykh tendentsii russkoi filosofii.* St. Petersburg, 1911.

Hans, Nicholas. *History of Russian Educational Policy, 1701-1917.* New York, 1964.

_____ *The Russian Tradition in Education.* London, 1963.

Harcave, Sidney. *First Blood:The Russian Revolution of*

1905. New York, 1964.

Iakovenko, B. V. *Ocherki russkoi filosofii*. Berlin, 1922.

Ivanov, Razumnik Vasilevich. *Istoriia russkoi obshchest-vennoi mysli*. 2 vols. 4th edition. St. Petersburg, 1914.

Johnson, W. H. E. *Russia's Educational Heritage*. Pittsburgh, 1950.

Kiss, Gabor. *Die Gesellschafts-politische Rolle der Studenten-Bewegung im vorrevolutionären Rußland*. Munich, 1963.

Koz'min, B. P. *Iz istorii revoliutsionnoi mysli v Rossii*. Moscow, 1961.

Leontovitsch, V. V. *Geschichte des Liberalismus in Rußland*. Frankfurt/Main, 1957.

Losskii, N. O. *Dostoevskii i ego khristianskoe miroponimanie*. New York, 1953.

——————— *History of Russian Philosophy*. New York, 1951.

Lukiianov, S. M. *O Vl. S. Solovieve v ego molodye gody. Materialy k biografii*. vol. I. Petrograd, 1916; vol. II, 1918; vol. III, 1921.

Maevskii, Vl. A. *Revoliutsioner-monarkhist:Pamiati L'va Tikhomirova*. Novy Sad, 1934.

Martov, L., Maslov, P., Potresov, A., eds. *Obshchestvennoe dvizhenie v Rossii v nachale XX veka*. 2 vols. St. Petersburg, 1909-1910.

Mochul'skii, K. V. *Vladimir Soloviev: Zhizn' i uchenie.* Paris, 1936.

Odinets, D. M. and Novgorodtsev, P. I. *Russian Schools and Universities in the World War.* Series of Economic and Social History of the World War, Carnegie Foundation for International Peace. New Haven, 1929.

Ognev, A. I. *Lev Mikhailovich Lopatin.* Petrograd, 1922.

Ognev, S. I. *Zasluzhennyi professor I. V. Ognev (1855-1928).* Moscow, 1948.

Oldenburg, S. S. *Tsarstvovaniie Imperatora Nikolaia II.* 2 vols. Belgrade & Munich, 1939-1949.

Orlov, V. I. *Studencheskoe dvizhenie v moskovskom universitete.* Moscow, 1934.

Ossip-Lourie. *La Philosophie russe contemporaine.* Paris, 1902.

Polivanov, M. P. "Russkoe zemstvo, ego istoriia i ideinoe znachenie." Manuscript in the possession of the author.

Radlov, E. L. *Ocherk istorii russkoi filosofii.* 2nd revised edition. St. Petersburg, 1920.

_____ *Vladimir Soloviev: Zhizn' i uchenie.* St. Petersburg, 1913.

Raeff, Marc. *Origins of the Russian Intelligentsia: The Eighteenth Century Nobility.* New York, 1966.

Rozhdestvenskii, S. V. *Istoricheskii obzor deiatel'nosti Ministerstva Narodnogo Prosveshcheniia. 1802-1902.* St. Petersburg, 1902.

_____ *Ocherki po istorii sistem narodnogo prosveshcheniia v Rossii v XVIII i XIX v.*, vol. I. St. Petersburg, 1912.

Sacke, Georg. *W. S. Solowjews Geschichtsphilosophie: Ein Beitrag zur Characteristik der russischen Weltanschauung.* Berlin, 1929.

Schultze, Bernardo, S. J. *Pensatori Russi di Fronte a Cristo.* 3 vols. n.p., 1947.

Semionov-Tian-Shanskii, D. *Otets Ioann Kronshtadtskii.* New York, 1955.

Shevyrev. S.P. *Istoriia imperatorskogo moskovskogo universiteta.* Moscow, 1885.

Shchipanov, I. Ia., ed. *Moskovskii universitet i razvitie filosofskoi i obshchestvenno-politicheskoi mysli v Rossii.* Moscow, 1957.

Smolitsch, I. *Geschichte der russischen Kirche, 1700-1917.* Leiden, 1964.

Tsetlin, L. S. *Iz istorii nauchnoi mysli v Rossii (Nauka i uchenie v Moskovskom universitete vo vtoroi polovine XIX veka).* Moscow, 1958.

Thaden, E. C. *Conservative Nationalism in Nineteenth-Century Russia.* Seattle, 1964.

Tikhomirov, N. N., ed. *Istoriia moskovskogo universiteta, 1755-1955*. Moscow, 1955.

Tkachenko, P. S. *Moskovskoe studenchestvo v ovshchestvenno-politicheskoi zhizni Rossii vtoroi poloviny XIX veka*. Moscow, 1958.

Venturi, Franco. *Roots of Revolution:A History of the Populist and Socialist Movements in XIX Century Russia*. London, 1960.

Veselovskii, B. B. *Istoriia zemstva za sorok let*. 4 vols. St. Petersburg, 1909-1911.

Veselovskii, B. B. and Frenkel, Z. H. *Iubileinyi zemskii sbornik, 1864-1914*. St. Petersburg, 1914.

Von Laue, T. H. *Sergei Witte and the Industrialization of Russia*. New York, 1963.

Vydryn, R. C. *Osnovnye momenty studencheskogo dvizheniia v Rossii*. Moscow, 1908.

Weintraub, V., Gerhardt, D., and zum Winkel, H. J., eds., *Orbis Scriptus Dmitrij Tschizewskij zum 70. Geburtstag*. Munich, 1966.

Zaionchkovskii, P. A. *Krizis samoderzhaviia na rubezhe 1870-1880 godov*. Moscow, 1964.

Zenkovskii, V. V. *Istoriia russkoi filosofii*. vol. II. Paris, 1950.

Zenkovskij, V. V. *Aus der Geschichte der Ästhetischen Ideen in Rußland im 19. und 20. Jahrhundert*.

The Hague, 1958.

Zernov, N. M. *The Russian Religious Renaissance of the Twentieth Century*. New York, 1963.

Ziegler, Theobold. *Der Deutsche Student am Ende des XIX Jahrhunderts*. 6th edition. Leipzig, 1896.

Articles

Alexeev, V. P. "Revoliutsionnoe studencheskoe dvizhenie 1869 gg. v otsenke tret'ego otdeleniia," *Katorga i ssylka*, book 10 (1924), 106-121.

Belokonskii, I. P. "K istorii zemskogo dvizheniia v Rossii," *Istoricheskii sbornik*, No. 1 (1907), 25-125.

Borozdin, A. K. "Studencheskoe nauchno-literaturnoe obshchestvo pri Sankt-peterburgskim universitete," *Istoricheskii vestnik*, LXXIX (Jan., Feb., March, 1900), 302-312.

Florovskii, Georges. "Review of the histories of Russian philosophy written by M. N. Ershov, *Puti razvitiia filosofii v Rossii* (Vladivostok, 1922); Gustav Shpet, *Ocherk razvitiia russkoi filosofii* (Petrograd, 1922); and B. Iakovenko, *Ocherki russkoi filosofii* (Berlin, 1922)," *Russkaia mysl'*, books VI-VIII (1923), 419-431.

Glinskii, V. V. "Universitetskie ustavy, 1755-1884," *Istoricheskii vestnik*, LXXIX (January/February, 1900), 324-351, 718-742.

Gusiatnikov, P. S. "Studencheskoe dvizhenie v 1905 g.,"

Voprosy istorii, No. 10 (1955), 74-81.

Haimson, Leopold. "Social Stability in Urban Russia, 1905-1917," *Slavic Review*, XXIII, No. 4 (December, 1964), 619-642, and XXIV, No. 1 (March, 1965), 1-22.

——————— "The Parties and the State:the Evolution of Political Attitudes," in Cyril Black, ed. *The Transformation of Russian Society*. Cambridge, Mass., 1960., pp. 110-145.

Kuskova, Ekaterina. "Kren naleva (iz proshlago)," *Sovremennyia zapiski*, XLIV (1930), 366-395.

Levin, Alfred. "Russian Bureaucratic Opinion in the Wake of the 1905 Revolution," *Jahrbücher für Geschichte Osteuropas*, Band XI (1963), 1-12.

Raeff, Marc. "Reactionary Liberal, M.N. Katkov," *Russian Review*, XI (July, 1952), 157-167).

Rubinshtein, M. M. "Filosofiia i obshchestvennaia zhizn' v Rossii (Nabrosok)," *Russkaia mysl'* (March, 1909), pp. 180-190.

Ruffmann, Karl-Heinz. "Russischer Adel als Sondertypus der europäischen Adelswelt," *Jahrbücher für Geschichte Osteuropas*, Band IX (September, 1961), 161-178.

Scheibert, Peter, "Die Peterburger religiös-philosophischen Zusammenkünfte von 1902 und 1903," *Jahrbücher für Geschichte Osteuropas*. Band II (Feb., 1965), 513-560.

Tolstoi, D. A. "Akademicheskaia gimnaziia v XVIII st.," *Zapiski Imperatorskoi Akademii Nauk*, LI (St. Petersburg, 1885), Appendix 1.

_____ "Akademicheskii universitet v XVIII st.," *Zapiski Imperatorskoi Akademii Nauk*, LI (St. Petersburg, 1885), Appendix 3.

_____ "Gorodskie uchilishcha v tsarstvovanie Ekaterine II," *Zapiski Imperatorskoi Akademii Nauk*, LIV (St. Petersburg, 1884), Appendix.

_____ "Vzgliad na uchebnoiu chast' v Rossii v XVIII st. do 1792," *Zapiski Imperatorskoi Akademii Nauk*, XLVII (St. Petersburg, 1883), Appendix 2.

Treadgold, Donald. "The Constitutional Democrats and the Russian Liberal Tradition," *American Slavic and East European Review*, X (April, 1951), 85-94.

Tyrkova-Williams, A. V. "The Cadet Party," *Russian Review*, XII (July, 1953), 173-186.

_____ "Russian Liberalism," *Russian Review*, X (January, 1951), 3-14.

Valk, S. N. "Studencheskii soiuz' i kazn' 8 maia, 1887 g.," *Krasnyi arkhiv*, vol. II (XXI) (1927), 226-231.

Weber, Max. "Rußlands Übergang zum Scheinkonstitutionalismus," *Archiv für Sozialwissenschaft und Sozialpolitik*, XXIII (n.f. 5) (1906), 165-401.

_____ "Zur Lage der bürgerlichen Demokratie in

Rußland," *Archiv für Sozialwissenschaft und Sozialpolitik*, XXII (n.f. 4) (1906), 234-353.

Zhivago, Sergei. "Akademicheskaia svoboda v germanskikh universitetakh," *Vestnik Evropy*, No. 12 (December, 1901), 469-531.